# American Adventurism Abroad

*30 Invasions, Interventions, and*
*Regime Changes since World War II*

MICHAEL J. SULLIVAN III

Westport, Connecticut
London

**Library of Congress Cataloging-in-Publication Data**

Sullivan, Michael J. 1941–
    American adventurism abroad : 30 invasions, interventions, and regime changes since World War II / Michael J. Sullivan III.
        p. cm.
    Includes bibliographical references and index.
    ISBN 0-275-97276-3 (alk. paper)
    1. United States—Foreign relations—Developing countries.  2. Developing countries—Foreign relations—United States.  3. United States—Foreign relations—1945–1989.  4. United States—Foreign relations—1989–   5. Intervention (International law)—History—20th century.  I. Title: United States foreign policy on the periphery.  II. Title.
    D888.U6S85 2004
    327.730172′4′09045—dc22        2003062254

British Library Cataloguing in Publication Data is available.

Library of Congress Catalog Card Number: 2003062254
ISBN: 0–275–97276–3

First published in 2004

Praeger Publishers, 88 Post Road West, Westport, CT 06881
An imprint of Greenwood Publishing Group, Inc.
www.praeger.com

Printed in the United States of America

The paper used in this book complies with the Permanent Paper Standard issued by the National Information Standards Organization (Z39.48–1984).

10  9  8  7  6  5  4  3  2  1

To Dan, Phil, and Liz
Adventurers for Peace

# Contents

# Tables

# Introduction

## INTRODUCTION: MAJOR ARGUMENT AND METHODOLOGY

American foreign policy since 1945 has mainly been motivated by the goal of being hegemon of the global capitalist economic system. As chief protector of transnational capitalism, the United States has replaced the United Kingdom, which played this role for more than a century before World War II. Although the 1947–91 Cold War presented an easy-to-understand threat to this objective, US diplomacy in these years was not primarily about keeping the USSR out of Western Europe (the original explanation for containment), but rather about projecting its own power, globally. It was not about making the world safe for democracy, the usual ideological justification, but rather about being the leader of the capitalist world, the upholder of the global economic system.

This motivation, which was evident in US policy toward Latin America before the Cold War, has continued on a worldwide stage in the post–Cold War era of globalization, and especially since 9-11-01. It is for this reason that today's generation can learn from the history to be described here. The 30 forceful American interventions into developing countries between the late 1940s and the late 1990s covered in this work foreshadow likely forms of involvement in the future, especially in George W. Bush's "war against terrorism" with no specific enemy and no identifiable end.

The *time frame* for this study is roughly the 50-year period from the "Truman Doctrine" of containing communism in Greece to Clinton's "humanitarian" intervention in Kosovo. Its special concern is with relatively low-level violent interventions (both military and covert), and only secondarily with major wars (like Korea and Vietnam) or more peaceable diplomatic or economic interjections (Blechman and Kaplan, 1978: 4–12; Blum, 1995: 19–20; Treverton, 1987: 17–28). The 30 cases chosen are drawn from 10 presidencies. Six studies are taken from the early Cold War years, 1945–60 (including Greece, Iran, and Guatemala); 14 are investigated from the "extremist" period, 1961–76 (including the Congo, Cuba, Cambodia and Chile); and 10 cases from the most-recent era, 1981–2000 (including Nicaragua, Afghanistan, and Haiti). This book's cases end with the Clinton administration, before the events of 9-11-01. But for reasons that will be explained throughout, its basic thesis is confirmed and reinforced by American foreign policy since that day.

This work divides the world into *five geographic regions* in the periphery of the global political arena (Sullivan, 1996: 6–10). (It does *not* focus on the heart of the Cold War in central Europe or its attendant concerns about nuclear weapons and the two Super Powers.) Two regions are the historic areas of America's pre–World War II "manifest destiny": the Western Hemisphere and eastern Asia. Eleven cases are drawn from Latin America and the Caribbean, the traditional sphere of US capitalist penetration since 1823. Seven studies are from east Asia, a continent harder to dominate for obvious geographic and demographic reasons, and the site of the two major wars (Korea and Vietnam), which will not be explicitly covered here.

Three other regions are identified as areas where the United States has, in the years since 1945, replaced European imperialists as the dominant power. Five cases are in the "Middle Eastern" Islamic world, the first area after World War II where the United States supplanted British-French influence. Four studies are from Africa, a continent where deference was given to Europe during the first 30 years after decolonization, but where the United States has shown greater attention since the end of the Cold War. The final three examples are drawn from southern Europe, on the periphery of the continent that forms the core of the global capitalist system. The 30 cases are itemized in Table 1A in a way that correlates the cases and their regions to the chapters in which they will be covered in this book.

Some of these cases are famous episodes whose main details are widely known and in which this narrative will stress interpretations; others are relatively obscure, and their basic facts will need to be elaborated. These two categories roughly relate to levels of intervention: those in the left column of Table 1B often involving significant force and presidential declarations of policy, those on the right being fuzzier and more covert.

## MAIN THESES

The main thesis of this work is that the primary *strategic* goal of the United States since 1945 has been to supplant the major imperial powers of the pre–World War II era—United Kingdom, France, Germany, and Japan—as the sole economic hegemon of the global capitalist system (Gilbert

**Table 1**
**Rise of the Global Hegemon: Fifty Years of US Foreign Policy in the Periphery: The 30 Cases**

### A. 30 Numbered Cases, divided by Regions and Text Chapters

| | Europe | Middle East | Africa | Asia | Western Hemisphere |
|---|---|---|---|---|---|
| | 1. Greece 47-49 | | | | |
| Ch. 1 | 2 . Italy 48 | | | 3. Philippines 46-53 | |
| Ch. 2 | | 4. Iran 53 | | | 5. Guatemala 54 |
| | | 6. Lebanon 58 | | | |
| | | | 7. Congo 60-65 | | 8. Cuba 61 |
| | | | | 10. Laos 63-73 | 9. British Guiana 62 |
| Ch. 3 | | | | 11. S. Vietnam 61-64 | 12. Brazil 64 |
| | | | | 14. Indonesia 65-66 | 13. Dom. Rep. 65 |
| | | 16. Kurdistan 71-75 | | 15. Cambodia 70 | 17. Chile 73 |
| Ch. 4 | | | 18. Angola 75 | 19. Australia 75 | |
| | | | | 20. East Timor 75 | |
| Ch. 5 | - - - No Interventions during Carter Administration - - - | | | | |
| | | | | | 21. El Salv. 79-91 |
| Ch. 6 | | | | | 22. Nicaragua 81-88 |
| | | 25. Afghanistan 80-88 | 24. Libya 81-86 | | 23. Grenada 83 |
| | | 27. Iraq 91 | | | 26. Panama 89 |
| Ch. 7 | 30. Yugo. 95, 99 | | 28. Somalia 92-94 | | 29. Haiti 94 |
| | n=3 | n=5 | n=4 | n=7 | n=11 |

### B. 30 Cases divided by Familiarity

| Famous (Familiar Cases) | Obscure (Less Familiar Cases) |
|---|---|
| Greece - 1947-49 civil war | Italy - 1948 election rigging |
| Iran - 1953 CIA coup | Philippines - 1946-53 counterinsurgency |
| Guatemala - 1954 govt. overthrow | Congo - 1961-65 civil war |
| Lebanon - 1958 military intervention | British Guiana - 1961-66 independence delay |
| South Vietnam -1961-65 aid, coup, deceit | Laos - 1961-73 secret war |
| Cuba -1961 Bay of Pigs invasion | Brazil - 1964 coup |
| Dominican Republic -1965 military intervention | Indonesia - 1965-66 Year Living Dangerously |
| Cambodia - 1970 incursion | Kurdistan - 1971-75 missionary work |
| Chile - 1973 overthrow of government | Angola - 1975 civil war |
| Nicaragua - 1981-88 contra war | Australia - 1975 parl. govt. ouster |
| Grenada - 1983 rescue of students | East Timor - 1975 genocide |
| Panama -1989 drug lord capture | El Salvador- 1979-92 counterinsurgency |
| Iraq - 1991 liberation of Kuwait | Afghanistan - 1981-88 support for *jihad* |
| Haiti - 1994 reinstall democratic govt. | Libya - 1981-86 bombings |
| Yugoslavia - 1995 Bosnia & 1999 Kosovo | Somalia - 1992-94 nation-building |
| n=15 | n=15 |

and Joris, 1981: 7; Tucker and Hendrickson, 1992: 2–6). This generally meant America's competing against the Soviet Union over which of the two post–World War II Super Powers would succeed Western Europe and Japan as leader of the *"Third World"* of developing nations in the Middle East, Africa, Asia, and the Western Hemisphere. (This thesis is only secondarily applicable in Latin America, where US hegemony began in the nineteenth century and is merely *consolidated* during the period covered in this work.)

A corollary to this thesis (which relates primarily to politics) is another pertaining more specifically to *economics*. The US objective, in most of the

30 cases, has primarily been to make the world safe *not* for democracy (as is often claimed), but rather to make the world safe for capital (Girling, 1980: 110–13; Kolko, 1988: 291–92; Shalom, 1993: 7). This is especially true in the periphery of the global capitalist system, where there is opportunity for the greatest economic growth and profit, and for demonstrations of the superiority of the system. To this end, US interventions in several of the 30 cases (e.g., the former French Indochina, the ex-Belgian Congo, British Guiana, 1990s Yugoslavia) are not limited to the protection of *specific* business investments of *American* corporations, but rather to upholding the economic system, the idea of capitalism itself.

In defense of this policy, it is often argued that safeguarding capitalism in a developing nation sometimes leads to an improved quality of life for a small number of local capitalists and some upper-middle-class managers and *in the long run* to democracy (or at least to "electoral" or "procedural" democracy). In the short run, however, economic hegemony by nations of the core over those in the periphery—a continuing goal in this current era of globalization and "war on terror"—leads to control not only of the weaker states' economic systems but of their politics as well. For many of the states to be studied here, the political systems that have been promoted to preserve capitalism range from one-party rule and military dictatorship to monarchies, colonies, and recurring civil wars (Chomsky and Herman, 1979: 3–4).

Table 2 summarizes these strategic and economic theses, and how they are reflected in each of the 30 cases.

## OTHER PATTERNS AND THEMES

In addition to these two theses, a number of patterns and themes are related to the methods and personalities involved in American foreign policy in the cases analyzed here.

Among the noteworthy *methods* adopted by the United States in its interventions are some that were nefarious and others that were more subtle.

The most notorious methods (Halperin et al., 1976: 3, 6–7; Nutter, 1999: 73–93; Langguth, 1978) include overt military interventions or, less politely, invasions entailing US combat troops in hostile situations (n = 10 cases on Table 3a); the provoking of coups resulting in the military takeover of government (n = 10); attempts at assassination of foreign leaders (n = 9); and the tolerance of overkill, sometimes to the point of genocide, by some of America's surrogates (n = 9).

Perhaps the most common example of this category (not shown in Table 3) is taking sides in civil wars with military arms and advisors. In nine countries covered in this book, this involved aiding *antigovernment* forces in efforts that could be described as state-sponsored terrorism on the part of the United States (the Miami Cuban exiles, the secret armies in Laos,

Table 2

Cases vs. Main Theses

| Case | a. Strategic (ex-colonial power replaced) | b. Economic (capitalism>democracy; non-democratic political form promoted) |
|---|---|---|
| 1. Greece '47-49 | UK | monarchists & fascists supported along with democrats; but only military in 1967-74 |
| 2. Italy '48 | Germany; (+UK, SU, '43) | 1-CDP-party dominant government, 1948-93 |
| 3. Philippines '46-53 | - - - | CIA-influenced elections, 1953-61; Marcos dictatorship, 1972-86 |
| 4. Iran '53 | UK, Russia | absolute monarchy of Shah Mohammed Reza Pahlavi, 1953-79 |
| 5. Guatemala '54 | - - - | military dictators, '59-85; Dulles law firm & United Fruit Co. key actors in '54 coup |
| 6. Lebanon '58 | France (+ UK in Suez) | ethnic-based managed democracy keeps capitalism in Christian control for 17 more yrs. |
| 7. Congo '61-65 | Belgium | Mobutu military dictatorship, 1965-97, yields klepto-capitalism |
| 8. Cuba '61 | (defends vs. USSR) | n.a. (US unsuccessful) |
| 9. British Guiana '61-66 | UK | ethnic-minority 1-party dominant government, 1966-92 |
| 10. Laos '61-73 | France | *troika* neutralist government has few democrats |
| 11. S. Vietnam '61-65 | France | Diem & later military leaders (Ky, Thieu) protect (primarily French) capital, 1954-75 |
| 12. Brazil '64 | - - - | military dictatorships, 1965-85; capitalist "economic miracle" |
| 13. Dom. Rep. '65 | - - - | civil war to restore crony capitalist Balaguer, 22 of next 30 yrs. (over elected soc.-dem. Bosch) |
| 14. Indonesia '65-66 | Netherlands | Suharto military dictatorship, 1966-98; crony capitalism |
| 15. Cambodia '70 | France | Lon Nol milit. dictatorship, '70-75; provokes civil war that brings *Khmer Rouge* genocide |
| 16. Kurdistan '71-75 | UK, Russia (see #4) | Shah of Iran, civil war in Iraq, preferred over self-determination (democracy) for Kurds |
| 17. Chile '73 | - - - | Pinochet military dictatorship, 1973-89; alleged "economic miracle" |
| 18. Angola '75 | Portugal | civil war, from 11/75 independence until 11/01 death of US's Savimbi |
| 19. Australia '75 | UK | elected government ousted, parliamentary democracy undermined, for US "security" interests |
| 20. East Timor '75 | Portugal | Indonesian "colony" preferred over self-determination (democracy) for Timorese |
| 21. El Salvador '79-91 | - - - | "progressive" juntas and "demonstration-elections" democracy |
| 22. Nicaragua '81-88 | - - - | civil war, 1981-88; subversion of 1984 election |
| 23. Grenada '83 | UK | n.a. (quick, one-year, transition to democracy) |
| 24. Libya '81,'86 | Italy; UK; USSR | n.a. (US unsuccessful) |
| 25. Afghanistan '80-88 | Russia, UK | civil war visited upon pre-industrial economy, 1980-88ff |
| 26. Panama '89 | - - - | n.a. (democracy restored after drug thug Noriega tolerated, 1981-89) |
| 27. Iraq '91 | UK | Kuwait monarchy upheld for Western capital |
| 28. Somalia '92-94 | UK, Italy; USSR | n.a. (US unsuccessful; civil war not ended in pre-industrial economy) |
| 29. Haiti '94 | - - - | Aristide's full term cut to make way for more pliant Preval |
| 30. Yugoslav.'95,'99 | USSR/Russia | ethnically partitioned, one-party nationalist govts. welcoming capitalist reconstruction |

- - - = not applicable (W. Hemisph., Phil. I.)

n.a. = not applicable (n=5: Cuba, Grenada, Libya, Panama, Somalia) the secessionists in Indonesia, the Kurdish insurgents in Iraq, the Union for the Total Independence of Angola, the Nicaraguan *contras,* the *muja-hedeens* in Iran and Afghanistan, and the Kosovo Liberation Army). In eight other cases, the United States helped existing governments, some-times in civil wars involving brutal counterinsurgency campaigns (Greece, the Philippines, Guatemala, the Congo, South Vietnam, Cambodia, El Sal-vador, and Indonesia [vs. East Timor]).

Among the less violent, though still dubious, tactics were manipulation of the constitutional relationship between head of state, head of govern-ment, and the legislative branch (n = 8 cases on Table 3b); and tampering with electoral processes (n = 9). Finally, in almost all cases, military and economic development aid has been used for narrow political gains; among the most blatant examples of this practice are the 19 noted in the third column of Table 3b.

Among the *personalities* encountered in these 30 cases, two themes emerge. One is the use of unsavory characters, or "thugs," as junior part-ners in many of the interventions. These span the spectrum from collab-orators with World War II Axis powers or with European colonial administrations (n = 6 on Table 4a) to CIA agents or informants who were, or became, among their countries' leaders (n = 14) to drug traffick-ers (n = 4). These examples are all part of a policy of preferring dictator-ships over democracies (n = 14), a corollary of the broader thesis involving capitalism, and a recognition of the unhappy means often needed to ensure the survival of America's preferred economic system in its peripheral re-gions (Lafeber, 1999).

A second theme relates to dealings with recalcitrant Third World leaders, or "pests." The most common technique was to defame disfavored leaders as "crazy," "unstable," "Hitler-like," and so forth. See the adjectives applied to 17 such leaders in the first column on Table 4b. Others became expend-able; either they were uppity American clients who had to be taught a harsh lesson (presumably as instruction for others), sometimes simply out of US presidential pique, or they were hapless, weak states or peoples who had to be sacrificed to larger strategic goals (n = 18).

Tables 3 and 4 are presented as a guide to the methods and personalities discussed in the cases cited.

It might also be noted that in most of these 30 cases there has been a reluctance by the United States to accept any "third way" in these devel-oping nations between left-wing "socialist nationalists" and right-wing "unreconstructed fascists" (Feinberg, 1983: 106–09; Gurtov, 1974: 202–07; Kwitny, 1984: 387–90). Transnational corporations, not governments, must organize these Third World economies; alternate models of development are rejected as not congenial to global capital. Not acceptable under this formula are social-democratic reformers with mixed economies where some private property is respected, and moderate capitalist governments

# Table 3
## Methods Employed in US Interventions

### a. Notorious

| i. invasions, n=10 | ii. coups, n=10 | iii. assassination attempts, n=9 | iv. overkill, n=9 |
|---|---|---|---|
| Lebanon | Iran | Congo: Lumumba | Iran (SAVAK) |
| Cuba (supported) | Guatemala | Cuba: Castro | Guatemala (Rios Montt) |
| Dom. Rep. | Congo | SVN: Ngo Dinh Diem | Laos (most bombed in history) |
| Cambodia | Laos | Dom.Rep.: Trujillo | SVN (strategic hamlets) |
| Grenada | S. Vietnam | Chile: Schneider,Allende | Indonesia ("Year: '65-66") |
| Panama | Brazil | Libya: Qaddaffi | Cambodia (Pol Pot) |
| Iraq | Indonesia | Iraq: Saddam Hussein | Angola (longest, deadliest war) |
| Somalia | Cambodia | Somalia: Aideed | E. Timor (annexation, genocide) |
| Haiti | Chile | Yugoslavia: Milosevic | El Salvador (death squads) |
| Yugoslavia | El Salvador | | |

### b. Subtle

| i. constitution manipulate, n=8 | ii. election tampering, n=9 | iii. political use of aid, n=19 | |
|---|---|---|---|
| Iran | Italy | Greece | Italy |
| Lebanon | Philippines | Philippines | Guatemala |
| Congo | British Guiana | Egypt | Congo |
| Laos | Dom. Rep. | British Guiana | Laos |
| Cambodia | Chile | S. Vietnam | Brazil |
| Chile | El Salvador | Indonesia | Cambodia |
| Australia | Nicaragua | Chile | El Salvador |
| Grenada | Haiti | Grenada | Panama |
| | Yugoslavia | Iraq (Coalition) | Haiti |
| | | Somalia | |

# Table 4
## Personalities Involved in US Interventions

### a. "Thugs" as Junior Partners

| i. collaborators, n=6 | ii. CIA "assets," n=14 | iii. drug traffickers, n=4 | iv. dictators, n=14 |
|---|---|---|---|
| Greece | Greece ('67-74 military) | Laos | Greece, '67-74 |
| Italy | Italy (CDPers, Andreotti, etc.) | Nicaragua (contras) | Philippines, '72-86 |
| Congo | Philippines (Macapagal, Magsaysay) | Afghanistan | Iran, '53-79 |
| Laos | Iran (Shah) | Panama | Guatemala, '59-84 |
| Indonesia | Guatemala (Castillo Armas) | | Congo, '65-97 |
| Croatia | Fertile Crescent (Jordan King) | | S. Vietnam, '54-75 |
| | Congo (Mobutu) | | Guyana, '66-91 |
| | Laos (Gen. Phoumi Nosavan) | | Brazil, '65-85 |
| | S. Vietnam (Conein collabators) | | Indonesia, '66-99 |
| | Chile (1970 coupsters) | | Cambodia, '71-75ff |
| | Australia (Gov. Gen. Kerr) | | Kurdistan (see Iran) |
| | Afghanistan (mujahedeen) | | Chile, '73-89 |
| | Panama (Noriega) | | E. Timor (see Indonesia) |
| | Haiti (Constant) | | Iraq (Kuwait, '91ff) |

### b. "Pests" to be Dealt With

| i. crazies, n=17 | | ii. expendables, n=18 | |
|---|---|---|---|
| weepy Mossadegh | communist Arbenz | Greece's Papandreou, left | Italy's Andreotti |
| long-winded, bearded Castro | labor leader Jagan | Phil.'s Marcos (after '86) | Christian Lebanese post- '76 |
| remote Ngo Dinh Diem | neurotic Qadros | Guyanese South Asians | non-Pathet Lao |
| communist sympathizer Bosch | immoral Sukarno | SVN's Diem, '63 | Dom. Rep.'sTrujillo, 5/61 |
| mercurial Sihanouk | incompetent Allende | "sideshow" Cambodians | Kurds, '75 and '91 |
| designer-glassed Ortega | "mad dog" Qaddaffi | Tshombe,'64; Mobutu,'97 | UNITA's Savimbi |
| drug-kingpin Noriega | Hitler Saddam Hussein | E. Timor, '76-99 | Afghan mujaheddin |
| warlord Aideed | defrocked Aristide | Nicaraguan contras | Panama's Noriega |
| war criminal Milosevic | | Haiti's Cedras, Constant | Yugoslavia's Kosovars |

sympathetic to labor unions or the poor (in the form of food subsidies or significant spending for health and education). Welfare must have a lower priority than repayment of international debt, or spending on infrastructure to entice investment from countries of the core.

It is a major contention of this study that these themes and patterns (of preferring right over center, embracing dubious personalities, and employing nefarious means) may have resulted in some short-term US foreign policy successes but nearly always have proved tragic for the local societies affected. Table 5 summarizes this conclusion for all 30 cases. Terrible disasters have been visited upon the local societies targeted by US interventions in about 26 of the 30 cases (all except Grenada, Libya, Panama, and Somalia). These range from the "mere" loss of democracy to the consolidation of authoritarianism where it was already the rule. In addition, more than 500 years of local politics have been stalled, interrupted, or diverted from their logical direction. Finally, in almost all instances, the overwhelming military technology accompanying American interventions into wars led to disproportionate destruction of life in these developing societies.

The left-hand column of Table 5 notes the losses of democracy, and (in italics) the *years of disruption* from the paths of more normal politics had the United States not intervened. These years range from less than 10 in three instances (Haiti 3, Greece 7, Nicaragua 8) to more than 30 years for five countries (Indonesia 32, Congo 38 +, Cuba 42 +, Italy 45, Iran 51 +; the " + " indicates the lack of democracy continues beyond the year 2003).

The right-hand side of Table 5 (wars, related *deaths*, etc.) totes up 28 instances (not including Italy and Australia) where US intervention either caused, or prolonged and exacerbated, almost 200 years of war involving several million deaths. To be sure, the United States does not bear primary accountability for some of these wars and deaths (five are exempted from the totals that follow: the two mentioned earlier in this paragraph, plus Lebanon, Kurdistan and Bosnia [not Kosovo]), but a case could be made for serious shared US responsibility for death tolls in the following ranges:

**0–900 deaths: Cuba 100, Grenada 100, Guyana 300, Libya 300, Brazil 500**　　　　　5 at 1,300

**1,000–99,000: Somalia 1,000, Panama 3,000, Chile 3,000, Dominican Republic 3,000, Haiti 4,500, Kosovo 10,000, Iran 21,000, Nicaragua 30,000, Philippine Islands 44,000, El Salvador 75,000**　　　　　10 at 194,000

**100,000–500,000: Congo 100,000, Iraq 100,000, Cambodia 150,000, Greece 160,000, Guatemala 200,000, East Timor 200,000, Indonesia 500,000**　　　　　7 at 1.4 million

**1–2 million: Angola 1 million, Afghanistan 2 million, South Vietnam and Laos 2 million**　　　　　4 at 5 million

**Total: 26 states with approximately 6.6 million deaths**

**Table 5**

**Cases vs. Local Disasters due to US Interventions**

| | i. loss of democracy/# yrs. politics disrupted (thru 2003) | *deferrals* | ii. wars, # deaths(=d.) |
|---|---|---|---|
| 1. Greece '47-49 | success until . . . . | *'67-74 mil. dictatorship=7 yrs.*| 160,000 d. in '45-49 civil war |
| 2. Italy '48 | 1-party-dominat CDP regime, 1948-93 = 45 yrs. | | NA |
| 3. Philippines '46-53 | CIA in elections, '53, '61 | *Marcos dictatorship,'72-86 = 14 yrs.* | 9,000 d. in '50-52, 35,000 d. in '69-86 |
| 4. Iran '53 | monarch, '53-79, Islamic Fund. rule, '79ff = 51+ yrs. | | 1,300 d. in '53; 20,000 d. in '78-79 |
| 5. Guatemala '54 | military rule, 1959-84 = 25 yrs. | | 200,000 d. in '61-96 (35-yr.) civil war |
| 6. Lebanon '58 | Christian rule artificially prolonged, '58-75 = 17 yrs. | *1975-91 civil war* | 150,000 d. in 16-yr. war |
| 7. Congo '61-65 | Mobutu, '65-97 + Kabilas, '97ff = 38+ yrs. | | 100,000 d. in '61-65 war; 2 million d. since 1998 |
| 8. Cuba '61 | Castro 1p-communist rule, '61ff=42+ yrs, but good qual. of life | | ~100 d. at Bay of Pigs |
| 9. Br. Guiana '61-66 | delay of independ., '62-66; 1-party minority rule, '66-92 = 30 yrs.. | | 300 d. in '63 strike, racial warfare |
| 10. Laos, '63-73 | Pathet Lao rule delayed, '62-75 = 13 yrs. | | most bombed country in history; 1 mill.d. or homeless |
| 11. S. Vietnam '61-65 | US-Indochina war, 1963/65-73/75 = 12 yrs. | | prelude to 10-yr.war, '65-75, with >2 million d. |
| 12. Brazil '64 | military dictatorships, 1965-85 = 20 yrs. | | ~500 dead or disappeared |
| 13. Dom. Rep. '65 | Trujillo's Balaguer, '66-78, '86-96 = 22 yrs. (of next 30) | | 3,000 d. in '65 |
| 14. Indonesia '65-66 | Suharto dictatorship, '66-98 = 32 yrs. | | 500,000 d. in '65-66 power transfer |
| 15. Cambodia '70 | end of stability, civil wars, 1970-98 = 28 yrs. | | 155,000 d. in '70-75; + 1.8 mill. d. in '75-79 |
| 16. Kurdistan '71-75 | loss of autonomy, 1975-91 = 16 yrs. | | ~200,000 d. in '74, '88 (especially), '91 |
| 17. Chile '73 | Gen. Pinochet dictatorship, '73-89 = 16 yrs. | | 1 mill. exiled, 3,000 d. in '73-74 |
| 18. Angola '74-75 | colonial war prolonged by US intervention into 1975-91 = 16 yrs. | | 1 mill. d. since 1975 |
| 19. Australia '75 | "normal" parl. govt. change removes Labor, '75-87 = 12 yrs. | | NA |
| 20. East Timor '75 | Indonesian colony, '75-99 = foreign rule for 24 yrs. | | 100,000 (of 600,000 pop.) d. in '75; + 2,000 d. in '99 |
| 21. El Salvador '79-91 | d'Aubuisson's ARENA rule succeeds CDP, 1986ff = 17+ yrs. | | 75,000 d. in '79-91 civil war |
| 22. Nicaragua '81-88 | contra v. Sandinista civil war, '81-88 = 8 yrs.(inclusive) | | 30,000 d. in '81-88 contra war. |
| 23. Grenada '83 | NO loss; in fact, improvement over Coard junta; and . . . | | "only" 100 d. |
| 24. Libya '81, '86 | ? Politics the same; 1986ff sanctions inconvenient only to elites | | < 50 d. before 259 in Pan Am 103 |
| 25. Afghanistan '81-88 | 1980-present civil war, occupation = 23+ yrs. | | 2 mill. d., 5 mill. refugees |
| 26. Panama '89 | NO, politics, democracy actually restored, but . . . | | 2,000-4,000 d. in "arrest" of Noriega |
| 27. Iraq '91 | Kuwait monarchy restored; '91ff sanctions consolidate Saddam | | 100,000 d. in war + 400,000+ d. fm. sanctions |
| 28. Somalia '92-94 | ? civilians fed, but civil war continues, and . . . | *600,000 d. in Rwanda, '94* | ~1,000 d. in US ops. |
| 29. Haiti '94 | Failure to oust '91-94 junta = 3 yrs. with . . . | | 4,500 d. |
| 30. Yugoslavia '95, '99 | ethnic-split Bosn. '95; autonom. Kosovo, '99, democ. Yugo., '00 | | 200,000 d in Bosnia, 10,000 d. in Kosovo |
| SUMMARY | NO/? = 4 (Grenada, Libya, Panama, Somalia) | *deferred = 4 (Greece, Phil., Lebanon, Somalia/Rwanda)* | NA = 2 (Italy, Australia) |
| TOTALS | >500 yrs, disrupted politics, including . . . | | ~180 yrs. exacerbated war, ~6,600,000 deaths |

Despite these appalling levels of death, destruction, and disruption related to American diplomacy, many of these interventions did not even result in any gains for US foreign policy. In about a third of the cases to be discussed—Guatemala, Iran, Cuba, Lebanon, Laos, South Vietnam, Cambodia, Chile, Libya, Somalia—it will be argued in the text that follows that American action actually produced long-term diplomatic losses.

In short, US foreign policy in the periphery of the global capitalist system in these 30 cases may have succeeded in securing the United States as hegemonic successor to earlier imperialist powers. However, it has been at a tremendous cost, especially for the societies besieged by American belligerence, and in lesser measure for the United States itself.

## REGIONAL PERSPECTIVES

### Europe (introduced in Chapter 1), n = 3 Cases

The case studies in this book will begin and end in Europe, the site where America's Cold War involvement in international politics started and where (until the "war on terrorism") the most recent post–Cold War military intervention occurred.

Chapter 1 covers the launching of the Cold War in 1947 with the "Truman Doctrine's" military aid in the Greek civil war, followed a year later by the CIA's not-so-covert collusion in the Italian elections of 1948. America's intervention expands in form and intensity as the Cold War moves to other regions around the globe over the next 40 years. Greece and Italy can be regarded as being on the Mediterranean periphery of Europe. The heart of the Cold War was in central Europe where the Berlin Wall and the "Iron Curtain" divided the continent into its Eastern and Western ideologies and spheres of influence. Greece and Italy, in southern Europe, are not on the fault line between the US and USSR military deployments during the Cold War. So the American military presence in them during the Cold War (unlike its bases in Germany, France, or the United Kingdom) was more akin to those to be analyzed in the other areas of the periphery of the global capitalist system.

In keeping with the thesis that US intervention is more about promotion of its place as hegemon of the global capitalist system, and only secondarily defensive vis-a-vis Soviet expansion, this book ends with Chapter 7's case studies of interventions in Bosnia and Kosovo, long after the demise of the USSR.

### Asia (introduced in Chapter 1), n = 7 Cases

The seven studies in Asia center around the containing of Communist China, culminating in the eight-year-long major war by the United States against (North) Vietnam, 1965–73. Lesser episodes related to that conflict are covered in the cases of Laos, South Vietnam, and Cambodia, in Chapters 3 and 4.

Further afield, but tangentially related to the same effort, are the cases involving the Philippines, Indonesia, East Timor, and Australia (in Chapters 1, 3, and 4). The "Vietnam Syndrome" kept the United States away from provocative military activity on the periphery of China in the years after 1975.

## Middle East (introduced in Chapter 2), n = 5 Cases

The Middle East will be defined here as that geographic region from Egypt into southwest Asia, where the most significant political issues are dominated by Islam. Three of this text's five Middle Eastern cases (in Chapters 2, 4, and 6) focus on Iran, Iraq, and the unfortunate Kurdish nation between these two states.

The intervention into Lebanon in Chapter 2 introduces the reader to the fertile crescent subregion of the Middle East, but the biggest conflict in this area (the Israel-Palestine dispute) is not a focus, for it is considered sui generis and has involved more diplomatic than forceful American attentions. Finally, Afghanistan (Chapter 6), often classified as part of South Asia, is considered Middle Eastern here because of the significance of Islam in America's involvement in its civil war and the subsequent 9-11-01 "blowback."

## Western Hemisphere (introduced in Chapter 2), n = 11 Cases

It is in the Western Hemisphere where the historic American policies of neo-colonialism and regime change are most in evidence. Long before the Cold War, the United States had established a record of intervening in the countries of Latin America and the Caribbean, toppling governments, installing friendly clients, and then withdrawing. Between 1890 and 1935, this occurred 38 times before President Franklin D. Roosevelt initiated the "Good Neighbor" policy, in pursuit of assuring the Pan-American republics' placement on the side of the United States in the upcoming war against Germany.

The first such return to more typical historic practice after World War II occurred in Guatemala in 1954 (Chapter 2). By this time, the Cold War had become globalized and the United States had the perfect excuse (containment of communism) for renewed intervention. In the next eight involvements (in Cuba, British Guiana, Brazil, Dominican Republic, Chile, El Salvador, Nicaragua, and Grenada), the anti-communist explanation was never far from the surface. But Chapter 7's moves into Panama and

Haiti required new justifications, and in reversion to America's historic role, they were readily found.

### Africa (introduced in Chapter 3), n = 4 Cases

Africa has been the continent of least American interest. For long periods of the time under consideration in this book, it was virtually ceded to Western European imperial powers (especially Britain and France) in a kind of Cold War division-of-labor vis-a-vis the USSR. But in two states with significant natural resources and weaker European colonial control—Congo and Angola—the United States has been more deeply involved since 1960 (Chapters 3 and 4).

There are also two rather insignificant Islamic countries in northern Africa (Libya and Somalia) which became the focus of American attention owing to the particular personal predilections of two US presidents (Reagan and Bush, in Chapters 6 and 7, respectively).

### POST-9-11 THOUGHTS

Much of *American Adventurism Abroad* was completed before the events of 9-11-01. Since that time it has become conventional wisdom that the world has changed and international politics will never again be the same. Indeed, the George W. Bush administration has done its utmost to create a new paradigm for American foreign policy, including a novel strategic doctrine of preemptive war, and a restructuring of government comparable to that at the start of the Cold War. The latter even includes a Department of Homeland Security, exposing the pretense that the Department of "Defense" was for something other than the projection of global power.

Thus, the basic thesis concerning American intervention in the Third World remains valid. The United States still aspires to be the global hegemon. Only the name of the enemy has been changed. Instead of "fighting communism," the U.S. is engaged in a "war against terrorism." Both of these rubrics, this book would assert, are essentially cover stories for a policy of global power projection in pursuit of world hegemony.

It remains to be seen whether the initial overwhelming support within the United States for the "war on terror" lasts as long as the bipartisan consensus for fighting communism did (about 20 years without discernible elite dissent until it broke over Vietnam). To date, the United States has not been as successful in getting state support for the "war on terror" in numbers comparable to the more than 50 partners in NATO (North Atlantic Treaty Organization), SEATO (Southeast Asia Treaty Organization), CENTO (Central Treaty Organization), and other alliances who formally embraced the "war on communism."

Accordingly, not many of this book's main themes regarding global hegemony and power projection have been affected. Its catalog of patterns and themes, methods and personalities adopted in pursuit of these goals remain viable as guides to American foreign policy today and in the future.

## INTRODUCTION BIBLIOGRAPHY

Blechman, Barry, and Stephen Kaplan. 1978. *Force without War: US Armed Forces as a Political Instrument.* Washington, DC: Brookings Institution.

Blum, William. 1995. *Killing Hope: US Military and CIA Interventions since World War II.* Monroe, ME: Common Courage Press.

Chomsky, Noam, and Edward S. Herman. 1979. *The Political Economy of Human Rights, vol. 1: The Washington Connection and Third World Fascism.* Boston: South End Press.

Feinberg, Richard E. 1983. *The Intemperate Zone: The Third World Challenge to United States Foreign Policy.* NY: W. W. Norton.

Gilbert, Tony, and Pierre Joris. 1981. *Global Interference: The Consistent Pattern of American Foreign Policy.* London: Liberation Press.

Girling, J. L. S. 1980. *America and the Third World: Revolution and Intervention.* Boston: Routledge, Keegan, and Paul.

Gurtov, Melvin. 1974. *The United States against the Third World: Antinationalism and Intervention.* NY: Praeger.

Halperin, Morton M., J. Berman, Robert Borosage, and C. Marwick (eds.). 1976. *The Lawless State: Crimes of the U.S. Intelligence Agencies.* NY: Penguin Books.

Kolko, Gabriel. 1988. *Confronting the Third World: United States Foreign Policy, 1945–1980.* Berkeley: University of California Press.

Kwitny, Jonathan. 1984. *Endless Enemies: The Making of an Unfriendly World.* NY: Penguin Books.

Lafeber, Walter. 1999. "The Tension between Democracy and Capitalism during the American Century," *Diplomatic History,* 23(2), Spring: 263–84.

Langguth, A. J. 1978. *Hidden Terrors.* NY: Pantheon Books.

Nutter, John Jacob. 1999. *The CIA's Black Operations: Covert Action, Foreign Policy, and Democracy.* Amherst, NY: Prometheus Books.

Shalom, Stephen R. 1993. *Imperial Alibis: Rationalizing US Intervention after the Cold War.* Boston: South End Press.

Sullivan, Michael J., III. 1996. *Comparing State Polities: A Framework for Analyzing 100 Governments.* Westport, CT: Greenwood Press.

Treverton, Gregory F. 1987. *Covert Action: The Limits of Intervention in the Post-War World.* NY: Basic Books.

Tucker, Robert W., and David C. Hendrickson. 1992. *The Imperial Temptation: The New World Order and America's Purpose.* NY: Council of Foreign Relations.

# PART I

# The Early Years: Embracing a New Role, 1945–60

Part I of *American Adventurism Abroad* covers the 15 years of American diplomacy after its ascendance to paramountcy in the periphery of the global capitalist world following the dropping of two atomic bombs to end World War II in August 1945. It introduces presidents Harry S Truman and Dwight D. Eisenhower and the two foreign policy "doctrines" that become associated with their names, as the United States moved to replace the UK and France as hegemon of the international capitalist system in such places as Greece, Iran, Suez, and Lebanon.

It describes how the United States moved from a political-economic form of containment of the USSR in Europe, to a more militarized type of containment of communism around the world. It raises the first questions as to whether the containment policy was used as a cover for a more robust replacing of the imperialist nations of Western Europe as sustainer of world capitalism in distant places beyond the main arena of the Cold War in central Europe.

Chapter 1 analyzes three cases under President Truman (1945–53) with an eye to showing the United States had designs on an expanded military presence on the periphery of Europe as early as 1943 (Italy), and laid the groundwork for a continuation of its imperial presence in Asia by granting a neo-colonial form of independence to the Philippines in 1946. The civil war in Greece provided the rationale for linking these two, and future, expansions under an ideological umbrella that virtually stifled all discussion of the matter in domestic politics for a generation.

Chapter 2 elucidates three episodes in the Eisenhower administration (1953–61), two of which (Iran and Lebanon) bring the United States into a new region, the Middle East, as successor hegemon in two areas of historic British and French imperialism. The third case (Guatemala) shows the United States consolidating its traditional role as dominant power in Latin America, but now under the new rubric of anti-communism.

By the end of 1960, the United States had established for itself a global presence, with a string of multilateral military organizations (OAS [Organization of American States], NATO, CENTO, and SEATO), as well as a number of smaller and bilateral alliances, which resulted in a circling of the "Sino-Soviet bloc" with American military bases from Canada, Iceland and Norway in the north Atlantic, around the Eur-Asian landmass through Turkey, Pakistan, and Thailand, out into the off-shore Pacific island states of the Philippines and Japan. This was indeed a new role for a country that just 15 years earlier had finished a war into which it had been reluctantly drawn, and from which it had briefly demobilized.

Part I, Chapters 1 and 2, covers 16 years, two presidencies and six cases, and provides introductions to four of the five regions of the world into which this book is organized.

## CHAPTER 1

# From World War II to the Cold War: The Truman Years, 1945–52

## INTRODUCTION

President Harry S Truman presided over the shifting of American foreign policy from World War II to the Cold War. After atomic-annihilating 200,000 civilians and obliterating two Japanese cities to bring a quick end to the war in 1945, the United States stood virtually unchallenged in global political paramountcy (Alperovitz, 1965). The other alleged "winners" of World War II—the UK, France, the USSR, and China—were physically devastated from five, six, or seven (in the case of China) years of war fought on their territories. The US military and industrial might was virtually unscathed, and practically supreme vis-a-vis any putative competitors. Indeed, as a result of its wartime mobilization, America was also in an absolutely stronger power position than when it entered the world war (late) less than four years earlier in 1941.

Within two years, however, a worthy foe emerged to challenge any thoughts of America's succeeding to the regional hegemonic roles of the Great Powers that dominated international politics before World War II. The clash would come from the USSR and would be about influence in the former German-controlled areas of eastern Europe. As part of the wartime division-of-labor against the Nazis, the Soviet Union (at great cost of blood and treasure: 20 million lives) drove the Germans not only out of Russia but also out of Poland, Hungary, Czechoslovakia, and other lands in central Europe. At the end of the war, the USSR also controlled the eastern quarter of Germany.

The United States objected to the Soviet Union imposing its economic and political systems (of socialism and one-party communism) on these liberated/conquered territories, but was not in any military position to do much about it. US armies remained in the liberated/conquered lands of Britain, France, the BeNeLux countries and the western three-quarters of Germany where America's economic and political forms of governance (capitalism and democracy) were imposed (or restored). By 1946, an "Iron Curtain" (to quote the rejected ex–prime minister of Britain, Winston Churchill) had been drawn down the center of Europe.

It is in the outlying areas of southern Europe that the first case studies of *American Adventurism Abroad* will begin. After 1946, the aim of US foreign policy was to allow no successful examples of alternative economic-political systems to exist beyond the Soviet-controlled areas of central and eastern Europe (Bills, 1990; Woods and Jones, 2001). As successor to Britain as hegemon of the global capitalist system (soon to be known as the "free world"), the United States under Truman would become involved in war in Greece and elections in Italy. Pursuant to the policy under which it took these actions, America also became engaged in a counter-insurgency in the Philippines. By the start of the next decade it was on the verge of war with China on the mainland of Asia.

To accomplish this massive turn-around in diplomatic orientation from the isolationist country that had to be literally bombed into participating in World War II, the United States would after 1947 reorganize its governmental structure into a vast national security state (Hogan, 1998; Leffler, 1992; Yergin, 1997). In addition to integrating its army, navy, and air force into one fighting force under a single Department of "Defense," a special Atomic Energy Agency was created to manage its new nuclear-weapons capacity, and a Central Intelligence Agency was formed to carry out "other" (i.e., covert) activities for which the president wanted "deniability."

The rubric under which this historic expansion of American government and diplomacy occurred was the "Truman Doctrine," the first of six presidential doctrines under which the United States over the next 50 years would spread its global reach from southern Europe and offshore Asia to all corners of the earth.

## INTRODUCTION TO THE EUROPEAN REGION

The case studies in *American Adventurism Abroad* will begin in Europe, the focal point of the Cold War where the metaphorical "Iron Curtain" divided the continent into its Eastern and Western ideologies and Soviet and American spheres. But in keeping with this book's focus on the periphery of the global capitalist system, it will not cover the meeting of the US and USSR armies in central Europe at the end of World War II, nor the subsequent division of Germany and Austria into their respective capitalist and communist sectors. Rather, Chapter 1 will begin with case studies of Greece and Italy, two states on the outer edges of the European land mass.

Greece and Italy are Mediterranean countries in southern Europe, not on the fault line between the American and Soviet military deployments in either World War II or the Cold War. But it was there that United States took the first actions that laid down its marker as successor to the UK and France as hegemon of the capitalist world, and protector of the international economic system.

As early as July 10, 1943, with the landing of American troops in Italy, the United States began reconstructing the lands it conquered in World War II in its own image without consulting either of its main allies (the USSR or the UK) in the war against Germany, Italy, and Japan. The scene in the Academy Award–winning movie *Patton*, showing that American general's parading troops beating UK Field Marshal Bernard Montgomery's into Sicily captures well the US spirit of the time.

By 1947 the British, thoroughly devastated despite their "victory" in World War II, and on the verge of losing an empire "upon which the sun had not set" in more than 100 years, was virtually begging for the United States to take over its role as hegemon in Greece. It was here that the United States seized the opportunity to enunciate the rationale for its growing presence throughout the globe. It is also here, in Greece, that this study of America's adventures in the global periphery begins with the first of its 30 case studies.

## CASE 1. GREECE, 1947–49

The US replacement of the United Kingdom as hegemon of the global capitalist system began in 1947 with Britain's *inviting* of the United States to assume its imperial role in Greece. The UK had been the dominant power there since 1821 when it midwifed that tiny nation's secession from the Ottoman Empire. For the next 126 years, the respective royal families intermarried and the UK controlled its client state's politics and presided over a strategic outpost of the British Empire in the eastern Mediterranean.

This cozy situation came to an end in 1941 when Hitler invaded Greece, provoking a civil war between collaborating fascist Greeks, pro-UK monarchist Greeks (whose leadership largely fled the country with the UK), and communist Greeks (who, in cooperation with Tito's partisans in neighboring Yugoslavia, led the armed resistance to the Nazis). By October of 1944, this National Peoples Liberation Army (ELAS) had driven out the Germans, and its political wing, the National Liberation Front (EAM), was poised to take control of the country. At this point the UK returned and, pursuant to an agreement with its ally, the USSR, was given a free hand to move against the Greek communists and to re-establish a pro-

British government in this theater of the World War II. (In return, the UK ceded similar rights of wartime control to the Soviet Union in Bulgaria and Romania [Fleming, 1961: 183–85; Smith, 1950: 225–30].)

In the fall of 1946, after the UK had installed a hard-line anti-communist government in 1945, the Greek civil war restarted, only now there was a fourth party. In addition to the fascists, monarchists, and communists, there were some "freedom-loving democrats" who wanted a republic without the trappings of the crown. By February 1947, with these various forces fighting amongst themselves, the Greek communists, with their experienced ELAS armed wing, were once again on the verge of taking control and overthrowing the pro-UK regime. Thoroughly devastated by World War II, and under a new Labor Government no longer committed to empire, Britain was in no position to intervene to protect the government it had installed during World War II. It came to the United States to plea for a bailout.

President Harry S Truman realized it would be difficult to get support for a new foreign adventure less than two years after the end of World War II, and in the midst of a major demobilization from that war. Thus, he was advised to "scare the hell" out of the country to get it to believe that it faced a threat comparable to Hitler's Germany (Kofsky, 1993; McWilliams and Piotrowski, 2001: 47, note 9). He found this threat in the "communist menace," which by this time, in the form of the Red Army in eastern Europe, had installed pro-Soviet governments in the lands it had liberated from Germany in Poland, Hungary, Bulgaria, and Romania (Czechoslovakia did not become fully communist until 1948).

In a speech to a joint session of Congress on March 12, 1947, Truman provided the rationale not only for an immediate American intervention in the Greek civil war, but also for a generation of fighting communism throughout the world. According to this *"Truman Doctrine"*:

nearly every nation must choose between two alternative ways of life.... One way of life is based upon the will of the majority, and is distinguished by free institutions, representative government, free elections, guarantees of individual liberty, freedom of speech and religion, and freedom from political repression. The second way of life is based upon the will of a minority forcibly imposed upon the majority. It relies upon terror and oppression, a controlled press and radio, fixed elections, and the suppression of personal freedoms.

I believe it must be the policy of the United States to support free peoples who are resisting attempted subjugation by armed minorities or by outside pressures. I believe that we must assist free people to work out their destinies in their own ways. ("Text . . . ," 1947: 2)

In hindsight, this "doctrine," which dominated US diplomacy for the next generation deserves some deconstruction. First of all, designating this departure from traditional American foreign policy as a "doctrine" was designed to give it a degree of mathematical, or theological, certitude that it did not deserve. The situation in Greece (not to mention "nearly every" other nation in the world) was more muddled than Truman presented. As already noted, there were not just two sides in the Greek civil war, but three or four. But Truman had to oversimplify the situation for domestic political purposes. The Republicans who controlled the Congress would not have gone along with such a fundamental shift in policy unless they were sure public opinion was persuaded it was necessary (Williams, 1962: 269–70).

The stark division of the world into two (and only two) warring camps was recalled by President George W. Bush who, in rallying the nation after 9-11-01, similarly divided the world into "evil-doers" and those who would resist terrorism: "either you are with us, or you are with the terrorists" ("A Nation Challenged," 2001: B4). Such Manichean oversimplification is apparently deemed necessary in a democracy to get a largely apathetic people behind a major change in foreign policy involving national commitment to war.

The "free institutions" that Truman described had not been present in Greece for some time. The minority party there was not "forcibly" imposing its will upon the majority, but had led the struggle against German occupation, had a membership between 10 and 20 percent of the population and was supported by a significantly larger segment; it had particularly strong representation in trade unions, youth movements, cultural and sporting groups, and perhaps a plurality of the population in Piraeus, Salonika, and Macedonia (Woodhouse, 1976: 75–76, 153, 193).

Even if the ELAS could be characterized as an "armed minority" (one of four now fighting), what were the "outside pressures" to which Truman referred. The USSR, in particular, had a history of *not* involving itself in Greek affairs, as seen in the October 1944 spheres of influence agreement with the UK in which Stalin sold out the Greek Communists. Moreover, by 1947, the Soviet Union was straining to retain even a modicum of influence in Yugoslavia, a country with which it had much longer, and stronger, historical ties (Djilas, 1962: 164).

Two other sentences in Truman's description of the war in Greece also warrant analysis:

I believe that our help should be primarily through economic and financial aid which is essential to economic stability and orderly political processes. . . . If Greece should fall under the control of an armed minority, the effect upon its neighbor, Turkey, would be immediate and serious. Confusion and disorder might well spread throughout the entire Middle East. ("Text . . . ," 1947: 2)

Truman was asking Congress to appropriate $400 million from the Fiscal Year 1948 budget for "economic and financial" aid for use in the Greek civil war; (the total would come to about $1 billion before its successful end in October 1949). The US intervention would not involve any *combat* troops, but there were about 500 military personnel in the American Mission to Aid Greece (AMAG), an indication that the line between "economic" and "military" aid was blurry from the start (Rossides, 1998). As condition for receiving this aid, AMAG Administrator Dwight P. Griswold forced the three non-communist armed parties into a coalition government in September 1947, and frequent changes of prime minister thereafter. He, and the American Ambassador Lincoln McVeigh, also approved the detention of some 4,000 "dissidents" (Blum, 1995: 38; Iatrides, 1980). Wielding overwhelming financial leverage in an otherwise bankrupt country, the United States by November of 1947 was able to take control of Greece's "national budget, taxation, currency issuance, price and wage policies, state economic planning . . . imports and exports . . . foreign exchange . . . military reconstruction and relief" (Amen, 1978: 114–15).

Among the recipients of direct American aid in addition to the "freedom-loving democrats" and monarchists, was a secret army unit with more than 200 former Greek collaborators from a World War II Nazi Security Battalion (Simpson, 1988: 81–82; Blum, 1995: 35–37). AMAG also helped to create the KYP, the intelligence apparatus that infiltrated the government and the military. Inclusion of such actors among the recipients of US largess led to a positioning of Greek politics on the right of the political spectrum for at least a generation, poisoning relations between many left-of-center Greeks and the United States for many years. This alienation culminated during the period of the Greek military dictatorship, 1967–74 (Close, 1993). (See Postscript to Chapter 3.)

Another interesting aspect of the aid Truman requested was that it would be not only for Greece, but for Turkey as well! There was no civil war, nor even political instability in Turkey, a country that had maintained a steady and successful neutrality for most of World War II. But Truman's warning about the Greek war spreading "throughout the entire Middle East" planted the seeds for what later became known as the "domino theory." More to the point, the US military had long-standing plans for establishing listening posts (i.e., bases) in this country on the southern border of the USSR, and the war in Greece provided the opportunity to get them (Kuniholm, 1980: 408–14; Iatrides and Rizopoulos, 2000).

In any event, the American intervention turned the tide in the Greek civil war. The three non-communist sides joined together to defeat the ELAS in a bloody struggle with more than 150,000 deaths and 800,000 refugees (Wittner, 1982: 283). At relatively little cost for US (no American blood shed), a possible communist regime was thwarted, and the United States replaced Great Britain as the hegemon in the eastern Mediterranean. By end of the war in 1949, Greece was firmly in the US camp in what was by this time a thoroughly polarized Cold War world (see Introduction to East Asian Region at end of this Chapter). In 1950, Greece was one of only 15 states that sent troops to Korea to "provide cover" (i.e., legitimacy) for the US war there. In 1952, Greece and Turkey were added to the "North Atlantic" Treaty Organization of "Western" European states containing Soviet communism (Jones, 1989).

But in some respects the intervention in Greece had a downside in that it provided a "successful precedent" that could be invoked in later years in circumstances where similar happy results could *not* be reproduced. In this case, and in a similar intervention into Italian electoral politics in 1948 (CASE 2), the United States did not embrace exclusively the far-right wing of local forces, but rather included significant factions from the middle as well. However, in subsequent years, particularly after criticism regarding the "loss of China" to communism in 1949, American interventions were less sophisticated, more polarized, and ultimately, less successful.

If the US had not intervened and the ELAS had won the civil war, this left-leaning Greek government would not have owed the USSR anything and Greek politics might have taken a more normal, certainly a more independent, course. But such an outcome could not be tolerated in the new world that Truman had defined in 1947. The center-right government America created in 1949 drifted more to the right over the next years of the Cold War as ties with the military grew stronger, eventually resulting in a coup and a seven-year dictatorship, 1967–74 (see Postscript to Chapter 3).

## CASE 2. ITALY, 1948

Within weeks of the announcement of the "Truman Doctrine" on March 12, 1947, the United States moved to institutionalize its new policy in both domestic and international bureaucracies. A massive economic aid program, the Marshall Plan, was created for all of Western Europe on the model of the modest $400 million requested for Greece. By the end of its five-year term (Fiscal Years 1948 through 1952), some $23 billion (in today's dollars) was disbursed to regenerate capitalism in what had been the heart of the capitalist world before the destruction of the world war started in 1939.

At home, pursuant to the "Truman Doctrine," the National Security Act of July 1947 unified the Army, Navy, and Army Air Corps in to the Department of "Defense" to be housed in the new, largest office building in the world, the Pentagon. The military commands were integrated under the Joint Chiefs of Staff (JCS) and its Chairman. Most important for *American Adventurism Abroad*, a new Central Intelligence Agency was created to correlate the various military intelligence operations, and to perform "whatever other tasks" the president might deem necessary in the war against communism. Finally, a National Security Council (NSC) was established in the White House, under the direction of the National Security Advisor to the President, to coordinate the various new bureaucracies with each other and with the more traditional departments that dealt with foreign policy: State, Treasury, Commerce, and so forth (Prados, 1991).

Following the example in Greece, Marshall Plan aid in the western (American, British and French) sectors of divided Germany was contingent upon their political, economic, and currency unification. In reply to this, the Soviet Union, in June 1948, cut off overland routes into its zone of occupation in eastern Germany (which included the capital city, Berlin). In order to keep supplies, and Marshall Plan aid, flowing to the western sectors of the divided capital city, the Berlin Airlift was organized to fly over this blockade with food and supplies for the next 11 months (Shlaim, 1993). Related to this allied military activity, the North Atlantic Treaty was signed linking the United States, UK, and France to eight other capitalist countries in Western Europe: Belgium, Netherlands, and Luxembourg (which were forced to merge in to the BeNeLux customs union as a condition for receiving Marshall Plan aid), Canada, Iceland, Norway, Denmark, and Portugal. The latter state, it might be noted, was a military dictatorship (and only tangentially in the "North Atlantic"), undermining the claim that the anti-Soviet alliance was one of "democracy" versus communism. Capitalism, and Marshall Plan economic aid and investment, was the true glue that bound the nations of what came to be called "the West" (or more grandiloquently, the "free world"). Most significant for this case study, however, was the inclusion of Italy as the 12th charter member of the alliance.

The addition of United States and Canada to the 10 Western European countries was an effort at creating a new "North Atlantic" community. By 1949, the "treaty" had morphed into a permanent "organization" (NATO) with headquarters in Paris. By 1951, as a result of events in Asia described later in this chapter, the "North Atlantic" Treaty Organization had expanded to include Greece and Turkey in the eastern Mediterranean. The "dominoes" alluded to in CASE 1 had begun to fall, but they were not falling to Soviet communism, but rather under the sway of the new global hegemon from across the Atlantic. It is in this context that CASE 2, Italy, 1948, must be placed.

American intervention in Italy began in July 1943, with the landing of its army in Sicily during World War II. Two months later, the occupying US troops took the surrender from Field Marshall Pietro Badoglio's Fascist Grand Council (which had overthrown the dictator Mussolini). In a maneuver that set the precedent for later Soviet policy in Eastern Europe, the United States refused to share administration of this conquered enemy with its wartime ally, the USSR (Ambrose and Brinkley, 1997: 24–25). On the advice of Winston Churchill, the United States installed war hero Badoglio as head of the government along with Fascist collaborator King Victor Emmanuel III as head of state. It also used the existing Italian army and declined to work through a leftist worker-peasant resistance movement, with thousands of armed partisans, which had held down six German divisions and liberated the north of Italy (Milan, etc.) before the United States had arrived in Rome (Kolko, 1968: ch. 2; Mammarella, 1966: 81–83; Chomsky, 1996: 14–15).

In short, the first territorial expansion of the Cold War was perpetrated by the United States as it established the pattern of excluding other allies from shared administration of occupied territories, a policy that Soviet Union replicated in Poland and eastern Europe, and United Kingdom adopted in Greece. More than 12,000 American troops are still in Italy to this day, although the "occupying forces" of World War II were converted long ago into "NATO military allies." Whatever the status, the US presence was instrumental in ensuring that the first independent post-war government in Italy would be in the western camp (Harper, 1986: 39).

The first free Italian national election after World War II was scheduled for April 18, 1948, and the campaign was conducted under the watchful eye of the US occupation forces (Hughes, 1979: 147). There were three main political parties: the Christian Democratic Party (CDP) under Alcide de Gasperi; the Italy Socialist Party (PSI) led by Pietro Nenni; and the Italian Communist Party (PCI) under Palmiro Togliatti; (the US Occupation Authority had outlawed the Fascist Party.) The two left-of-center parties were quite popular in the political context of 1946–48. Italian food production was two-thirds of what it was before the war; its Gross National Product was one-half of that in 1938. The left's program of recognizing workers' rights, and aiding small and medium businesses in preference to concentrated heavy industries, was appealing to many. In the June 1946 referendum that abolished the monarchy and established a republic, the vote for the constituent assembly resulted in the PSI getting 20.7 percent of the vote, and the PCI 18.9 percent. A grand coalition government was formed under the leadership of the CDP Prime Minister de Gasperi whose party got 35.1 percent of the vote (Mammarella, 1966: 116). Within a year, however, with the United States threatening to withhold some $418 million in food aid, the two left-wing parties were dismissed from the government (Mammarella, 1966: 117–18). The Christian Democrats were then promptly rewarded with a $100 million loan (tied to purchases from the United States), and the cancellation of the nation's $1 billion debt to the United States (Blum, 1995: 29; Kolko and Kolko, 1972: 151).

In preparation for the 1948 election, the PSI and PCI combined in to the Popular Democratic Front, and was drawing 40–45 percent of the vote in public opinion polls (Harper, 1986: 156). It was time for the United States to move more brazenly, employing for the first time its newly-created powers under the 1947 National Security Act. Following the dictates of the first NSC directive, Number 1/1 of November 14, 1947, the United States threw its full support behind the CDP government. Economic aid was increased six-fold under the new Marshall Plan—from $100 million in Fiscal Year 1947 to $600 million in the first months of 1948 (Miller, 1983). Also, for the first time, a modest amount of secret moneys—some $10 million in "unvouchered funds"—was funneled via the new CIA into the campaigns of the Christian Democrats and allied right-wing candidates (liberals, monarchists, even former fascists) (Karabell, 1999: 38–40).

At the United Nations, the United States proposed Italian membership in that body, something not yet suggested for Germany or Japan, none of which had yet signed peace treaties with the Soviet Union. The United States also recommended Italian trusteeship over its former African colonies Libya and Ethiopia, a wholly unrealistic proposal, and the return of Trieste, in Yugoslavia, to Italy. In each of these diplomatic ploys, the USSR was maneuvered into casting a veto, moves that hurt the prospects of the Italian Communist Party and enhanced that of the pro-American parties (Miller, 1986).

At home, a government-orchestrated campaign resulted in more than 10 million Italian-Americans sending (mass-produced, prewritten, postage-paid) letters to their countrymen suggesting links between the "correct vote" and monetary remittances from the new world and future immigration prospects of relatives (Martinez and Suchman, 1950). The newly-formed Voice of America and US Information Agency produced and distributed films starring Frank Sinatra, boxer Rocky Graziano, and Italian-American labor leaders extolling the virtues of the American, as contrasted with the Soviet, way of life. They also circulated Greta Garbo's 1939 Hollywood film that satirized life in Russia called *Ninotchka*; it was shown to more than 15 million Italians in the weeks before the election and was regarded as particularly effective (Blum, 1995: 31). Finally, on March 15, 1948, President Truman announced in no uncertain terms that economic aid to Italy would be terminated in the event of a Communist victory.

The American campaign blitz succeeded. By polarizing the electorate into viewing the contest as one between the US and USSR, the CDP won 48.5 percent of the vote and an absolute majority of seats in the parliament. The Popular Front saw their pre-election poll numbers plummet to 31 percent on election day. But the result boded ill for Italian democracy. Using the technique of secret funding to nonleftist parties during subsequent elections from the 1950s through the early 1970s, the United States ensured that the Christian Democrats continued to be the dominant partner in every coalition for the next generation, although it never again reached 48 percent of the popular vote. The secret American funding stopped in the 1970s, but the CDP continued to be in every government (though not necessarily with the prime minister's post) until the end of the Cold War. The Communist Party, meanwhile, consistently drew between 30 and 35 percent of the vote over the years—the second largest party—but never once was admitted into a ruling coalition.

In short, the United States in Italy created in 1948 and sustained for 46 years (until 1994) not a true democracy, but a "one-party dominant" form of political system designed to keep the country's second largest party from ever having share of government (Sullivan, 1996: 80). The result was a weak polity in which Italy had 52 governments in 46 years, as the CDP and its allies rotated the major cabinet ministries amongst themselves in an increasingly corrupt system. One CDP leader with ties to the CIA and the Mafia, Giulio Andreotti, was prime minister seven times before he was abandoned by the United States as expendable in the 1990s (Stanley, 1999: 3). A similar system was set up, financed, and maintained in occupied Japan starting with the elections there in 1951 and 1954, and where the Liberal Democratic Party played the part of Italy's CDP (Pempel, 1990).

## CASE 3. PHILIPPINES, 1946–53

American influence over the composition of governments in Greece and Italy in the late 1940s followed a pattern established earlier when the United States gave "independence" to its largest colony, the Philippine Islands, in 1946. The practice of prescribing acceptable governments for less powerful peoples can be defined as *"neo-colonialism,"* a policy that involves indirect control over another country wherein the dominant power does not exercise outright political administration over the weaker state, but through its overwhelming economic influence, and other forms of intervention, can dominate politics in the smaller state to the point of virtually picking the head of government and key members of the cabinet. It involves techniques that the United States perfected in the Western Hemisphere earlier in the century as will be explained in the introduction to that region in Chapter 2. The situations in the Philippines, Italy, and Greece are interesting because the addition of anti-communism to the rationale for action provided the template for America's going global with its historic hemispheric policy of neo-colonialism.

The United States has had a proprietary interest in the Philippine Islands ever since they were acquired after victory in the Spanish-American War in 1898 (Karnow, 1990: 125–30). That war was started to liberate Cuba from Spain, but US victory also brought American colonial control over Spain's other imperial "possessions": Puerto Rico, Guam, and most significantly, the Philippines, a huge archipelago of 7,000 islands 500 miles off the coast of China. The victory over the Spanish fleet in Manila Bay took about four hours (the United States had the ironside *USS Olympia;*

Spain had only wooden ships). The war in Cuba lasted about four months and was termed a "splendid little war" by Secretary of State John Hay. But the battle to subdue the Filipinos was a bloody four-year "war of pacification," 1899–1902, in which 500,000 (out of a population of 7.5 million) of the natives perished, as compared with only 4,165 Americans (Poole and Vanzi, 1984: 132). This was typical of the overkill employed by imperial powers to subjugate colonies during this era. Whether it was right and proper, or even worth the effort, was a matter of some debate in the United States at the turn of the century (Brands, 1991: 20–35). Many thought it the next logical step in the "manifest destiny" of America's westward movement. The issue was not decided until President William McKinley announced he was inspired by Almighty God "to take . . . and to educate the Filipinos, and uplift and civilize and *Christianize* them" (Zinn, 1995: 306, italics mine; the Philippines had been forcefully converted to Catholicism by Spain 400 years earlier).

The United States gave the Philippines their independence in 1946, but entangled them in so many economic and military base agreements that the power relationship between the two countries met the definition of "neo-colonial" (Shalom, 1981: xiii–xvii; Pomeroy, 1974). Before the transfer of power, the United States supervised an election for a congress in which ten winning candidates were rejected because they were members of the *Hukbalahap* ("Peoples Army" in Tagalog), a peasant-based, communist-led movement that fought against Japan during World War II. These "Huks" advanced a program of land reform and industrialization that the United States had largely thwarted during its 43 years of colonial rule, and so in this respect were a threat to the United States as well as to Japan; the United States fought against them as well as against the Japanese during the war (Kerkvliet, 1977; Shalom, 1981: 7–8).

Between the April 1946, election and July 4th "independence day," the carefully-vetted Philippine congress granted the United States land for 23 military bases (Berry, 1989), and equal rights in the development of the nation's natural resources and the operation of its public utilities. The United States was also given absolute free trade rights on the islands for the next eight years whereas export quotas were established for the Filipinos for cordage, sugar, and other goods (Cullather, 1994: 38). In addition, the independence transition included a military aid pact that prohibited the Philippines from getting arms from any other country (Friedman, 2001). Most significant for what would follow, the new Philippine army moved into areas sympathetic to the Huks, destroying villages and killing more than 500 peasants. The Huks felt they had little alternative but to take up arms again just as the new government was coming to power (Taruq, 1952: ch. 23–24; Pomeroy, 1974: 78).

Over the next seven years, 1946–53, the United States spent more than $200 million in helping the first two Philippine governments prosecute a counter-insurgent war against the Huks. At its height, in 1950–52, some 9,000 people, mainly civilian supporters of the Huks, were killed in a brutal campaign reminiscent of the 1899–1902 pacification (and presaging a similar effort in Vietnam in the 1960s). As part of its campaign, the US military aid group selected Ramon Magsaysay as head of the Philippine defense and intelligence establishment. More importantly, the newly-formed CIA dispatched Lt. Col. Edward G. Lansdale (the model for *The Ugly American* in a later incarnation) to oversee a program of psychological warfare in Philippine politics (Lansdale, 1972: 24–30, 69–85; Smith, 1976: 95–106). In 1953, he successfully maneuvered Magsaysay into the presidency, funneling money into his campaign through CIA front organizations and playing dirty tricks (e.g., drugging opponent's drink before he gave a public speech to make him appear incoherent [Karnow, 1990: 346–53; Blum, 1995: 41]). Magasysay himself died in mysterious circumstances in 1957.

The 1946–53 patterns of suspicious American involvement in Philippine politics and Filipino dependence on the United States to suppress militant left-wing opposition, have continued to the present time. The CIA was instrumental in the election of President Diosdado Macapagal, 1961–65, a man who was on the Agency's payroll for many years (Karnow, 1990: 362–65; 444), and during whose term two American bases, Clark Air Field and Subic Bay Naval Base, expanded (in support of the war effort in Vietnam) to become the largest in Asia. His daughter, Gloria Macapagal Arroyo, is president at the time of this writing (2004).

In 1972, the United States acquiesced in President Ferdinand Marcos's "constitutional coup" regime during which martial law was declared and elections were called off for the next 14 years (Bonner, 1987: 112). It did not object when Marcos's left-of-center opponent, Benigno Aquino, was assassinated on the airport tarmac as he returned from a trip to the United States in 1981. The stated reason for US tolerance of the Marcos dictatorship was the rise of the New Peoples Army (NPA), descendants of the Huks who reorganized in 1969 and launched a 17-year insurgency in which some 35,000 were killed. As in the earlier 1946–53 war, the US fear of communism, in this case at the height of the Vietnam War in a country of historic American control, led to its initial approval of Marcos's uncompromising approach to any opposition on his left. (Aquino, in addition to calling for a return to democratic elections, advocated negotiating with the NPA.) Despite the US-Marcos hard line, NPA armed strength grew from a few hundred in 1972 to more than 15,000 by 1986 (Bonner, 1987: 442). Its popular supporters were estimated to be in the hundreds of thousands.

As the Cold War waned, however, the Philippines became less important to America. Indeed, by 1986, Marcos had become an expendable embarrassment who had to be pressured into retirement by a show of US military force in support of the widow Cory Aquino's electoral win that year (Blitz, 2000: 80–84). Mrs. Aquino's "people power" electoral revolution redirected popular support away from the insurgency and toward support of the new government. In 1991, when a volcano destroyed Clark Air Field, the United States chose not to rebuild it, and quietly accepted the Philippine Senate's request to vacate all its other bases as well.

On balance, America's neo-colonial policy in the Philippines in the 50 years after its 1946 "independence" could be deemed a success. Throughout the ideological struggle against communism, the United States retained a loyal client, and its influence lingered on even after its ouster from the bases. Its West Point–educated military client, Fidel Ramos, ruled as president for most of the 1990s, and when the global "war on terrorism" was declared after 9-11-01, the Philippines was the first state outside of the Middle East to allow US troops (back) in to their country.

One significant thing about the US involvement in the Philippines, 1946–53, is that it began *before* the announcement of the "Truman Doctrine" in March 1947 and was in high gear before the triumph of the communists in China in October 1949. To understand this American policy more fully, it might be helpful at this point to place this study of the United States in the Philippines in the larger context of US policy in Asia between World War II and the height of the Cold War.

## INTRODUCTION TO THE EAST ASIAN REGION

In 1941, the United States was at war with the most important military power in Asia: Japan. Ten years later, in 1951, the United States was at war with the most important military power in Asia: China. Was something wrong with American diplomacy in Asia during these times? No, not if one accepts the premise that the goal of US foreign policy was to be hegemon of the global capitalist system, and that Japan and China, respectively, represented the major obstacles to America's achieving this objective in that region at those times. The case of US intervention in the Philippines should be seen in the context of this goal and how it became operationalized on a global scale after the start of the Cold War in Europe in 1947.

The US approach to East Asia has historically been cautious as far as the mainland was concerned; it focused more on the larger Pacific islands and, more tentatively, on the peninsulas (Korea, Indochina) of mainland China. After the 1898 Spanish-American war, the United States gained the Philippine Islands as a colony and, in the Taft-Katsura Agreement of 1905, Washington and Tokyo acknowledged each other's rights in the Philippines and Korea, respectively.

After World War II, the United States and USSR replaced Japan as occupying powers in a divided Korea. Given China's historic interest in this former tributary nation, the seeds were sown for one of the Cold War's major confrontations—the Korean War, 1950–53—in which American troops directly clashed with those of China. This event will not be discussed at length here, in keeping with this book's emphasis on matters peripheral to the larger wars and countries involved in the Cold War. But the United States reaction to victory of the communists in the Chinese civil war in 1949 was a watershed event that led directly to their fighting each other one year later, so a brief summary of the antecedents is in order.

Although the two armed parties in China—the Communists under Mao Tse Tung and the Kuomingtang (Republican) Party under Chiang Kai Shek—had been fighting each other on and off for more than 20 years, the total takeover of the mainland by the communists on October 1, 1949, came as a surprise to the United States. Along with the Soviet testing of an atomic bomb that summer (several years before it was expected to happen), it led to America's decision—in National Security Council Document NSC-68 of April 14, 1950 (*before* the Korean War)—to call for the expansion of containment from a primarily political-economic program aimed at the Soviet Union in Europe to a global, militarized policy aimed at the "Sino-Soviet bloc."

The Chinese and the Russians had historically been enemies and in 1950, despite both being ruled by communists, still had many outstanding border claims and national differences. But they signed a 10-year friendship pact in January 1950, and in solidarity the USSR boycotted the United Nations when that supposedly universal organization refused, upon exercise of the American veto, to admit the new "People's Republic of" China as a member. (The UN, under US pressure, allowed the Kuomingtang government, in exile on island of Taiwan, to retain the "Republic of" China seat until 1971.)

The decision to expand containment from Europe to Asia led to the US involvement in Korea when the communist northern half of that divided state attacked the south on June 25, 1950. Although there is little evidence that either the USSR or China was behind this decision (Merrill, 1989; Cumings, 1990), the United States interpreted the assault as the start of a global offensive by the communist allies. Taking advantage of the Soviets' boycott of the United Nations, the United States maneuvered that organization into going to war to repel the North Korean aggression. It got 14 other countries to contribute troops (some only in token amounts) to what was essentially an American war against North Korea. When the US/UN commander, General Douglas MacArthur, went beyond his mandate of "repelling aggression" and in October 1950, sent troops across the North/South demarcation line and up to the border of China, the latter responded with 300,000 troops to drive back the advancing Americans.

As noted above, the details of the US-China war in Korea will not be discussed here. Suffice to say, the US intervention in Korea led to American collaboration with France in its colonial war in Indochina, and to support for a similar British counterinsurgency in Malaya. The three wars were seen as part of the division of labor by the leading capitalist countries in their global struggle against communism. By the end of the Korean War, pursuant to the policy laid down in NSC-68, the United States had formed military alliances to "contain Chinese communism" with Japan (1951), Australia and New Zealand (ANZUS) (1951), South Korea (1953), and the Republic of China (i.e., Taiwan) (1954). Also, following the recommendations of NSC-68, spending for "defense" in the United States tripled—from about $15 to $45 billion annually—an amount from which it has never receded by more than 10 percent, adjusting for inflation, to this day.

Thus, the US intervention into Korea must be understood in the context of America's expansion into new areas of the world in the wake of its World War II rise to Super Power status (Thompson et al., 1981; Buckley, 2002). The American decision to project its power beyond the Pacific on to the mainland of Asia—and to transform its Philippine colony into a neo-colonial staging area in this pursuit—was reinforced during the Korean War. A year after this war ended, the Philippine capital, Manila, was chosen as the headquarters for the new South East Asia Treaty Organization (SEATO), the vehicle through which the United States replaced France as the dominant Western power in Indochina (see the introduction to *Southeast* Asia in Chapter 2). By that time the United States had its man Magsaysay in the presidency, and the bases agreement and the multilateral treaty provided the infrastructure for building American hegemony in a new area of the world.

## CHAPTER 1 BIBLIOGRAPHY

### Truman Foreign Policy

Alperovitz, Gar. 1965. *Atomic Diplomacy: Hiroshima and Potsdam*. NY: Simon and Schuster.

Bills, Scott. 1990. *Empire and Cold War: The Roots of US-Third World Antagonism, 1945–1947*. NY: St. Martin's Press.

Hogan, Michael J. 1998. *Harry S Truman and the Origins of the National Security State*. NY: Cambridge University Press.

Leffler, Melvyn P. 1992. *A Preponderance of Power: National Security, the Truman Administration, and the Cold War*. CA: Stanford University Press.

Woods, Randall B., and Howard Jones. 2001. *Dawning of the Cold War: The United States's Quest for Order*. Chicago: Ivan R. Dees Publishers.

Yergin, Daniel. 1977. *Shattered Peace: The Origins of the Cold War and the National Security State*. Boston: Houghton-Mifflin Co.

### CASE 1. Greece, 1947–49

Amen, Michael M. 1978. *American Foreign Policy in Greece, 1944/1949: Economic, Military, and Institutional Aspects*. Frankfurt, West Germany: Peter Lang.

Blum, William. 1995. "Greece 1947 to Early 1950s: From Cradle of Democracy to Client State," Chapter 3: 34–39, *Killing Hope: US Military and CIA Interventions since World War II*. Monroe, ME: Common Courage Press.

Close, David. 1993. "The Reconstruction of a Right-Wing State," pp. 156–90, *Origins of the Greek Civil War, 1943–50*. London: Longman's Publishing Group.

Djilas, Milovan. 1962. *Conversations with Stalin*. London: Harcourt Brace World.

Fleming, D. F. 1961. *Cold War and Its Origins, 1917–1960*. NY: Doubleday.

Iatrides, John O. (ed.). 1980. *Ambassador MacVeagh Reports: Greece, 1933–1947*. NJ: Princeton University Press.

Jones, Howard. 1989. *"A New Kind of War": America's Global Strategy and the Truman Doctrine in Greece*. NY: Oxford University Press.

Kofsky, Frank. 1993. *Harry S Truman and the War Scare of 1948: A Successful Campaign to Deceive the Nation*. NY: St. Martin's Press.

Kuniholm, Bruce R. 1980. *The Origins of the Cold War in the Near East: Great Power Confrontation and Diplomacy in Iran, Turkey, and Greece*. NJ: Princeton University Press.

McWilliams, Wayne C., and Harry Piotrowski. 2001. *The World since 1945: A History of International Relations*. Boulder, CO: Lynne Riener Publishers.

"A Nation Challenged: President Bush's Address on Terrorism before a Joint Meeting of Congress," *New York Times*, September 21, 2001.

Rossides, Eugene T. 1998. *The Truman Doctrine of Aid to Greece: A Fifty Year Retrospective*. NY: American Academy of Political Science/American Hellinic Institute.

Simpson, Christopher. 1988. *Blowback: America's Recruitment of Nazis and Its Effects on the Cold War*. London: Weidenfeld and Nicolson.

Smith, Howard K. 1950. *The State of Europe*. London: Angus and Robertson.

"Text of President Truman's Speech on New Foreign Policy," *New York Times*, March 13, 1947.

Wittner, Lawrence S. 1982. *American Intervention in Greece, 1943–49*. NY: Columbia University Press.

Woodhouse, Christopher M. 1979. *The Struggle for Greece, 1941–1949*. Brooklyn Heights, NY: Beekman/Esanu.

## CASE 2. Italy, 1948

Ambrose, Stephen E., and Douglas G. Brinkley. 1997. *Rise to Globalism: American Foreign Policy since 1938*. NY: Penguin Books.

Blum, William. 1995. "Italy 1947–1948: Free Elections, Hollywood Style," Chapter 2: 27–34, *Killing Hope* (see CASE 1).

Chomsky, Noam. 1996. *What Uncle Sam Really Wants*. Tucson, AZ: Odonian Press.

Harper, John L. 1986. *America and the Reconstruction of Italy, 1945–48*. Cambridge: Cambridge University Press.

Hughes, H. Stuart. 1979. *The United States and Italy*. Cambridge, MA: Harvard University Press.

Karabell, Zachary. 1999. "Italy: A Secret Agency for an Open Election," Chapter 3: 37–49, *Architects of Intervention: The United States, the Third World, and the Cold War, 1946–1962*. Baton Rouge: Louisiana State University Press.

Kolko, Gabriel. 1968. *The Politics of War: The World and United States Foreign Policy, 1943–1945*. NY: Random House.

Kolko, Joyce, and Gabriel Kolko. 1972. *Limits of Power: The World and United States Foreign Policy, 1945–1954.* NY: Harper and Row.

Mammarella, Giuseppe. 1966. *Italy after Fascism: A Political History, 1943–1965.* South Bend, IN: Notre Dame University Press.

Martinez, E. Edda, and Edward A. Suchman. 1950. "Letters from America and the 1948 Elections in Italy," *Public Opinion Quarterly,* Spring: 111–25.

Miller, James Edward. 1983. "Taking Off the Gloves: The United States and the Italian Elections of 1948," *Diplomatic History,* 7 (Summer): 34–55.

Miller, James Edward. 1986. *The United States and Italy, 1940–50: The Politics and Diplomacy of Stabilization.* Chapel Hill: University of North Carolina Press.

Pempel, T. J. (ed.). 1990. *Uncommon Democracies: The One-Party Dominant Regimes.* Ithaca, NY: Cornell University Press.

Prados, John. 1991. *Keeper of the Keys: A History of the National Security Council from Truman to Bush.* NY: William Morrow.

Shlaim, Avi. 1983. *The United States and the Berlin Blockade, 1948–49: A Study in Crisis Decision-Making.* Berkeley: University of California Press.

Stanley, Alessandra. 1999. "Ex-Premier Andreotti Acquitted of Mafia Murder Conspiracy," *New York Times,* September 25.

Sullivan, Michael J. III. 1996. *Comparing State Polities: A Framework for Analyzing 100 Governments.* Westport, CT: Greenwood Press.

## CASE 3. Philippines, 1946–53

Berry, William E., Jr. 1989. *US Bases in the Philippines: Evolution of the Special Relationship.* Boulder, CO: Westview Press.

Blitz, Amy. 2000. *The Contested State: American Foreign Policy and Regime Change in the Philippines.* Lanham, MD: Rowman and Littlefield.

Blum, William. 1995. "The Philippines 1940s and 1950s: America's Oldest Colony," Chapter 4: 39–45, *Killing Hope* (see CASE 1).

Bonner, Raymond. 1987. *Waltzing with a Dictator: The Marcoses and the Making of American Policy.* NY: Times Books.

Brands, H. W. 1991. *Bound to Empire: The United States and the Philippines.* NY: Oxford University Press.

Cullather, Nick. 1994. *Illusions of Influence: The Political Economy of United States-Philippine Relations, 1942–1960.* CA: Stanford University Press.

Friedman, Hal M. 2001. *Creating an American Lake: US Imperialism and Strategic Security in the Pacific Basin, 1945–1947.* NY: Greenwood Publishing Group.

Karnow, Stanley. 1990. *In Our Image: America's Empire in the Philippines.* NY: Ballantine Books.

Kerkvliet, Benedict J. 1977. *The Huk Rebellion: A Study of Peasant Revolt in the Philippines.* Berkeley: University of California Press.

Lansdale, Edward G. 1972. *In the Midst of Wars: An American's Mission to Southeast Asia.* NY: Harper and Row.

Pomeroy, William. 1974. *An American Made Tragedy: Neo-Colonialism and Dictatorship in the Philippines.* NY: International Publications.

Poole, Frederick K., and Max Vanzi. 1984. *Revolution in the Philippines: The United States in a Hall of Cracked Mirrors.* NY: McGraw-Hill.

Shalom, Stephen Rosskam. 1981. *The United States and the Philippines: A Study of Neo-Colonialism.* Philadelphia: Institute for the Study of Human Issues.

Smith, Joseph Burkholder. 1976. *Portrait of a Cold Warrior: Second Thoughts of a Top CIA Agent*. NY: G. P. Putnam's Sons.

Taruc, Luis (Huk leader). 1952. *Born of the People*. NY: International Publications.

Zinn, Howard. 1995. *A People's History of the United States, 1492–Present*. NY: Harper Perennial.

## Introduction to East Asia

Buckley, Roger. 2002. *The United States in the Asia-Pacific since 1945*. NY: Cambridge University Press.

Cumings, Bruce. 1990. *The Origins of the Korean War. Volume II: The Roaring of the Cataract*. NJ: Princeton University Press.

Merrill, John. 1989. *Korea: The Peninsular Origins of the War*. Newark: University of Delaware Press.

Thompson, James C., Jr., Peter W. Stanley, and John Curtis Perry. 1981. *Sentimental Imperialists: United States Foreign Policy in East Asia*. NY: Harper and Row.

# CHAPTER 2

# The Expanding Empire under Eisenhower, 1953–60

## INTRODUCTION

The Eisenhower presidency marks America's first moves beyond the "manifest destiny" regions of the Western Hemisphere and Pacific Asia, and the World War II sites of Europe and East Asia. As diplomacy shifts from Truman to Eisenhower, a difference in styles between the two political parties becomes evident. Despite Truman's interventions in Greece, Italy, and the Philippines, the opposition Republican Party could never forgive him for the "loss" of China (the United States never really "had" any control of this country), or the "draw" in the Korea (North Korea was repulsed from the South, but not otherwise defeated). Accordingly, the GOP developed an almost rabid rhetorical style of anti-communism that the Democrats could never quite match.

Under the influence of his moralistic Secretary of State John Foster Dulles (Hoopes, 1973), Eisenhower often drew upon the imagery of his "crusade" in Europe during World War II to describe the new Republican foreign policy. The pair frequently expanded upon Truman's "mere containment" of the Soviet Union to embrace a more general ideological battle against communism throughout the world (Parmet, 1972; Broadwater, 1992). Truth be said, however, the actual Eisenhower-Dulles policy was somewhat more modest than the rhetoric (Immerman, 1999).

Two of the three cases in this chapter—Iran and Lebanon—are from the Middle East, a region where US foreign policy during the late 1950s led to the announcement of the "Eisenhower Doctrine" to prevent communism from spreading to that area of the world. The other case in this chapter, Guatemala, represents a consolidation of America's traditional role in the Western Hemisphere, but in pursuit of a new rationale: anti-communism (Rabe, 1988). Also, during this time, the first steps were taken into an area (South East Asia) that would be the site of the most extreme example of American adventurism in the next decade (Bowie and Immerman, 1998; Divine, 1981).

## INTRODUCTION TO THE MIDDLE EAST

The Middle East will be defined in this book as that region of the world between Europe, Africa and Asia where Islam is the predominant cultural force. For purposes of this study, it consists of two subregions: the northern tier and the fertile crescent, which are the sites, respectively, of two of this chapter's three cases.

The northern tier consists of those Muslim, but non-Arab, states bordering on the Black Sea, the Caspian Sea, and the USSR. The US move into Turkey was described in Chapter 1 as almost an afterthought to America's involvement in the Greek civil war. The intervention in Iran, which was much more considered, will be analyzed in this chapter. Afghanistan, a third state in the northern tier, will be covered in Chapter 6.

The fertile crescent is that swath of land in the eastern Mediterranean encompassing (from northeast to southwest) the Arab nations of Iraq, Greater Syria, historic Palestine, and parts of northeast Egypt. This area had been under the control of the Ottoman Turks for some 400 years before they were driven out by the British and French during World War I. After World War II, the dominant position of these European powers was replaced by that of the United States, particularly during the events involving the Suez Canal and Lebanon to be recounted in this chapter.

Finally, Saudi Arabia dominates the Arabian peninsula, a third subregion that links the fertile crescent and the northern tier geographically, culturally, and (through its dominance of the oil trade), economically. It is politically and religiously the heart of the Islamic world and has historically not been open to much outside penetration. Despite a special relationship dating to the 1930s, the United States has not intervened militarily in Saudi Arabia except on only the tightest of leashes, as will be see in Chapter 6, CASE 27 involving Iraq in 1991. That intervention, however, led directly to the events of 9-11-01 in which 15 of the 19 terrorist bombers came from Saudi Arabia.

One state in this region will *not* figure prominently in this book. Israel, carved out of British Palestine, is considered a special case due to the overwhelming impact of US domestic politics on American policy there, and due to the intrinsic momentum of Israel's own situation vis-a-vis its Arab neighbors. More to the point, there have been no American interventions, as this term is defined in this study (see Introduction), into Israel.

## CASE 4. IRAN, 1953

On May 1, 1951, Iranian Prime Minister Mohammed Mossadegh nationalized the Anglo-Iranian Oil Company. The AIOC was a joint-country venture that had the monopoly over the development of that resource that accounted for 95 percent of Iran's foreign currency, but from which the UK derived the bulk of the profits. Between 1945 and 1950, of £275 (pounds-sterling) of revenue, the British government received £125 million (or 45 percent) in taxes, the Company (of which the British government was majority shareholder) received £100 million (36 percent) in profits, and the government of Iran only £50 million (18 percent) in royalties. These distributions followed the terms of a 60-year treaty Britain had imposed upon Iran in 1933. (Elm, 1992: 38, 98–99).

The Truman administration criticized the nationalization as a matter of principle, and participated in a UK-led worldwide boycott of any purchase of the "stolen" oil. For the next two years, it attempted to mediate between the UK and Iran, being more motivated by the impact of the dispute on the Cold War than by the monetary terms of the dispute that were felt to be negotiable (Cottam, 1988: 62–69). Most significantly, it avoided pressures from Britain for covert actions against Mossadegh's government (Karabell, 1999: 59–61). This policy changed, however, upon the Republicans' taking office in 1953.

As noted in this chapter's introduction, since the start of the Cold War, the GOP had adopted an extremely aggressive line against communism, criticizing the incumbent Truman for not doing more to live up to the words of his "Doctrine." It was the Republican leader of the Senate, Arthur Vandenberg, who told the president that he would have to "scare hell out of the American people" (Williams, 1962: 269–70) if he wished to have the major planks of the containment policy adopted by the Congress. There was even a wing of the party that felt containment was "cowardly," and that the policy of the United States should have been to "roll back" communism in places it already existed rather than merely holding the line against further expansion. Although this faction of the party did not produce a president until Ronald Reagan, it always had enthusiastic supporters including, in the campaign of 1952, Vice President Richard Nixon, and Eisenhower's chief foreign policy advisor, John Foster Dulles.

Upon taking office, Dulles was named Secretary of State, and his brother, Allen, the head of the CIA. The United States soon began escalating its disapproving rhetoric of the Iranian government, portraying Mossadegh as unstable, weepy, and a madman. More ominously, a plan was made to use the CIA for the first time to do one of those "other tasks" alluded to in its charter: overthrow another government. The covert action, dubbed "Operation Ajax," was accomplished in six days, August 16–22, 1953, as the CIA took advantage of instability within Iran.

Mossadegh had been in a shaky situation for about a year as elements of his ruling coalition began to desert him. His Iranian National Front (INF) in 1951 had commanded a strong majority of the parliament behind a platform of social reform: redistributing land, including that owned by the clergy; taxing big merchants in the bazaar; diverting more power from the constitutional monarch (the Shah, Mohammed Reza Pahlavi) to the elected parliament, and so on. By 1953, this program had begun to threaten many vested interests in the country. About the only one of Mossadegh's original policies most sectors of society still endorsed was the nationalization of the oil, which was accepted as a simple matter of sovereignty. The army was split on the constitutional issue, with most of the officers loyal to the Shah and the rank and file soldiers divided.

The coup began on August 16th when the Shah, acting in his constitutional position as head of state, sent a colonel to dismiss the Prime Minster; the plan was to name Interior Minister General Fazlollah Zahedi as the new premier (Abrahamian, 1982: 278–80.) But Mossadegh arrested the colonel and a frightened Shah fled to Rome. Crowds organized by the Tudeh (Communist) Party, the largest remaining support group in Mossadegh's INF, took to the street in celebration. At this point, Kermit Roosevelt, head of the US CIA team in Tehran, took advantage of the situation to act as agent provocateur. He paid others to join the crowds and attack statues of the Shah as well as mosques. The result was to discredit the left-wing party and to spread fear that Mossadegh was planning to abolish the monarchy, a prospect worrisome to the army. Then, on August 19th, Roosevelt organized another gang, of pro-Shah supporters, to attack the first group. As the two mobs fought in the streets, army tanks fired upon Mossadegh's home and seized the fleeing prime minister. Three days later, the Shah returned from exile, with Zahedi who would prove to be a pliant prime minister as the Shah assumed near absolute powers for himself.

A year after the coup, in September 1954, a new treaty was signed under which it was admitted that Iran owned all the oil. However, it would be marketed, and hence effectively controlled, by an international consortium in which Britain would have only 40 percent control. The US share of these oil royalties also would be 40 percent, divided among five American corporations: Esso/Exxon, Mobil, Standard Oil of California, Texaco, and Gulf; France and the Netherlands shared the final 20 percent of revenues (Yergin, 1991: 476–78; Kwitny, 1984: 181). In addition to the financial windfall for American corporations, the US had begun to replace the UK as the region's political hegemon (Watt, 1984: 127; Nirumand, 1969: 100–08; Heiss, 2000).

There is much debate today as to whether this successful CIA coup was as great a victory as was portrayed when the Shah was in power (Gasiorowski, 1991; Ramazani, 1982: 146–47). For the cost of about 1,300 killed in mob rioting, and $20 million in bribes to high-ranking army officers and members of the street crowds (a fraction of the $1 billion expended in Greece and in Italy), the United States in addition to getting an equal share of the downstream profits had purchased a loyal ally for the next 26 years (Roosevelt, 1979: 190–95; Wilber, 1986: 187–91).

Under the Shah, Iran signed on to the Baghdad Pact and CENTO when these became American priorities in the Middle East in 1955 and 1959. It also allowed America to build bases in the northern part of the country to eavesdrop on Soviet electronic communications and missile testing sites. During the 1970s—when the Shah was the designated regional policeman under the "Nixon Doctrine"—Iran proved to be a boon to America's military-industrial complex, purchasing $22 million worth of US arms. The replacement of a rudimentary parliamentary democracy under a constitutional monarch (Iran's situation from 1946–53) with an absolute despot for the next 26 years was thus considered by those most intimately involved a small price to pay (Molotsky, 2000: 52; Risen, 2000: 15). America's isolation from the Iranian scene in the 25 years since 1979 (to 2004 publication date) has not yet equaled those 26 years of "good times."

In the long run, however, by so polarizing the political situation within Iran—outlawing the Tudeh Party, marginalizing other centrist forces, and creating the repressive overkill machinery of the SAVAK secret police—America's Shah prepared the way for the Islamic Fundamentalist revolution of 1979 (Rubin, 1980). Along with the seizure of the US Embassy and the holding of some 50 Americans hostage for 444 days, this revolution represented one of the greatest failures in the history of American foreign policy (Sick, 1985: vii; Bill, 1988: 243). For more than a generation now the policy of the United States toward Islamic Iran has been an ineffective economic boycott, plus occasional resorts to state-sponsored terrorism, with the CIA helping to support raids from exile by forces of the *Mujaheddeen-e-Khalq*.

Thus, the long-term result of the CIA coup of 1953 has been to destroy totally any hope of America's allegedly preferred form of politics (multiparty democracy) in Iran. Instead, the country has reeled from 26 years of absolute monarchy (with no elections or civil liberties), to 25 years of essentially nonparty Islamic Fundamentalism (albeit with regular elections among religiously vetted, "independent," candidates). Any semblance of the parliamentary politics that prevailed in 1946–53 has disappeared.

Finally, a case could even be made for a link between the 1953 coup and the 9-11-01 terrorist attack upon the United States (Zahrani, 2002: 93). The 1953 coup provoked, ultimately, the 1979 revolution (during which 20,000 died) and the hostage crisis. The US reaction to this humiliation resulted in America's tilting toward Iraq in the Iran-Iraq war of 1980–88, emboldening Iraq's president to think he would have US acquiescence in his invasion of Kuwait in 1990 (CASE 27). The American war in the Persian

Gulf to reverse this action required the stationing of US troops in Saudi Arabia, which culminated in the Saudi-led al Qaeda attack upon the United States on 9-11-01.

## INTRODUCTION TO THE WESTERN HEMISPHERE

The concept of "neo-colonialism" was introduced in Chapter 1 when discussing the Philippines, the American colony given its "independence" in 1946. But the practice had been pioneered by the United States in its diplomacy in the Western Hemisphere, especially since the turn of the century when the American military invaded with regularity to topple governments and install others that would be more favorable to US economic interests operating in their countries (Aguilar, 1966; Whitaker, 1954). To put these interventions into some perspective, it helps to divide the phenomenon into three geographic regions, and three periods of time.

The regions are South America, Central America, and the Caribbean; the time frames are pre-1890; 1890–1935; and post-1945. A Congressional study made during the high point of American interventionism in Vietnam identified 115 occasions before World War II when the United States inserted military troops into other countries; 64 of these interventions were in the Western Hemisphere including 31 times in Central America, 21 times in the Caribbean, and 12 times into South America (United States, Library of Congress, 1969). Obviously there is a pecking order guiding where the "Colossus of the North" chooses to exercise its power within its sphere of influence, and the "banana republics" of central America and the small islands of the Caribbean top the list; there is a hesitancy to get involved in the larger countries further south.

Chronologically, more than half, or 38, of these 64 interventions occurred between 1890 and 1935. The first date represents the end of the Indian wars in the continental US and the start of America's drive for overseas possessions and influence (e.g., Hawaii, Samoa, the Philippines). The second year marks the start of President Franklin D. Roosevelt's "Good Neighbor" policy, and the end of US intervention in Latin America (for a while) in pursuit of assuring the Pan-American republics' placement on the side of the United States in the coming war against Germany. The years in between are characterized by US gunboat diplomacy in the region, justified ideologically by President Theodore Roosevelt in his 1904 "Corollary" to the "*Monroe Doctrine*" of 1823. That earlier pronouncement proclaimed this hemisphere "off limits" to military penetration by the Great Powers of Europe. *Roosevelt's Corollary* deemed it open to such intervention by the United States in the interests of order, stability, and prosperity (Galeano, 1973; Blasier, 1985).

Since World War II, there have been more than a dozen forceful US interventions in to the republics of this hemisphere, depending on how such "interventions" are defined. American troops never left Guantanamo Bay, Cuba (1898 arrival) or the Panama Canal Zone (1903), even during the days of the "Good Neighbor," so these two sites might be considered already invaded (or occupied) at the start of this survey. There are also to be covered in *American Adventurism Abroad* the four overt military invasions in to the Dominican Republic, Grenada, Panama, and Haiti (CASEs 13, 23, 26, and 29), plus the six covert involvements in Guatemala, Cuba, British Guiana, Brazil, Chile, and Nicaragua (CASEs 5, 8, 9, 12, 17, and 22). Finally, there are the American military support groups thrust into El Salvador and Honduras during the wars in central America in the 1980s; and the military "advisors" sent to Colombia, Ecuador and other Andean countries relating to the "drugs war" of the 1990s. (The commitment to Colombia has increased since 9-11-01 as the drug-enemies have been redefined as "terrorists.")

Until the end of the Cold War, the rationale for most of these American interventions was "containment of communism." Related to the "Truman Doctrine," the Rio Treaty was signed on September 2, 1947, binding the nations of this hemisphere to that goal. One year later, in the manner of what was being done in Europe, the treaty was given bureaucratic form in the creation of the Organization of American States (OAS), headquartered in Washington, DC. When added to NATO, SEATO, CENTO and other Cold War alliances, the OAS provided institutional protection for the North American home base in the militarized, global war against communism. Looked at from a longer perspective, it simply provided a new rationale for traditional US hegemonic behavior in its historic sphere of influence.

## CASE 5. GUATEMALA, 1954

As in the case of Iran, the CIA-engineered overthrow of the government in Guatemala, on June 27, 1954, was regarded as a great success at the time. The coup stopped a social revolution that had been building in Guatemala since the ouster of dictator Jorge Ubico in 1944. In November 1950, Jacobo Arbenz was elected—by a 3-to-1 margin!—over Miguel Ydigoras, a former general in Ubico's army and the candidate of the country's landowners, the Catholic Church hierarchy, and American business interests. Prominent among the latter was United Fruit, the country's largest landowner, and chief shareholder in the land's only railroad—a quasi-colonial creation whose tracks ran only from interior banana plantations to the coast (Adams, 1970).

Arbenz's electoral platform called for an expansion of the 1944 reform movement that had allowed for the first time in Guatemala's history workers to unionize and strike, and parties (including the Communist Party) to organize and run in democratic elections. The next step for

Arbenz—in a country where 3 million of its 4 million people were peasants, but only 2 percent of the population owned 75 percent of the land—would be to address the agricultural sector of the economy (Gleijeses, 1991). In protest against the direction in which the country was moving, Ydigoras went into exile in El Salvador after the election. With similar motivation, Carlos Castillo Armas, a disgruntled former Army colonel, fled to Nicaragua and was given a retainer by Truman's CIA. But plans for any additional counter-reaction went no further under the Democratic administration (Cullather, 1999: 30–32; Immerman, 1982: 118–22).

In June 1952, President Arbenz issued Decree Number 900, a rather modest reform measure, applying only to *uncultivated* land on estates greater than 224 acres. Under this criteria only 22 *latifundia* (vast estates, some the size of Rhode Island), accounting for 13 percent of all arable land in the country, would be subject to expropriation. It would affect less than one-half of one percent of all private holdings, but among those targeted was the United Fruit Company. UFC owned 500,000 acres, of which 75,000 were under active cultivation. Arbenz's decree envisioned taking, with fair compensation—the declared value of the land on UFC's tax returns: $1.2 million—about 400,000 of these acres and distributing their ownership to the 100,000 peasants who had historically lived on them (Melville and Melville, 1971).

As in the Iranian situation, relations became worse after the Republican administration took power in 1953. For one thing, the two men now responsible for US diplomacy, the Dulles brothers, had come to Washington from Sullivan and Cromwell, United Fruit's Wall Street law firm (Dosal, 1989). John Foster in particular considered such nationalizations of private property (even if not being used, and even if with compensation) to be immoral and tantamount to communism (Karabell, 1999: 110, citing the Secretary of State's "Moral Initiative" speech of November 18, 1953). And Allen, in short order, reinstated the CIA's ties with ex-Col. Armas in Nicaragua. By the fall of 1953—flush from the successful venture in Iran—Eisenhower had authorized the covert campaign against Guatemala (Immerman, 1982: 134–37).

Headquarters for "Operation PBSUCCESS" were established in Miami, and Nicaraguan dictator Anastasio Somoza provided a site for the training of about 300 Guatemalan exiles in the use of weapons, explosives, and radio transmission. About a dozen World War II vintage airplanes, stationed in the US Canal Zone, were also committed to the cause. As part of an elaborate propaganda offensive, the CIA next attempted to convince—with thousands of pamphlets, and several secret radio transmitters—conservative elements in Guatemalan society that the reformist Arbenz was a "communist." Although only four members of Arbenz's majority coalition of 51 in the Guatemalan Congress were communists, and although that party held only a few *sub*-Cabinet posts, clandestine radio broadcasts directed by agent David Atlee Philips blanketed the country with the message that Arbenz was "dominated by the Soviet Union."

From Washington, the CIA's Deputy Director, Frank Wisner, worked with Edward Bernays, a Madison Avenue PR man detailed to United Fruit, to orchestrate stories in the international media about the impact of this insidious communist infiltration. One CIA operative on the scene, E. Howard Hunt (later of Watergate fame), got the local archbishop, Mariano Rossell y Arellano, to denounce Arbenz from the pulpit. Throughout Latin America, the USIA distributed 100,000 copies of a pamphlet entitled "Chronology of Communism in Guatemala," and 200 articles citing it were written and planted in scores of newspapers (Schlesinger and Kinzer, 1982: 167–68; Hunt, 1973: 99; Phillips, 1977: 34–35).

The Guatmalan military was a particular target of this propaganda war. Eisenhower had cut off weapons sales to Guatemala, convincing its military that it would have trouble getting arms and equipment. This forced President Arbenz to go to Czechoslovakia for resupply, further evidence of his "Soviet bloc ties." On the diplomatic front, Secretary of State Dulles convinced a conference of American states meeting in Caracas to pass a resolution declaring that "international communism" was "incompatible with the concept of American freedom." He could not, however, get an endorsement from the Organization of American States for US military intervention.

Finally, on June 18, 1954, the CIA radio stations reported an "attack" from Honduras by a small rebel army under former-Col. Armas. Planes dropped leaflets demanding Arbenz resign. When he refused, air attacks were unleashed for a week, targeting ports, fuel depots, ammunition dumps, and several cities. But the "invasion force" was no match for the 7,000-man Guatemalan Army. Totaling no more than 300 mercenaries, trained and equipped by the CIA at a cost of about $20 million, in eight days it never got closer to the capital than 100 miles (Zepezauer, 1994: 12–13). But at this point President Arbenz was betrayed by General Carlos Diaz and the Army's General Staff. Perhaps convinced by the months of anti-communist psychological warfare, and possibly by $60,000 in bribes (Blum, 1995: 80), the generals told Arbenz that the army would not defend the country unless he resigned.

Arbenz fled into exile and General Diaz prepared to step into office. But US Ambassador John Puerifoy threatened him with more bombing unless he turned power over to ex-Col. Armas's advancing "army." Accompanied by a CIA officer, Enno Hobbing, who arrived in Guatemala City with a draft constitution reversing the nationalizations, banning all political parties, and workers' unions, Armas took over. Within a month some 72,000 "suspected leftists" were arrested and thrown in jail, many never to be seen again. The new regime also disenfranchised three-quarters of

Guatemala's voters by barring illiterates from the electoral rolls. Opposition newspapers were closed down and subversive books—including *Les Miserables*—were burned (Schlesinger and Kinzer, 1982: 60, 221–22; Cook, 1981: 231; Blum, 1995: 81). A generation-long reign of terror had begun.

In 1957 Armas was assassinated and the army selected Ydigoras, the loser of the 1950 election, to replace him. When progressive forces began to organize to restore their aborted reform movement, the military stepped in to run the country for the next 25 years, 1959–84 (Streeter, 2000). With no other outlet for their political ambitions, the left resorted to arms, beginning one of the longest civil wars in Latin American history. It lasted from 1961 to 1996 and provoked a savage counterinsurgency that resulted in some 200,000 deaths and several hundred villages being destroyed (Peckenham et al., 1983).

The military rule during this time was particularly harsh; Guatemala's governments were among the worst of countries cited for human rights violations when the State Department began publishing such reports in the 1970s. In fact, its generals refused to accept US military aid during the Carter years because they resented the respect-for-human-rights conditions attached to receipt of the aid. Guatemala felt it needed an unfettered hand to prosecute a war that bordered on the genocidal in that most of the victims were from its large minority Mayan Indian ethnic group, the very people that Arbenz had attempted to empower (Aybar de Soto, 1978; Jonas, 1991). The situation was especially oppressive during the junta of evangelical Christian Efrain Rios Montt (March 1982–August 1983), which, given a relatively free pass under the new policies of the Reagan administration, engaged in "large scale torture, disappearances, and extrajudicial executions," and massacres of the entire populations of villages in Huehuetenango and Alta Verapaz in 1982 (Amnesty International, 1983: 142; 1984: 158).

Thus the 1954 American intervention in Guatemala, though a short-term victory for American foreign policy, was a longer term failure. This judgment is made not only on human rights grounds, but also in geostrategic and propaganda terms. Because the Guatemala coup was thought by many to be a model for successful American adventurism in the region, the precedent was applied in Cuba seven years later at the Bay of Pigs. The result was the "loss" of that country to communism for more than 40 years (see CASE 8). The propaganda embarrassment of these two episodes came after the details of the CIA chicanery in both countries were revealed in Senate hearings in 1975 (see below CASE 18). The fallout from these events also bedeviled Reagan's central American policy in the 1980s, causing its illegal resorts to secrecy and, eventually, the Iran-*contra* affair (see CASE 22).

But, thanks to the 1954 coup, the United States retained a dependable anti-communist ally in the Organization of American States at the height of the Cold War. Capitalism had been preserved, though at the expense of democracy; right-wing military regimes were preferred to center-left reformists. The Guatemalan intervention thus represented the first post-OAS, Cold War, example of that American tradition from the years of gunboat diplomacy, 1890–1935: neo-colonialism. In those earlier years, the United States toppled governments and installed more favorable leaders without establishing direct political control in the manner of the European imperialists in Africa and Asia. With the Cold War and the establishment of the OAS, a new rationale (anti-communism) had been found for an old US practice: intervening in the affairs of its smaller neighbors to the south. Guatemala, 1954, was the first example of this recycled policy; *American Adventurism Abroad* will present eight more before the end of the Cold War.

## CASE 6. LEBANON, 1958

The fertile crescent, described earlier in this chapter, includes within it the historic cities of Baghdad, Damascus, Beirut, Amman, Jerusalem, and Cairo. This case study will focus on one major US military intervention: "Operation Blue Bat," the landing of 15,000 marines in Lebanon on July 15, 1958. But this act was the culmination of two years of events—starting in Egypt, ending in Iraq—in which poor, unfortunate Lebanon served as a proxy and locale for the playing out of larger strategic games.

Lebanon, in 1958, was a tiny country of 1.5 million people divided roughly (no *actual* census had ever been taken) into about 50 percent Christians (of four main types: Maronite, Melchite, Greek Orthodox, Armenian Orthodox) and 50 percent Muslim (of three main types: Sunni, Shiite, and Druze). According to the 1943 National Pact under which France left Lebanon during World War II, a power-sharing system was set up under which the Maronites (the largest Christian group) would have the presidency and control of the army and hence the most power; the Sunnis (the second largest Muslim group, but the wealthiest,) would hold the prime ministership; and the Shiites (the most populous, but poorest, Muslim group) the speakership of the national assembly. The parliament was a weak creation, compared to the strong presidency, and strictly proportioned according to the 1943 French population *estimates* of the seven major religious groups. In support of these different "confessions," the geopolitical ambitions of various external powers were played out in the 1950s (Gerges, 1994). In general, Egypt had the strongest ties with the Sunnis, Syria and Iran competed for influence among the Shiites, and the United States was most sympathetic to the Christians.

It is a main thesis of *American Adventurism Abroad* that an American strategic goal since 1945 has been to replace the UK and France as hegemon in various parts of the world. In the Middle East, that would mean the US succeeding the UK in Iraq and Palestine (Ovendale, 1996), and ousting France from Syria and Lebanon (Lesch, 1992: 95, 105). It would, thereby, become arbiter of the global trade in oil flowing from the more important farther reaches of the region: the Persian Gulf (Gendzier, 1996: 369–71). The move into Iran in 1953 (CASE 4) was a function of this strategy on its eastern flank and northern tier; the United States had been the predominant external actor in the Saudi Arabian heart of the Arab world to the south since the 1930s (Polk, 1969: 238).

The first step for the United States in this scenario was the removal of Britain and France from the Suez Canal in Egypt in 1956 (Freiberger, 1992: 157; Louis and Owen, 1989: 11). As with many other episodes in the Cold War, this move took on the coloration of protecting this area from encroaching Soviet influence. In September 1955, Gamal Abdel Nasser's new revolutionary nationalist regime in Egypt signed an agreement to buy planes and tanks from the USSR. Before this deal, the United States had been the primary financier in building the Aswan Dam on the Nile River in southern Egypt. But Nasser balked at continued American assistance for this vast project when future financing was tied to Egypt's not buying any more weapons from Eastern bloc countries. Nasser also resented Dulles's criticism of his foreign policy of nonalignment in dealing with the Cold War's two Super Powers as "immoral" (Finer, 1964: 43).

On July 26, 1956, one week after the United States formally withdrew its financing for the dam, Nasser announced that Egypt would nationalize the Suez Canal. This engineering marvel, which gave Europe shortened shipping access to Asia, was built by the UK and France in 1870–80 (under a lease from Ottoman Turkey, then the reigning power). It had been operated by the two European nations ever since that time even as political control of the region shifted from the Ottomans to Egypt. As with the nationalization of Iran's oil, the capitalist world responded to the indigenous Arab government's taking control of this "natural resource" with a boycott of Egypt's economy. The UK and France (in secret from the US) also made plans, with Israel, to retake the canal from Egypt by force. (Israel joined in because it had been refused passage through this international waterway by Egypt, technically still in a state of war with Israel since the end of their 1948 belligerency.)

When those three nations invaded Egypt on October 29, 1956, the world was plunged in to a crisis. At the United Nations Security Council, the United States surprised its NATO allies by joining with the Soviet Union in condemning the British-French-Israeli aggression. Without American diplomatic (and economic) support, the operation could not be sustained, and within weeks the invading forces were withdrawn. Egypt was now in control of the canal, and an era of European hegemony over one of the trading world's most important water routes had ended (Hahn, 1991).

Now the competition began as to whether the US or the USSR would succeed the West Europeans as the major political power in Egypt. For the years of this case study, and until Nasser died in 1971, the answer to that question would be the Soviet Union, which backed Nasser's call for a pan-Arab movement as a way of removing capitalist imperialism from that region of the world. The policy of the United States became one of containing the spread of Nasser's revolutionary nationalism beyond the boundaries of Egypt. Nasser's vision (which he attempted to implement in Egypt since its 1952 revolution) foresaw leftist republican regimes replacing monarchies more integrated into international capitalism. In this context, on January 5, 1957, the United States announced the *"Eisenhower Doctrine,"* which promised to protect the "territorial integrity and political independence" of any states in the Middle East threatened by "international communism" (Little, 1996: 34).

This policy was soon challenged as Nasser moved to woo Syria into a federation of nationalist Arab republics that would be aligned with neither east nor west in the Cold War. In February 1958, they formed the United Arab Republic, the first step in Nasser's pursuit of a 20-state pan-Arab union. The new UAR was promptly rewarded with Soviet diplomatic support for their effort. But the United States, in response, moved closer to the monarchies in Saudi Arabia, Jordan and Iraq, and to Middle Eastern republics with more Western orientations: first Christian Lebanon, and later Jewish Israel.

The presence of Israel in the midst of the Arab world has always complicated the US plan for hegemony in the region. Due to a domestic political situation with significant numbers of Jewish voters clustered in states with many electoral votes, and relatively few politically involved Arab-Americans, the United States could not treat Israel as "just another actor" in this region's international politics. Thus, Israel does not figure prominently in any of the five Middle Eastern case studies in this book. After 1956, especially after 1967, US support for Israel is taken as a given. In any case, in the wake of its rebuff at Suez, Israel is not where the next round of Great Power maneuvering for influence was played out. It was, rather, in Lebanon (Allin, 1994: 48–49).

According to the 1943 National Pact that served as its constitution, Lebanon was to be independent, and aligned with neither the West (i.e., Christian France) nor the East (in the context of 1943, the Muslim Arab world). But Lebanon's historic separation from Greater Syria by France in 1860 (in a protectorate agreement with the Ottoman Empire), concentrated power in the Christian community, and meant that France would have predominant economic influence in the country. Then, in 1919, both Lebanon *and* Syria were granted to France under the League of Nations Mandates imposed on Ottoman territories after World War I. In further institutionalizing the separation of Lebanon from Syria in 1943, France carved out in the Muslim Middle East a Christian-dominated enclave similar to what Britain was doing vis-a-vis the Jews when it separated Palestine from TransJordan in 1920s.

In 1956, the Christian Lebanese president, Camille Chamoun, was the only Arab leader not to break relations with France and Britain at the time of the Suez crisis. In 1957, he embraced the "Eisenhower Doctrine," the only Arab leader explicitly to do so except for the King of Iraq who had earlier (in 1955) cast his lot with Britain in the Baghdad Pact. Nasser regarded Chamoun as a puppet of the West and a year later was supporting Lebanese political groups more committed to pan-Arabism in low-level civil wars for control of the various religious communities there. According to the National Pact constitution, the president of Lebanon was supposed to serve one six-year term. As the 1958 election approached, using the civil unrest as the excuse, Chamoun moved to extend his term. This provoked, in May 1958, an intensification of the wars among the various paramilitary forces allied with the respective religious factions. The official military of Lebanon, under General Fuad Chehab, remained neutral: the national army did not want to be drawn into domestic politics (Karabell, 1999: 160–61).

The United States preferred that Chamoun step down when his term ended, but sent signals that it would respond to a request for help if the "independence and integrity" of Lebanon (as opposed to the political fortunes of Chamoun) were at stake. The crisis began to subside in June when the United Nations sent in an Observer Group (UNOGIL), and Chamoun backed off from holding on to the presidency, contenting himself with picking his successor from within the Maronite Christian community.

Then on July 14, 1958, the King of Iraq was overthrown and killed in a coup d'etat. His successor, General Abdul Karim Kassem, voiced support for the secular, pan-Arabist ideology of the UAR and for similar forces among the Muslims in Lebanon. The next day the United States responded to the coup in Iraq by invading Lebanon. Although there was no evidence that Iraq, Syria, or Egypt were planning any military moves in to Lebanon, Eisenhower declared that the "independence of Lebanon" was in peril. The UK made a similar dispatch of troops to shore up the King of Jordan; shortly thereafter he was put on the CIA payroll for the next 20 years (Blum, 1995: 90), ensuring Jordan's place in the Western camp, but exposing the king to charges that he was a "kept ... client of Washington" (Kaplan, 1975: 202). The King of Saudi Arabia and the Shah of Iran supported the United States and UK, furthering the polarity between the republicans and the monarchies in the Muslim Middle East. Republican Christian Lebanon, with 15,000 American troops patrolling the streets of Beirut and the shores of Tripoli, became even more the odd man out.

But the US insertion of marines into Lebanon was more of a political than a military operation. They came under no hostile fire and served mainly to "stabilize" the political situation, ensuring that Chamoun departed from power, and that he was succeeded by Chehab, a Christian general with whom the United States felt comfortable. The other religious communities, outgunned by this American show of support for the Christians, went along with this "resolution" of the crisis. From the perspective of this book's cases, this represents the first time US troops—as contrasted with military aid or CIA covert operations—were openly pressed into political service on behalf of another government. Although they stayed in Lebanon for only three months, the invasion set a precedent for the more extreme commitments of the 1960s. Meanwhile, Maronite Christian rule, and a pro-Western diplomatic orientation, were assured for another generation (Biska, 1987: 106).

By 1975, a greater Muslim birth rate, plus the immigration of (mainly Muslim) Palestinians from both sides of the Jordan River (i.e., from the Israeli-occupied west bank in 1967 and from the east-bank Jordanian heartland in 1970) had shifted Lebanon's population balance from the alleged 50–50 percent of 1943 to 65–35 percent against the Christians. The civil war, which was thwarted by the United States in 1958, resumed. This time, in addition to its Christian vs. Muslim aspect, it included Lebanese vs. Palestinian, and Sunni vs. Shiite vs. Druze dimensions within the Muslim community as well. It raged for the next 16 years, 1975–91, and resulted in the occupation of parts of Lebanon by Syria (in the east, after 1976) and by Israel (in the south, after 1982), further shrinking the enclave France had carved out for European influence in 1860, 1919, and 1943. It also brought the United States back, briefly and tragically, in 1982–83 (Korbani, 1991; Kennedy and Haas, 1994: 21–22). By this time, however, Lebanon no longer seemed threatened by Soviet communism or radical Arab nationalism. Egypt under Nasser's successor, Anwar Sadat, had moved in to the western camp in the 1970s, and a new balance of power in Lebanon (policed by Israel in the south and Syria in the east, and greased with Saudi financial assistance) had stabilized the situation there. For the United States, a Christian-dominated Lebanon had become expendable.

Viewed from the longer perspective, the events of 1952 to 1991 resulted in the United States replacing the United Kingdom as the predominant power in Egypt, Palestine (now Israel and Jordan) and, after the 1991 Gulf War, two-thirds of Iraq. France had definitively departed from Syria and Lebanon, being replaced in their southern border regions by Israel. The US movement toward hegemony in the region, begun at Suez in 1956, was becoming completed by the turn of the century. The "war against terrorism" confirmed this trend after 9-11-01. Geopolitics, more than the advancement of any particular American capitalist assets, defined these past 40 years of American foreign policy in this region. Further afield, in the Persian Gulf area, there were specific oil holdings; the American rise to hegemony in the fertile crescent can be seen as additional protection for them.

To be sure, the United States suffered a short-term loss of influence in Egypt under Nasser, 1958–71, and from Syria and Iraq ever since 1958. But as noted earlier in this case study with respect to Syria, and as will be seen with Iraq (in CASE 27), the control of these two countries over even their own lands has become more and more truncated. But the one state that has suffered the most in all this time has been Lebanon. In many respects an arbitrary creation in the first place, it is today an independent country in name only. More than 150,000 died in its civil war, 1975–91, a conflict that might have been prevented had Lebanese politics been allowed to take its natural course in 1957–58. Instead the ambitions of various outside powers—Egypt, Syria, Israel, Iraq, Iran, and the United States—were played out within that unhappy land, and it has been the biggest loser of all.

## INTRODUCTION TO THE SOUTHEAST ASIA SUBREGION: INDOCHINA-I

Before leaving the Eisenhower administration and the 1950s, one other geographic area deserves explicit mention: Southeast Asia, or Indochina. This section thus updates the Introduction in Chapter 1 to the *East* Asia Region, and anticipates the later cases of Laos, South Vietnam, and Cambodia in Chapters 3 and 4.

Indochina is that area between India and China where the United States replaced France as the dominant Western power in the 1950s. It is far beyond either America's "manifest destiny" region of Pacific Asia at the turn of the century, or the Korean war theater of battle earlier in the decade. The Korean peninsula is in northeast Asia and is historically linked with Japan and China, two countries with which the United States has had some historic involvement. The Indochina peninsula is 1,800 miles distant from Korea and in an area of historic French, not American, interest. But after the end of the Korean War, US policies at conferences in Geneva and Manila led to a clear attempt to expand its influence into this region. This move was implemented with some restraint, however, involving an American boycott of the conference at Geneva where accords were signed creating an independent Vietnam, and a US effort to muddle its role in subverting this decision by creating, in Manila, the multilateral South East Asia Treaty Organization (SEATO) as the successor to France's military presence in Indochina.

The US replacement of France in Indochina thus was more subtle than its actions in Suez or Lebanon in the 1950s, but ultimately more fateful. With the spread of the Cold War into Korea, a division of labor between the United States and France had developed: the Americans would carry the heaviest load in the fight against communism in Northeast Asia (Korea, Taiwan), the French would have responsibility in Southeast Asia (Vietnam, Laos, and Cambodia) (Gardner, 1988: 86–87; Lee, 2000). France had in fact been fighting "international communism" there since 1946 when it moved to crush the incipient nationalist movement that had taken root during the Japanese occupation in World War II. Its leader Ho Chi Minh had actually declared an independent Vietnamese Republic at the end of that war in 1945. But the French imperialists returned with a vengeance and by the time of the Korean conflict, were in the fourth year of a brutal war to get their colony back. In 1950, they were defeated in several battles on the northern frontier, including one at Lang Son where they lost 60 percent of their men and tons of ammunition, prompting one observer to call it France's "greatest colonial defeat since Montcalm had died at Quebec" (Fall, 1961: 30).

Until the outbreak of the Korean war and the militarized globalization of containment, the United States was lukewarm in support of France's efforts to reestablish colonialism in Indochina, although the initial approval of some aid for the French was made on February 17, 1950, *before* the writing of NSC-68 (Irving, 1975: 100). But after 1950, the United States began financially subsidizing the French effort in a major way; by 1954 it was picking up 80 percent of the cost of their war. Cheering from the sidelines, by 1954 the United States was more enthusiastic about the French venture than France itself where public opinion was beginning to crumble under the burden of eight years of fruitless effort (Sullivan, 1978: 44; Herring, 1986: 18–27; Irving, 1975: 98–107).

The Indochinese nationalist movement combined the efforts of Vietnamese, Cambodians, and Laotians from the three nations that were conquered by France in 1883 at the start of the modern era of European colonialism. It was led by the Vietnamese whose population was five times that of the other two nations combined and was called the Viet Minh after its leader, Ho Chi Minh. Ho was a nationalist who had studied socialism, communism, and democracy in Paris as a student during World War I. At the 1919 Versailles Conference, he attempted to press the cause of self-determination for Vietnam; after all, such national freedom was being granted to ten other nations emerging from the Austrian, Prussian, and Russian empires in Europe. But Ho was turned away, a rebuff that led to his becoming one of the founders of the French Communist Party a few months later. Before returning to Vietnam to lead the nationalist movement in the 1930s, he traveled and studied in the Soviet Union and China becoming more committed to the doctrines of Marx and Lenin as a means of furthering his primary goal of advancing a Vietnamese nation free from French colonialism (Halberstam, 1971: 31–35).

The turning point in this struggle came in the spring of 1954, when Ho's nationalist forces surrounded a French garrison at Dien Bien Phu (Fall,

1967). After a 55-day siege, France gave up, on May 8, 1954. The formal surrender of its colonial holdings occurred at the conference in Geneva attended by Great Powers UK, USSR, and China (the latter's presence causing the United States to boycott), plus Canada, Poland, and India (in keeping with the *troika* diplomatic formulations common during this period). According to the *"Geneva Accords,"* France agreed to depart its colony, and to recognize *three* countries: Laos, Cambodia, and Vietnam. The two smaller nations were given immediate and total independence. But Vietnam was to be *temporarily* divided, along the 17th parallel line of latitude in recognition of the military distribution of forces at the end of the war that included the French and many Vietnamese collaborators holding areas in the south. An election to determine the government of a unified Vietnam was scheduled to be held in two years. Such partition at the end of a war was not unusual during this era; it followed the pattern of post–World War II international politics in Germany, Austria, China, and Korea (Cable, 1986).

It was assumed that Ho Chi Minh and his communist and nationalist followers in control of the northern half of the country would gather there, whereas anti-communist and other political forces would regroup in the southern areas. It was also expected that Ho—the leader of the eight-year independence struggle against the French—would probably win any free election for president; indeed, Eisenhower estimated he would get 80 percent of the vote. (Eisenhower, 1963: 372; Brown, 1975: 107). It was about this time that the American president issued his famous "falling dominoes" remark, predicting that if Indochina went communist, so too would Thailand, Malaysia, Indonesia, the Philippines, Australia, and so on (Hess, 1998: 45–46).

As a result, the United States was determined that such a vote would never be held. Days before the Geneva Accords were to be signed, a Vietnamese politician named Ngo Dinh Diem, who had sat out the war in a Catholic monastery in *New Jersey* (and thus was free from any taint of collaboration with France), slipped back into the southern zone of Vietnam. Under American and French pressure, Vietnamese Head of State Emperor Bao Dai appointed Diem leader of the governing administration in the south. He was soon given "technical support" by a small team of US (CIA) advisors led by Col. Edward Lansdale, fresh from his success in the Philippines (Lansdale, 1972: 159; Leary, 1984; Schulzinger, 1997: 81–84; Kolko, 1985: 87).

Between 1955 and 1960, the US military-political advisory group grew into the hundreds, but Eisenhower was careful to keep the total of such Americans in "South" Vietnam under 1,000, the number of military personnel that would be in keeping with the Geneva Accords' stipulation for the removal of "all outside forces" from Indochina (see CASE 11). But in all other respects, the United States, which was not a signatory to the

Accords, set about to undermine its premises. As a symbol of US distancing from this agreement, Secretary of State Dulles refused to shake the hand of Chinese Foreign Minister Chou en-lai and pointedly left the conference early, before the signing of the final accords.

In addition to this abrupt departure, and to supporting a political movement behind Diem as leader of the anti-communist forces in the south, the United States also established an organization modeled on NATO that was designed to protect his regime from the "communist" threat from the north. But SEATO—the *South East Asia Treaty Organization*—was no NATO. Unlike NATO whose fifteen members agreed to come to the defense of one another if any one of them was attacked, SEATO was comprised of eight countries who promised to come to the defense of three *other* entities that were not signatories: the newly created countries of Laos, Cambodia, and "the free territory under the jurisdiction of the State of Vietnam"; that is, *South* Vietnam (Gettleman et al., 1985: 52). Moreover, the main signatories of SEATO were not even geographically *in* southeast Asia. Among its eight members were: the United States, United Kingdom, and France (hardly Asian countries); Australia and New Zealand (Asian in geography, but whose politics reflected those of the UK and US); the Philippines (ex-American colony, and still dominated by the United States; Pakistan (located in south*west* Asia and looking for protection from India); and Thailand (the only state actually in southeast Asia and possibly worried about communism). In any event, when Diem refused to allow the elections promised in the Geneva Accords to be held in the south of Vietnam, SEATO became the prime international instrument pledged to the protection of his regime.

The reaction of the nationalist-communists in the north under Ho Chi Minh (and his diplomatic supporters in Moscow and Peking) was to try, for three years, to pressure the West and Diem into having the elections. When this was unsuccessful, Ho encouraged communists in the south to organize, in December, 1960, all anti-Diem forces under the banner of the National Liberation Front, and to begin a political-military struggle to overthrow the regime there. Ho's government in North Vietnam pledged to support this effort. The civil war among Vietnamese for control of all of Vietnam had begun.

## CHAPTER 2 BIBLIOGRAPHY

### Eisenhower Foreign Policy

Bowie, Robert R., and Richard H. Immerman. 1998. *Waging Peace: How Eisenhower Shaped an Enduring Cold War Strategy.* NY: Oxford University Press.

Broadwater, Jeffrey. 1992. *Eisenhower and the Anti-Communist Crusade.* Chapel Hill: University of North Carolina Press.

Divine, Robert A. 1981. *Eisenhower and the Cold War.* NY: Oxford University Press.

Hoopes, Townsend. 1973. *The Devil and John Foster Dulles*. Boston: Atlantic Monthly Press.

Immerman, Richard H. 1999. *John Foster Dulles: Piety, Pragmatism, and Power in US Foreign Policy*. Wilmington: Scholarly Resources.

Parmet, Herbert S. 1972. *Eisenhower and the American Crusades*. NY: Macmillan.

Rabe, Stephen G. 1988. *Eisenhower and Latin America: The Foreign Policy of Anti-Communism*. Chapel Hill: University of North Carolina Press.

## CASE 4. Iran, 1953

Abrahamian, Ervant. 1982. *Iran: Between Two Revolutions*. NJ: Princeton University Press.

Bill, James. 1988. *The Eagle and the Lion: The Tragedy of American-Iranian Relations*. New Haven, CT: Yale University Press.

Cottam, Richard. 1988. *Iran and the United States: A Cold War CASE Study*. PA: University of Pittsburgh Press.

Elm, Mostafa. 1992. *Oil, Power, and Principle: Iran's Oil Nationalization and Its Aftermath*. NY: Syracuse University Press.

Gasiorowski, Mark. 1991. *United States Foreign Policy and the Shah: Building a Client State in Iran*. Ithaca, NY: Cornell University Press.

Heiss, Mary Ann. 2000. *Empire and Nationhood: The United States, Great Britain, and Iranian Oil, 1950–1954*. NY: Columbia University Press.

Karabell, Zachary. 1999. "Iran: Succeeding John Bull," Chapter 3: 50–61, *Architects of Intervention: The United States, the Third World, and the Cold War, 1946–1962*. Baton Rouge: Louisiana State University Press.

Kwitny, Jonathan. 1984. *Endless Enemies: The Making of an Unfriendly World*. NY: Penguin.

Molotsky, Irvin. 2000. "Kermit Roosevelt, 84, Director of CIA's 1953 Coup in Iran" (Obituary), *New York Times*, June 11.

Nirumand, Bahman. 1969. *Iran: the New Imperialism*. NY: Monthly Review Press.

Ramazani, Rouhollah. 1982. *The United States and Iran: The Patterns of Influence*. NY: Praeger.

Risen, James. 2000. "How a Plot Convulsed Iran in '53 (and in '79)," *New York Times*, April 16: 1, 14–15.

Roosevelt, Kermit. 1979. *Countercoup: The Struggle for the Control of Iran*. NY: McGraw-Hill.

Rubin, Barry. 1980. *Paved with Good Intentions: The American Experience and Iran*. NY: Oxford University Press

Sick, Gary. 1985. *All Fall Down: America's Tragic Encounter with Iran*. NY: Random House.

Watt, D. Cameron. 1984. *Succeeding John Bull: America in Britain's Place*. London: Cambridge University Press.

Wilber, Donald N. 1986. *Adventures in the Middle East*. NJ: Princeton University Press.

Williams, William Appleman. 1962. *The Tragedy of American Diplomacy*. NY: Delta.

Yergin, Daniel. 1991. *The Prize: The Epic Quest for Oil: Money and Power*. NY: Simon and Schuster

Zahrani, Mostafa T. 2002. "The Coup That Changed the Middle East: Mossadeq v. the CIA in Retrospect," *World Policy Journal*, Summer: 93–99.

## Introduction to the Western Hemisphere

Aguilar, Alonso. 1966. *Pan-Americanism from Monroe to the Present: A View from the Other Side.* NY: Monthly Review Press.

Blasier, Cole. 1985. *The Hovering Giant.* PA: University of Pittsburgh Press.

Galeano, Eduardo. 1973. *The Open Veins of Latin America: Five Centuries of the Pillage of a Continent.* NY: Monthly Review Press.

U.S. Library of Congress. Legislative Reference Service. Foreign Affairs Division. 1969. *History of Commitment of US Armed Forces without Congressional Declaration of War.* Washington, DC: US Government Printing Office.

Whitaker, Arthur P. 1954. *The Western Hemisphere Idea: Its Rise and Decline.* Ithaca, NY: Cornell University Press.

## CASE 5. Guatemala, 1954

Adams, Richard. 1970. *Crucifixion by Power: Essays on Guatemalan National Social Structure, 1944–1966.* Austin: University of Texas Press.

Amnesty International. 1983, 1984. *Reports.* London: Amnesty International Publications.

Aybar de Soto, Jose. 1978. *Dependency and Intervention: The CASE of Guatemala in 1954.* Boulder, CO: Westview.

Blum, William. 1995. "Guatemala 1953–1954: While the World Watched," Chapter 10: 72–83, *Killing Hope: US Military and CIA Interventions since World War II.* Monroe, ME: Common Courage Press.

Cook, Blanche Wiesen. 1981. *The Declassified Eisenhower.* NY: Doubleday.

Cullather, Nick. 1999. *Secret History: The CIA's Classified Account of Its Operations in Guatemala, 1952–1954.* CA: Stanford University Press.

Dosal, Paul. 1993. *Doing Business with the Dictators: A Political History of the United Fruit Company in Guatemala, 1899–1944.* Wilmington, DE: Scholarly Resources Books.

Gleijeses, Piero. 1991. *Shattered Hope: The Guatemalan Revolution and the United States, 1944–1954.* NJ: Princeton University Press.

Hunt, E. Howard. 1973. *Give Us This Day.* New Rochelle, NY: Arlington House.

Immerman, Richard H. 1982. *The CIA in Guatemala: The Foreign Policy of Intervention.* Austin: University of Texas Press.

Jonas, Susanne. 1991. *The Battle for Guatemala: Rebels, Death Squads, and US Power.* Boulder, CO: Westview Press.

Karabell, Zachary. 1999. "Guatemala: Ike and Armas," Chapter 6: 108–35, *Architects of Intervention* (see CASE 4).

Melville, Thomas, and Marjorie Melville. 1971. *Guatemala: The Politics of Land Ownership.* NY: The Free Press.

Peckenham, Nancy, Marvin E. Gettleman, Jonathan Fried, and Deborah T. Levanson (eds.). 1983. *Guatemala in Rebellion: Unfinished History.* NY: Grove Atlantic.

Phillips, David Atlee. 1977. *The Night Watch: Twenty-five Years of Peculiar Service.* NY: Atheneum.

Schlesinger, Stephen, and Stephen Kinzer. 1982. *Bitter Fruit: The Untold Story of the American Coup in Guatemala.* NY: Doubleday.

Streeter, Stephen M. 2000. *Managing the Counterrevolution: The United States and Guatemala, 1954–1961.* Athens: Ohio University Press.

Zepezauer, Mark. 1994. "Hit #4: Guatemala," pp. 12–13, *The CIA's Greatest Hits,* Tucson, AZ: Odonian Press.

## CASE 6. Lebanon, 1958

Allin, Erika G. 1994. *The United States and the 1958 Lebanon Crisis: American Intervention in the Middle East.* Lanham, MD: University Press of America.

Biska, Michael. 1987. "The 1958 American Intervention in Lebanon: A Historical Assessment," *American-Arab Affairs,* Winter: 106–19.

Blum, William. 1995. "The Middle East 1957–1958: The Eisenhower Doctrine Claims Another Backyard for America," Chapter 13: 89–99, *Killing Hope* (see CASE 5).

Finer, Herman. 1964. *Dulles over Suez: The Theory and Practice of His Diplomacy.* Chicago: Quadrangle Books.

Freiberger, Steven Z. 1992. *Dawn over Suez: The Rise of American Power in the Middle East, 1953–57.* Chicago: Ivan R. Dee Publisher.

Gendzier, Irene. 1996. *Notes from the Minefield: US Intervention in Lebanon and the Middle East, 1945–58.* NY: Columbia University Press.

Gerges, Fawaz. 1994. *The Superpowers and the Middle East: Regional and International Politics, 1955–67.* Boulder: University of Colorado Press.

Hahn, Peter. 1991. *The US, Great Britain, and Egypt, 1945–56: Strategy and Diplomacy in the Early Cold War.* Chapel Hill: University of North Carolina Press.

Kaplan, Stephen S. 1975. "United States Aid and Regime Maintenance in Jordan, 1957–1973," *Public Policy,* 23(2) Spring: 189–217.

Karabell, Zachary. 1999. "Lebanon: To the Shores of Tripoli," Chapter 8: 151–172, *Architects of Intervention* (see CASE 4).

Kennedy, David M., and Richard N. Haass. 1994. *The Reagan Administration and Lebanon.* Washington, DC: Georgetown University Institute for the Study of Diplomacy, CASE No. 340.

Korbani, Agnes. 1991. *US Intervention in Lebanon, 1958 and 1982.* NY: Praeger.

Lesch, David W. 1992. *Syria and the United States: Eisenhower's Cold War in the Middle East.* Boulder: University of Colorado Press.

Little, Douglas. 1996. "His Finest Hour? Eisenhower, Lebanon, and the 1958 Middle East Crisis," *Diplomatic History,* 20 (Winter): 27–54.

Louis, W. Roger and Roger Owen (eds.). 1989. *Suez 1956: The Crisis and Its Consequences.* NY: Clarendon Press.

Ovendale, Ritchie. 1996. *Britain, the United States, and the Transfer of Power in the Middle East, 1945–1962.* London: Leicester University Press.

Polk, William R. 1969. *The United States and the Arab World.* Cambridge, MA: Harvard University Press.

## Introduction to Southeast Asia

Brown, Weldon A. 1975. *Prelude to Disaster: The American Role in Vietnam 1940–63.* Port Washington, NY: Kennikat Press.

Cable, James. 1986. *The Geneva Conference of 1954 and Indochina,* NY: St. Martin's Press.

Eisenhower, Dwight D. 1963. *The White House Years: Mandate for Change, 1953–1956.* NY: Doubleday.

Fall, Bernard B. 1967. *Hell in a Very Small Place: The Siege of Dien Bien Phu.* Philadelphia: Lippincott.

Fall, Bernard B. 1961. *Street without Joy: Indochina at War, 1946–1954.* Harrisburg, PA: Stackpole.

Gardner, Lloyd. 1988. *Approaching Vietnam: Fm. World War II to Dien Bien Phu, 1941–54.* NY: W. W. Norton.

Gettleman, Marvin E., Jane Franklin, Marilyn Young, and H. Bruce Franklin (eds.). 1985. *Vietnam and America: A Documented History.* NY: Grove Press.

Halberstam, David. 1971. *Ho.* NY: Vintage Books.

Herring, George C. 1986. *America's Longest War: The United States and Vietnam, 1950–1975.* Philadelphia: Temple University Press.

Hess, Gary R. 1998. *Vietnam and the United States: Origins and Legacy of War.* NY: Twayne Publishers.

Irving, R. E. M. 1975. *The First Indochina War: French and American Policy 1945–1954.* London: Croom Helm.

Kolko, Gabriel 1985. *Anatomy of a War: Vietnam, the United States, and the Modern Historical Experience.* NY: Pantheon Books.

Lansdale, Edward G. 1972. *In the Midst of Wars: An American's Mission to Southeast Asia.* NY: Harper and Row.

Leary, William M. 1984. *The Central Intelligence Agency: Perilous Missions.* University: University of Alabama Press.

Lee, Steven Hugh. 2000. *Outposts of Empire: Korea, Vietnam, and the Origins of the Cold War in Asia, 1949–1954.* Montreal: Mc-Gill–Queen's University Press.

Schulzinger, Robert D. 1997. *A Time for War: United States and Vietnam, 1941–75.* NY: Oxford University Press.

Sullivan, Marianna P. 1978. *France's Vietnam Policy: A Study in French-American Relations.* Westport, CT: Greenwood Press.

# PART II

---

# The Extremist Years, 1961–76

The years 1961–76 mark the high-water point of US foreign policy in the periphery, culminating in the eight-year US war in Indochina (1965–73). Through the study of 14 cases, Part II reveals a difference in attitude toward government activism between the Democratic and Republican parties. But the common thread throughout all four of the presidencies in these years (Kennedy, Johnson, Nixon, and Ford) was commitment to the bipartisan Cold War consensus of controlling the capitalist world under the guise of containing communism.

More activist by party ideology and tradition, the 1960s Democratic presidents John F. Kennedy and Lyndon B. Johnson (1961–69) were more predisposed to act upon the GOP rhetoric of the 1950s, moving into the heart of Africa (Congo), bringing the world to the brink of nuclear war (Cuba), and unleashing America's longest and most violent war (Vietnam). In the home hemisphere, Chapter 3 also includes cases involving tiny British Guiana and massive Brazil, as well as an historic target of US military intervention, the Dominican Republic. Related to the containment of communism in Asia, there are studies of Laos, South Vietnam, and probably the most important "domino" of all, but one of the least recognized, Indonesia.

By nature more skeptical of government, the Republican presidents covered in Chapter 4 (Richard M. Nixon and Gerald R. Ford) spent the next eight years (1969–77) "tidying up" after the Democratic excesses. But they still reflected the extremist ethos of the era by continuing to strive for the same expansive goals by subtler, more restrained means. The Cambodian "sideshow" was part of Nixon's "Doctrine" of getting regional surrogates to do the policing of America's far-flung, although informal, empire. So too was the support of the Iraqi Kurds on behalf of Iran's Shah. Chile was this administration's application of the historic habit of hemispheric hegemonism. Under Ford, three of the more obscure examples of neo-colonial meddling occurred as the United States attempted to select pliant governments in the unlikeliest of venues: Angola, Australia, and East Timor.

Part II, Chapters 3 and 4, covers 16 years, four presidents, and 14 cases, and introduces the last region (Africa) covered in *American Adventurism Abroad*.

# CHAPTER 3

# The Kennedy-Johnson Idealist Extensions, 1961–68

## INTRODUCTION

John F. Kennedy (age 42) ran for president in 1960 projecting a contrast to the elderly, retiring Eisenhower (age 72) and promising to "get this country moving again" (White, 1961). In foreign policy, his inaugural address promised to "pay any price, bear any burden, meet any hardship, support any friend, oppose any foe . . . to assure the survival and success of liberty"("Text," 1961). The logical conclusion of this renewed national vigor was to bring American military presence to continents it had never been before (Africa: Congo), and more deeply to areas where it was already committed (Southeast Asia: Laos, South Vietnam). There would also be more militant prosecution of the Cold War in the Western Hemisphere core zone of influence (Cuba, British Guiana, Dominican Republic).

Kennedy also adopted what many saw as a more sophisticated approach to diplomacy than that offered by the seemingly distracted Eisenhower and his moralistic Secretary of State Dulles. Drawn from the supposed brightest minds from the best schools (Halberstam, 1972), the Kennedy foreign policy team promised to move beyond nuclear saber-rattling and to adopt a more flexible response the military threats (Taylor, 1959). There was also to be a more enlightened approach to the use of foreign aid for economic development, symbolized by the extraction of the foreign aid function from the Department of State and the creation of the new, free-standing Agency for International Development (A.I.D.). In the context of Latin America, this meant the Alliance for Progress that would, in theory, stress long-range economic development over short-term political gains in its programs (Hilsman, 1967; Paterson, 1989; Walton, 1973).

But three years later, the shift from Kennedy to Johnson signaled a more aggressive, and less nuanced, approach to anti-communism both in the home hemisphere and further afield in Asia (Brands, 1995; Cohen and Tucker, 1994; Rostow, 1972). In Latin America there was a step back from the economic carrots of Kennedy's Alliance for Progress aid program and a step up in both covert political and overt military operations (in Brazil and the Dominican Republic). In Asia, there was movement beyond the SEATO area of concern to involvement with a huge domino in a new geographic periphery: Indonesia, in the former Dutch East Indies.

The contrast between Kennedy and Johnson can be seen in seven of the eight cases in this chapter where policies begun under Kennedy became significantly more polarized under Johnson (in Cuba, it was impossible for relations to have become more hostile). As far as Latin America was concerned, a virtual *"Kennedy-Johnson Doctrine"* was established: no more Cubas. As regards Southeast Asia, LBJ's excess became his legacy.

## INTRODUCTION TO THE AFRICAN REGION

The first case in this chapter brings the United States to Africa, a new continent in America's quest for global hegemony. For much of the Cold War period, Africa was ceded to Britain and France in a division of labor with respect to containment of the Soviet Union. However, when two of Europe's weaker imperial powers, Belgium and Portugal, left their colonial possessions in the 1960s and 1970s, the United States moved in to fill the Great Power vacuum that was left in Congo and Angola. It is no coincidence that these two states are extremely rich in natural resources, and geographically proximate to the Atlantic Ocean. (Two other less significant and more remote African countries (Libya and Somalia), where the reasons for American attention are more peculiar, will be covered in Part IV.)

## CASE 7. CONGO, 1961–65

Three days before John F. Kennedy was inaugurated (on January 20, 1961), Patrice Lumumba was executed in the Congo. Although this CIA-related assassination occurred during the last days of the Eisenhower administration, the Agency's commitment to Joseph Désiré Mobutu, the Army Chief who delivered Lumumba to his executioners, began earlier. The first contacts were in 1959 in Belgium, and the relationship grew until his seizure of control of the Congo at the culmination of its civil war in 1965 (Borstelmann, 1997: 156). It then persisted for 32 more years until he was overthrown in 1997. Although the initial American interest in the Belgian Congo began in the 1950s, it was under Kennedy and Johnson that the commitment expanded to embrace one of the most notorious dictators of the twentieth century (Kelly, 1993). From the perspective of this book's analysis of the methods and tactics of American foreign policy in the periphery, the association with Mobutu entailed the first acknowledged assassination complicity, and the longest (up to this time) covert involvement in a civil war.

When Belgium gave its largest colony independence on July 1, 1960, it was not inevitable that the United States would be the successor imperial power in that land. But in hindsight it seems natural that just as the UK and France transformed their explicit imperial relationships with African colonies into more sophisticated economic controls around this time, the United States would soon develop similar ties with the colonies left behind by Belgium and Portugal, two European powers too weak to continue even a neo-colonial presence in Congo and Angola once they decided to leave (Smith, 1974:37–43).

In the Congo, the United States initially found itself in the ideological middle—between the UN- and Soviet-backed legitimately elected Prime Minister Patrice Lumumba on the left, and Moise Tshombé's movement of collaborators with colonial Belgium for a secessionist mineral-rich Katanga province on the right. In this context, the American positioning of itself behind the originally apolitical Army Chief of Staff Mobutu appeared to be a centrist position and the United States succeeded in the short term in both replacing the departing colonial power and thwarting any putative Soviet strategic designs in the center of the African continent (Atwood, 1967; Weissman, 1974: 15–28).

At the time of Belgium's departure from Congo, there were three geographic centers of political power in this huge territory the size of Western Europe: (1) the capital Leopoldville, in the southwestern corner of the country near the tributary of the Congo River on the Atlantic Ocean, politically-important base of President Joseph Kasavubu; (2) Stanleyville, further up the Congo River into the northeast, home of the leftist supporters of Lumumba; and (3) Katanga province in the southeast, site of the lucrative *Union Miniere* copper company, and of secessionist, pro-Belgian politicians like Tshombé. These geographic and ideological divisions also corresponded to ethnic (or "tribal") differences, with the BaKongo, Bangala and Lulua dominant in the west; Lumumba's Tetela in the northeast; and the BaLunda and BaLuba in the southeast (Merriam, 1961).

These ethnic differences were probably more significant in the political motivations of the locals than the ideologies imposed upon them by the external Great Powers caught up in their own Cold War and for whom the spectrum of politicians in Congo consisted of left- and right-wingers plus an allegedly apolitical army that held ultimate power. On the left, there was Prime Minister Lumumba who shocked his colonial patrons (who had presided over the elections that brought his party to power) by dismissing the Belgian officer corps left behind to lead his 25,000-man army. In hostile response Belgium, after consulting with the United States, backed a secessionist movement led by Tshombé in the southeast, where most of the country's mineral wealth (copper, cobalt, uranium, and gold in Katanga; diamonds in Kasai) was to be found (Gibbs, 1991).

When Lumumba tried to get help from the United Nations to rein in the renegade province, he was dismissed by President Kasavubu on September 5, 1960, in what many describe as Congo's "first" coup because there is some debate as to whether the country's constitution allowed the president (as contrasted with the parliament) to make such a change (Kwitny, 1984: 63). When Lumumba responded by arming his supporters, he was pursued by "government" forces in what in hindsight can be seen as the start of a five-year civil war. Kasavubu then named Mobutu as interim head of the government on September 14th, in what some refer to as "Mobutu's coup" owing to the pressure the army chief put upon the Head of State. In this context, he was supported by the US CIA chief on the scene, Lawrence Devlin, who also recommended the "permanent disposal" of not only Prime Minister Lumumba, but also of his supporters in the cabinet, including Deputy Prime Minister Antoine Gizenga (Kalb, 1982: 97).

The details of CIA complicity in Lumumba's assassination four months later are murky, but began to be confirmed during Senator Frank Church's Intelligence Committee investigations in 1975. From this source, one learns that as early as an NSC meeting of August 18, 1960, Eisenhower instructed Agency Director Allen Dulles that the United States had to do "whatever is necessary to get rid of him" (Kwitny, 1984: 62; US Senate, 1975: 57). The two September coups, encouraged by US Ambassador Claire Timberlake and his deputy Frank Carlucci, were the first steps in this process (Weissman, 1979: 267). Dulles cabled CIA Chief Devlin to take "even more aggressive action if it can remain covert . . . [and] . . . targets of opportunity present themselves to you" (US Senate, 1975: 16).

Among the more bizarre efforts to eliminate Lumumba, the CIA's Special Assistant for Scientific Matters, Joseph Schneider, investigated biological material that could produce a disease "indigenous to the area" and that could kill an individual "or incapacitate him so severely that he would be out of action" (US Senate, 1975: 21). Another CIA scientist, Dr. Sidney Gottlieb, was assigned to produce a poison to be injected into Lumumba's toothpaste to incapacitate him and eliminate him from "any possibility of resuming governmental position" (Kwitny, 1984: 67).

When these efforts failed, however, the plan was hatched to turn Lumumba over to his main political enemy, Tshombé. Pursuant to this strategy the new Kasavubu-Mobutu government army captured Lumumba on December 2, 1960, and after holding him for six weeks, put him on the plane to Katanga on January 17, 1961. After being met at the airport by Tshombé's soliders and their Belgian advisors, he was never seen again. Recently, Belgian sources have revealed more details of that country's complicity in this scheme: viz., that two Belgian police officers were the ones who shot Lumumba, cut up his body, and threw pieces of it into a bin of sulphuric acid (Namikas, 2000: 26; DeWitte, 2001).

Lumumba was assassinated just before John F. Kennedy became president; but under JFK, US involvement in Congo's continuing civil war only intensified (Mahoney, 1983: 65–66). Aid to the regime of President Kasavubu and Army Chief Mobutu reached some $400 million over the next four years during which 100,000 died as the pair attempted to put down continued rebellions in the northeast and southeast. During this time, all the main Congolese politicians except for Gizenga were receiving payments from American intelligence agents, who also had hundreds of white mercenaries on the scene helping various sides in the civil war (Prouty, 1974: 129–30; Weissman, 1974: 105, 205).

In the northeast, Lumumba's followers regrouped under Gizenga and fought on for about a year; in the southeast Tshombé lasted for almost three years, as he supplemented his Belgian advisors with some 500 soldiers of fortune from the white racist regimes in South Africa and Rhodesia. In the center, Kasavubu and Mobutu appointed as Prime Minister Cyrille Adoula, recommended on the basis of his affiliation with the CIA-subsidized Congolese trade union movement dating from the days of Belgian rule. During Kennedy's years, the United States worked through the UN to funnel money to this "central government," which never really controlled more than half the country. It was successful, however, in capturing Gizenga in January, 1962, and in co-opting (by naming as prime minister) Tshombé in 1964. At this time, the United Nations considered the job done and departed; but also by this time, Johnson had succeeded Kennedy as US president and a more unilateral American resolution of the Congo civil war was adopted.

The followers of Lumumba/Gizenga had regrouped in an organization called the *Simbas,* or Lions (and which included among its members Laurent Kabila, the man who eventually became president in 1997). As prime minister, Tshombé relied not only upon Mobutu's army, but also upon the mercenaries with which he was originally associated in the southeast plus, upon CIA recommendation, some additional anti-communist Cuban pilots from Miami looking for action in the wake of the failed Bay or Pigs invasion (Weissman, 1979: 272–73). Using particularly these mercenary forces, Tshombé moved to end the rebellion of the "leftists" in the northeast in the fall of 1964. From the American perspective, the center (Kasavabu and Mobutu) was using the right to subdue the left; Tshombé and his expatriate army would be discarded when the job was done.

A critical episode occurred in November, 1964, when the *Simbas* seized as hostages several hundred white (mostly European) expatriates, but also including 39 Americans, working in the eastern part of the country. The United States flew in 600 Belgian paratroopers in a rescue mission; they were accompanied by Tshombé's mercenary forces that moved in on the ground. In the operation, 30 hostages were killed, including a renowned American missionary doctor, Paul E. Carlson. But all the rest, including 37 Americans, were freed. After briefly securing the area, however, the US-European military force pulled out, and the fighting between the rebels and Tshombé's white mercenaries resumed.

For the next several months, a war raged in the northeast quadrant of Congo. In response to the presence of anti-communist Cuban exiles in the employ of the government, Fidel Castro sent a small contingent of Cuban military advisors including, for a brief period, Ché Guevara. But they were soon withdrawn, the Africans being deemed insufficiently Marxist to merit such help from the vanguard party (Kwitny, 1984: 84–85). Meanwhile, back in the capital, Americans were the prime movers in a coup on November 25, 1965, in which Army Chief Mobutu finally overthrew both Kasavubu and Tshombé and took over the running of the government and the winding up of the war in the northeast (Stockwell,1978: 187–88).

With the accession to power by Mobutu, America achieved a compliant client in the strategic heart of Africa (Congo borders nine other states) for the next 32 years. For many of these years this was considered one of the great success stories in US keeping of Soviet influence out of central African during the Cold War (Schatzberg, 1991). As time passed, however, the embrace of the dictator became an embarrassment to the United States (Jackson, 1982: 47–50). Mobutu eliminated the political opposition and channeled all the country's productive enterprises into firms controlled by his friends and family members, making himself one of the richest men on the planet ($5 billion in net worth) by the time of his overthrow in 1997. Meanwhile, the Congo's 40 million people became one of the world's most impoverished (UN Human Development Index rank of 152, out of 174 countries).

Even with this dismal record, it took a seven-month civil war with help from four of Congo's neighbors to oust an ailing, aging Mobutu and install the old *Simba*, Kabila, in 1997. But neither this government nor its successor (his son, Joseph Kabila), have been able to bring the country under the control of a central government. As of this writing (2004), more than 2 million people have died, and two additional neighboring countries have joined, in the various post-Mobutu wars of succession. The legacy of America's man in Africa has been a disaster for the unfortunate citizens of that entire region (Wrong, 2000).

### CASE 8. CUBA, 1961

Another secret CIA operation begun under Eisenhower, but which reached its climax under Kennedy was the Bay of Pigs invasion of April

17, 1961. Cuba, then, is the first, and most significant, of four Western Hemisphere cases of American adventurism in the Third World involving Presidents Kennedy and Johnson in the brief four-year period, 1961–65; the others are British Guiana, Brazil, and the Dominican Republic (CASEs 9, 12, and 13). In each of these interventions, the motivation was to defend America's preeminent position in the home hemisphere against real or imagined threats of Soviet-inspired communism. Although the anti-communist rationale reflects the post-1947, post-OAS justification for US intervention in this region, the practice of American interference in the politics of neighboring states to the south can be traced back to the Monroe Doctrine of 1823 and the Roosevelt Corollary of 1904.

In addition to geostrategic hegemony, in all four cases capitalism is chosen over democracy as the goal to be preserved. In Cuba the methods are the most extreme, involving attempts at invasion and assassination, as well as a legacy of state-sponsored terrorism carried out by Cuban exiles from Miami (Blum, 2000: 79–80, 108–11). As in Guatemala, it was primarily the ideology of capitalism that was seen at stake here rather than any specific economic interests—although there were some of these: American sugar companies, Mafia-run casinos, and so forth. But the risky activities to be described next cannot have been undertaken for such dubious pecuniary concerns. The consequences of US policy in Cuba in 1961 were drastic: bringing the world to the brink of nuclear war during the missile crisis of October 1962 (Walton, 1973: 104), and even (some would assert) causing the assassination of President Kennedy himself. In any case, the events of 1961–63 were followed by more than 40 years of one-party dictatorship in Cuba and, in the long run, diplomatic embarrassment and isolation for the United States.

The 1961 invasion at the Bay of Pigs on the south shore of Cuba by 1,500 exiles armed and trained by the CIA in central America was inspired by the successful overthrow of the government of Guatemala in 1954 (*Operation Zapata*, 1981: xi). Flush with the alleged lessons of that "success," the United States began plotting against Fidel Castro soon after he came to power on January 1, 1959, and particularly after his promulgation of the Agrarian Reform Law on May 17, 1959 (Welch, 1985). It was on March 17, 1960, that Eisenhower officially approved a memorandum titled "A Program of Covert Action Against the Castro Regime," which led to the invasion; but it was under Kennedy that the final execution of the $100 million "Operation Zapata" was carried out 13 months later.

The complete Eisenhower plan for "regime change" in Cuba was called "Operation Pluto" and included such harassments as cutting back on Cuba's sugar export quota to the United States, a propaganda offensive against Castro using shortwave broadcasting facilities from offshore Swan Island, building up of political forces inside Cuba more acceptable to the United States, and development of the aforementioned paramilitary force outside of Cuba. Small, militant anti-Castro groups were funded to carry out acts of sabotage against sugar mills, power stations, water mains, and public transportation. It was during this time, the Church Committee discovered in 1975, that Richard Bissell, the Agency's Deputy Director of Operations, hatched the first CIA plans to assassinate Castro, along with such other outlandish schemes to discredit him as contaminating the air of his radio station with an LSD-like spray that would cause his lengthy speeches to become incoherent, and the placing of depilatory powder in his cigars to make his beard fallout. The cost for these activities in Fiscal Year 1960 was $15 million, from which the first $150,000 for a Mafia assassination of Castro was also committed (Prados, 1996: 178–79; Karabell, 1999: 182–87; US Senate, 1975: 73–83).

But all of these dirty tricks, which failed to dent Castro's support among his people, paled in comparison to the plan for "Zapata," the amphibious invasion of exile troops that was supposed to inspire, and link up with, a simultaneous indigenous rebellion. As has been amply documented, the operation was a total disaster (Higgins, 1987: 154–73; Vanderbroucke, 1984: 490–91). Secrecy, a crucial element of success, had been breached early on. Air support, also critical in an amphibious operation, was more controversial. Among the questions it has inspired are: had Eisenhower indicated the United States would provide such and Kennedy vetoed it? or, more likely, had eager CIA operatives gone beyond their mandate and promised coverage higher-ups in the US government had never approved? (Karabell, 1999: 175–77; *Operation Zapata*, 1981: xii–xiii). In any case, when the exiles' force landed on the Cuban beaches, they were met by Castro's army, which promptly killed about 100 of them and captured most of the rest. Among the dead were four American pilots flying cover for the operation, shot down by Castro's air defenses.

Within a week of the failure at the Bay of Pigs, Kennedy met with the leaders of the Cuban exiles in the White House and promised that the United States would continue its efforts to oust Castro, only now it would have to be by stealthier means (Hinckle and Turner, 1981; Branch and Crile, 1975: 50). To indicate his seriousness of commitment, Kennedy put Col. Edward G. Lansdale (of Southeast Asian fame) in charge of "Operation Mongoose" and committed a budget of $50 million per year, three times that of the first years of "Pluto." This largess created an operations headquarters in Miami under a new station chief, Theodore Shackley, who ran a virtual state within a state with a staff of several hundred Americans directing thousands of Cuban agents. With a fleet of hundreds of motorboats based throughout the Florida Keys, the exiles engaged in sea and air commando raids on oil refineries, railroad bridges, sugar cane fields, and other key parts of the Cuban economic infrastructure (Prados, 1996: 211; US Senate, 1975: 139–48).

More ominously, the operation also included as many as 33 attempts to assassinate Castro, prompting Lyndon Johnson later to opine that Kennedy had been "running a damned Murder Incorporated in the Carib-bean" (Weiner, 1998: 27). Some of these abortive hits employed the Mafia still smarting from the closing down of its casinos and brothels by the new, revolutionary regime. In one case, a link has been made between William Harvey, head of CIA's Task Force W, which supervised the Miami station, and Mafioso Johnny Rosselli (Zepezauer, 1994: 23; Prados, 1996: 212–14; US Senate, 1975: 126–31, 153). Similar ties of these people with Lee Harvey Oswald and Jack Ruby cause many to see a connection be-tween the Kennedy administration's attempts to assassinate Castro, and the assassination of Kennedy himself two years later. But all of this activity ended with the Cuban missile crisis in October 1962.

After the Bay of Pigs and its proof of American government involve-ment in efforts to overthrow him, Castro turned to the USSR for protection against a future invasion. The Soviet Union responded with a promise of "defensive" missiles, with potential nuclear warhead capacity. When sites for these weapons began to be prepared in Cuba, and Soviet ships carrying missiles were sighted sailing across the Atlantic, the scene was set for the crisis, the high point of the Cold War for many observers (Fursenko and Naftali, 1997). The details of this nuclear stand-off are well known (Na-than, 2000) and not the focus of this book in that they involve a direct Soviet-American conflict. Suffice to say, after 13 tense days, the American naval blockade worked, forcing the Soviet ships to turn around and return home without offloading their deadly cargo. As far as the themes of this book are concerned, the most significant result was that in return for the removal of the Soviet missiles, the United States promised not to support any more invasions of the island. The United States would limit its future opposition to the Castro regime to economic sanctions and diplomatic isolation.

For Cuba, the long-term consequence of Kennedy's policies has been the extreme longevity of Castro's rule (Paterson, 1994: 262–63), probably the oldest, most enduring regime in the world at the time of this writing. Although a one-party dictatorship, Castro himself has been surprisingly popular with the majority of the Cuban people. His socialist programs of health and education, subsidized until 1989 with Soviet aid, delivered a standard of living higher than that of most other countries in central America and the Caribbean. As of the late 1980s, Cuba was rated first in Latin America according to Ruth Sivard's respected Economic and Social Ranking, and scored 98 out of 100 on Morris D. Morris's Physical Quality of Life Indicator (Sullivan, 1991: 227–28).

For the United States, the events of 1961–63 led to a long-term "loss" of Cuba to the US sphere of influence in its own "backyard" (Morley, 1988: 305–10). This embarrassment has become greater as the years passed and more of the OAS allies (and even the Pope, in 1998) resumed diplomatic and economic relations with Cuba. It is at the point today that the United

States, not Cuba, is the party most isolated from the rest of the world regarding the investment and tourism opportunities being seized by Canadians, Mexicans, and Europeans on the Caribbean's largest island (Kaplowitz, 1988).

Domestically, the power of the Cuban exile community in Miami has had significant "blowback" effects in the US political arena, above and beyond its obvious impact on Florida's presidential electoral vote. Veterans of the Bay of Pigs fiasco were prominent in the 1972 Watergate break-in of Democratic Party headquarters and the resulting disgrace of President Nixon. Even after the end of the Cold War, provocative over-flights of Cuban territory by the Miami-based "Brothers to the Rescue" in 1995 led to a deadly response by Castro's air defense and, ultimately, to the passage of the Helms-Burton Act. Under its terms, the United States now has a policy of sanctions not only against Cuba but even against its own NATO allies if their corporations do business involving any former American properties nationalized by Castro. In short, US diplomacy toward the island is essentially frozen, held in thrall to the nation's lasting grievances from setbacks suffered 40 years ago.

## CASE 9. BRITISH GUIANA, 1961–66

The American involvement in British Guiana, 1961–66, is not widely noted due to the small (population 560,000) colony's relative insignificance in world politics. But because the US intervention followed a classic pattern in its methods and motivation, it is worth a brief mention in *American Adventurism Abroad* (Fraser, 1994). It is also noteworthy for being the first step in the America's replacing the UK as the major power in the black, English-speaking states of the Caribbean Basin (see also CASE 23: Grenada, 1983).

Dr. Cheddi Jagan, a mild-mannered dentist and leader of Guiana's Peoples Progressive Party (PPP), was thrice elected president under the British colonial administration—in 1953, 1957, and 1961—and he was headed to be his country's leader at the time of its scheduled independence in 1963. With a power base rooted in the labor unions of plantation workers made up mainly of South Asian Indians—the largest ethnic group with 47 percent of the population—Jagan was easily the most popular politician in the country. But the new Kennedy administration, reeling from its embarrassing defeat at the Bay of Pigs, felt it could not tolerate the presence of another leftist government on the fringes of the Caribbean and so proceeded to polarize the political situation there (Parekh, 1999).

There were two other political parties in British Guiana: the Peoples National Congress (PNC) under Forbes Burnham, drawn largely from the African 35 percent of the population who were mainly employed in the unionized civil service, police and the military; and the United Front (UF), led by a Portuguese businessman, Peter D'Aguiar, and which drew its support from the 13 percent of the people who were European or of mixed race; the remaining 5 percent were Amerindians not involved in politics (Spinner, 1984).

Unlike in the Congo (CASE 7), where the United States affiliated with the center against the Soviet-backed left and Belgian-linked right, in Guiana, the USSR was not a player, and the British saw Jagan as a left-centrist alternative to Castroite revolution; his PPP was also moderate in its appeals to a broad multiracial coalition of supporters. The US allied itself with what it thought was the more economically right-wing party, Burnham's PNC, which was also more politically extreme in that it made blatant racist appeals in attempts to increase the participation of the black minority. The chosen instrument of US interfering was not the covert use of force as in most of the past cases to this point, but rather a more subtle tinkering with the modalities of the colony's electoral processes, and the use of CIA front organizations in the labor movement as its preferred means of entry into Guiana's politics.

In the August 1961 parliamentary election, which democratically reconfirmed (for the third time) the popularity of Jagan as the destined independence leader, his PPP got 43 percent of the vote and 20 seats in the 35-seat representative assembly; the PNC got 41 percent of the vote and 11 seats; the UF had 16 percent of the vote and 4 seats (Singh, 1988: 29). The election was held under the UK's traditional First-Past-the-Post system, a staple throughout the British Empire and in most Anglo-Saxon societies (including the United States), where candidates run in geographic districts and the person with the most votes wins, even if the percentage is less than 50 percent in multiparty races (Sullivan, 1996: 58).

American intervention in British Guiana over the next two years was designed to pressure Britain into delaying the scheduled 1963 independence, and to having another vote. This election, however, would be conducted under the more European Proportional Representation (PR) electoral system, in which candidates would run on party lists and seats would be allocated on the basis of overall party strength nationwide. As a result of two CIA-financed strikes to be described below, the planned 1963 independence was postponed, and another election was held in December 1964, in which the size of the parliament was raised from 35 to 53. Under the new PR voting system, the PPP still had the highest percentage of votes, 46 percent (more than before), but was allotted only 24 seats. The PNC got 41 percent of the vote (as earlier), but now had 22 seats. The UF with 12 percent of the vote won 7 seats (Kibbe, 2002: 29). The British Governor General asked PNC leader Forbes Burnham to form a coalition government with the UF, and when this happened, promptly put independence back on schedule—for 1966.

How did the United States get Britain to delay the date of independence and change its electoral system? There were two crucial labor actions, in February 1962 and April 1963. In the first, the PNC, the UF and the colony's Trades Union Council sponsored a general strike to protest an austerity budget being promoted by the PPP government. The TUC was led by Richard Ismael, who several months earlier had been promised by Assistant Secretary of State William Burdett help for strengthening his unions of black civil service workers as a bulwark against Jagan (Kibbe, 2002: 20). The vehicle for this help would be the Public Services International (PSI), a London-based secretariat for international unions of government employees. The PSI was channeled money from its US affiliate, the American Federation of State, County, and Municipal Employees (AFSCME). More CIA funds came via a conduit known as the Gotham Foundation. On the scene a CIA operative named Gene Meakins worked for the TUC putting out a weekly newspaper and daily radio program of anti-Jagan propaganda (Blum, 1995: 110–11, 442; Fraser, 2000: 596–97). The strike led to rioting and arson that burnt down the center of the capital city, Georgetown, and took on racial overtones as the largely black police force stood by while protesters attacked the shops of South Asians (Jagan, 1966: 252–69). The unrest led the United States to complain to Britain that the colony was not ready for independence, and to argue that it should be delayed until "stability" could be restored.

But Britain did not succumb to these and other American entreaties over the next year, and in 1963 was still planning on independence before the end of the year. Then in April 1963, another general strike was called by the TUC. In between the two strikes, its leader Ismael traveled to the United States for training at the new American Institute for Free Labor Development. The AIFLD was established by President Kennedy in 1962 as a way of channeling money to anti-communist labor unions in Latin America; among its guiding spirits were Secretary of Labor Arthur Goldberg, George Meany, the head of the AFL-CIO (AFSCME's parent organization), and the new, post–Bay of Pigs, CIA Director John McCone (Kwitny, 1984: 341). It was an adjunct to Kennedy's Alliance for Progress plan for capitalist development in Latin America, supposedly a more benign form of intervention than sponsored invasions (Romualdi, 1967: 346–52).

Again the CIA and PSI were involved in funneling moneys to the strikers. The funds not only went for food and supplies but also for radio time for Ismael. This time the strike lasted 80 days, the longest in Guiana's history (Jagan, 1966: Chapters 13–14). The total amount of external funding reached more than a million dollars. In addition to Ismael, five other graduates of the CIA-funded AIFLD sat on the strike committee and Meakins was on the strikers' negotiating team. This time open racial warfare broke out and 300 people died (Rabe, 1999: 90; Fraser, 2000: 605). The government and economy were brought to a standstill. In the midst of the strife, the UK allowed Cuban and Soviet ships to bring emergency supplies to the government. It was in this context that President Kennedy met with British Prime Minister Harold Macmillan at Birch Grove, England, and referred to Latin America as "the most dangerous area in the world" (Rabe, 1999: 91). Shortly thereafter, the UK called off the independence for that year, and decreed the system of proportional representation for a new election.

The results of this tainted election have been noted above. But the PNC did not merely win this vote; as the incumbent government, it proceeded to rig the political system to ensure minority-African, one-party rule for the next 26 years. Ironically for the United States, soon after independence Burnham embraced an economic ideology of "cooperative socialism" (Rabe, 1999: 94–95; Kibbe, 2002: 29), but by this time American attention had moved from "the most dangerous area in the world" to Vietnam. The issue of control over the minor economic fruits of this tiny land on the northeast coast of South America in which the United States had less than $50 million in investments, was ignored for a generation.

It was only after the Cold War ended that the United States tolerated truly free elections and multiparty democracy in independent Guyana. When this occurred, in 1992, the election was won by none other than Cheddi Jagan, now in his 80s. After his death, his 77-year-old widow won the country's second free election, in 1997 ("Guyana: Hello Again," 1997). In the interim, under corrupt, racist one-party rule endorsed by the United States, Guyana went from one of the strongest economies in Caribbean basin in the 1960s, to Number 83 of 142 countries in Ruth Sivard's Economic and Social Ranking, 18th out of 24 states measured in the Western Hemisphere (Sullivan, 1991: 226).

## INDOCHINA-II

Whereas intervention in the Western Hemisphere was part of an historic pattern of US interference in the region, the Kennedy administration's policies in Southeast Asia represented a significant expansion of American activism in to a new part of the world: Indochina. At first JFK tried to remove the most contentious issue, Laos, from the foreign policy agenda by finessing a neutralist agreement in negotiations in 1961–62, and limiting the US commitment to the anti-communist cause there to sub-rosa activities. In reaction to this, however, greater military attention was given to the more significant "domino," South Vietnam (Warner, 1995; Toye, 1968). The next two cases follow up on the Introduction to Indochina events of Chapter 2. In keeping with the focus of this book, however, the major war of the United States in Vietnam, 1965–73, will not be analyzed here; rather, the focus will be on the low-level counter-insurgency operations in South Vietnam before that time and on the "secret war" that was waged next door in Laos.

## CASE 10. LAOS, 1961–73

Laos was the first country covered by the 1954 Geneva Accords where the political arrangements established by the Great Powers began to unravel. For the next 20 years, power there reflected the struggles of three groups: the right under General Phoumi Nosavan, with links to Thailand and the US CIA; the neutralist-center under Prince Souvanna Phouma, installed as prime minister as part of the 1954 Accords; and the left under Prince Souphanouvong, with ties to North Vietnam and the USSR. The last two of these personalities were half-brothers, representing rival wings of the historic royal family that had collaborated with the French colonialists, especially in resisting Japan during World War II. After 1950, however, Souphanouvong founded the Pathet Lao ("Lao Nation") party and allied with the Vietminh against France; his was the only group in the country serious about social change from its royal-feudal system (Langer and Zasloff, 1970). During the 1950s, the US policy was to favor the right, and barely tolerate the center only when politics came under pressure from the left, all the while consolidating its replacement of France as the hegemonic power in the region.

The 1954 Accords set up a coalition government dominated by centrist and right-wing forces, headed by the neutralist Souvanna Phouma, but also including a few members of the left. Under its terms, parts of the Pathet Lao military were integrated into the national armed forces; others remained unreconciled and continued a low-level, largely ineffective, insurgency against the new government. In the 1958 elections for the National Assembly, the Pathet Lao won 13 of 21 contested seats, increasing its numbers there to about one-third of the total. In reaction, and in anticipation of American disapproval of increased leftist power, the assembly forced out Prime Minister Souvanna Phouma. He was replaced with Phoui Sananikone who soon used his majority in the assembly to dissolve it altogether and to call off future elections in an effort to "to counteract communist influence and subversion" (Blum, 1995: 140).

Over the next two years, the United States engineered other (nonelectoral and unconstitutional) governmental changes, using hundreds of millions of dollars in aid to manipulate the currency, bribe politicians in the Laotian parliament, and to withhold the pay of troops who did not support the US-picked candidates for prime minister. On one occasion, in January 1959, as a condition of aid, the government renounced Laos's Geneva Accords neutrality. Finding itself forced out of government and legitimate politics, the Pathet Lao representatives took up arms again, rejoining their compatriots who had never put them down in 1954. By

May 1959, the recombined forces were waging a major insurgency against the right-wing government. In response, American aid to Laos rose to $50–55 million per year, a huge amount for such a small country (population: 3 million); on a per capita basis it was the largest American aid recipient in the world. The money paid for 65 percent of the government's expenditures, including the entirety of the budget for the 25,000-man army (Goldstein, 1975: 132–37; Hess, 1998: 68–70). Two results were widespread corruption within the army and rampant inflation in the Laotian economy.

In response, the CIA created what it hoped would be a more trustworthy army of 9,000 Hmong tribesmen that would be used to outflank the official military and to destabilize governments that were uncooperative with the United States. Ethnic Lao comprised only about half of the people of Laos; the Sino-Tibetan Hmong represented about 13 percent of the population. Though numbering less than 400,000, the Hmong under their leader Vang Po and his CIA/Special Forces advisors, were highly motivated to assert their identity vis-a-vis Laotians, and even more so with respect to the more historically repressive Vietnamese (Hamilton-Merritt, 1993: 39–46; Moore, 1965).

The situation regressed in 1960 when three coups occurred. In April, General Nosavan backed the reinstallation of Sananikone, who wanted to intensify the war against the Pathet Lao. In August, a coup led by Army Colonel Kong Le brought back Souvanna Phouma and attempted to reconcile the center with the left. In December, General Nosavan struck back, inserting another member of the royal clan, a distant cousin Prince Boun Oum, as prime minister. Although these CIA-linked men once again controlled the capital, Kong Le and Souphanouvong joined forces to control 70 percent of the countryside (Fall, 1969: 170–99; Karabell, 1999: 213).

It was in this context that lame-duck president Eisenhower warned Kennedy in their foreign policy transition briefing that Laos represented the worst foreign policy crisis on the incomer's agenda (Schlesinger, 1965: 299). But Kennedy, after initially considering increasing the US military commitment to Boun Oum, was sobered by his experience at the Bay of Pigs. In the midst of that crisis, on April 16, 1961, he decided to opt for a more diplomatic solution to America's problems in Laos. Following the 1954 precedent, a conference of Great Powers was convened in Geneva and Kennedy sent Averell Harriman as his special ambassador to work out the details of an American extrication from the situation. In the Declaration on the Neutrality of Laos of July 23, 1962, a tripartite government of national unity under a restored Souvanna Phouma was set up, and the neutrality of the country vis-a-vis the growing conflict next door in Vietnam was legally reestablished (Dommen, 1964). Although the arrangement prevailed in the capital, Vientiane, for a while, it did not reflect realities in the rest of the country. The CIA and its Hmong and rightist-Laotian allies, led by Vang Po and General Nosavan, continued to control many mountainous areas, whereas the Pathet Lao retained dominance of the strategic Plain of Jars.

This situation deteriorated further in April 1964, when General Nosavan engineered yet another coup to drive out the left-wing members of the three-party government. This move should be seen as a piece with increased CIA activities in Vietnam and part of the expanding American war there under new President Lyndon B. Johnson (see, e.g., the OPLAN 34A commando assaults in CASE 11). The CIA-aided Hmong army in Laos began to triple its size to some 30,000 as additional mercenaries were recruited from Thailand, the Philippines, Taiwan and South Korea (Prados, 1996: 269–74; Branfman, 1976: 48–55; Blum, 1995: 141). Known as the *Armée Clandestine* and modeled after the French Foreign Legion, this "secret army" was soon supported by some 3,000 American Special Forces in country helping with logistics, and launching low-level sabotage and terror attacks in North Vietnam (Castle, 1993: 42–43).

In addition, there were 4,000 CIA contract workers and other soldiers of fortune on the payroll of the legendary "Air America" based in Thailand and flying in supplies on a regular basis (Robbins, 1985: Chapters 5 and 8; Prouty, 1974: 190–93). Headed by Charles Pierce Gabeler, who later became head of air operations for the entire CIA, this "private" airline fielded more than 140 aircraft, most of them DC-3 and C-123 transports flown by retired American military pilots (Pace, 1998: 23). To finance this "off-the-books" operation, in addition to laundering money through an expanded A.I.D. program, the CIA and its secret army trafficked in opium and refined heroin in a laboratory in northern Laos. By 1970, this Golden Triangle area of Laos, northern Thailand, and northeast Burma had become the source of 70 percent of the world's illicit opium, morphine, and heroin (McCoy et al., 1972: 244–48; Robbins, 1985: Chapter 9).

As the North Vietnamese increased their use of the southeast corner of Laos for the "Ho Chi Minh Trail" of supplies to the communists in the south of Vietnam, the American bombing of Laos began in earnest. From 1965 to 1973—as part of "Operation Rolling Thunder" under Lyndon Johnson, and then secretly under Richard Nixon—more than 2 million tons of bombs were dropped on Laos, more than were visited upon Germany and Japan combined during World War II (Branfman, 1972). To this day, Laos remains the most bombed country in history with an estimated one million people (one-third of the population) killed or made homeless during this "secret" war. In the words of one American official, the bombs were "aimed at the systematic destruction of the material basis of civilian society" (Nashell, 1997: 40). By the time the communists finally won the war, Laos had become a land of nomads and refugees with most villages and farms destroyed (Stevenson, 1972). This carnage was largely attributable to the introduction of American military technology in to an otherwise low-level conflict; that scale of devastation never could have been wrought if the Laotians had been left to fight on their own.

But, US activities in Laos were largely conducted in secret, at least as far as the American people were concerned; (the inhabitants of that unhappy country certainly knew they were being bombed). Some would say that this kind of stealth operation was preferable to the kind of war America waged next door in South Vietnam; and many supporters of the current "war on terror" see it as a model for a war fought with specialized troops with minimal political oversight and few questions asked. But Laos was a little, landlocked country, with no inherent strategic significance apart from the war surrounding it in Vietnam. It could not serve as the template for a solution in Vietnam (as will be seen in the next case), not to mention a war against terrorism with "global reach."

## CASE 11. SOUTH VIETNAM, 1961–65

The low-profile way the United States handled the situation in Laos could have provided a precedent for Vietnam, if the goal was to keep the conflict from overwhelming US domestic politics. But the stakes in Vietnam were larger (15 times as many people, historic dominant nation of the entire peninsula, etc.). Moreover, right-wing critics in the United States would not countenance another "sell-out," as the 1962 agreement in Laos was often termed.

After its official founding on December 20, 1960, the National Liberation Front quickly began to gain support in the villages of South Vietnam, militarily conquering some, politically infiltrating others. Armed followers of this communist-led, but broadly based, movement grew from 2,000 hard-core cadre in 1959 to 7,000 in 1960, 10,000 in 1961 (Hess, 1998: 67). Although some of the NLF leaders were from the north (or were pre-1954 southerners returning from the north), the movement was overwhelmingly southern in composition (O'Ballance, 1981: 43). Their policy of taking land owned by absentee landlords and turning it over to the peasants who worked on it, and of providing education and health services that the government had ignored, proved popular. It was also becoming more obvious that South Vietnamese President Ngo Dinh Diem was not his own man, but a puppet of the Americans. Under Eisenhower, $1.2 billion in military and economic aid moneys had been spent to keep him in power, an absolute sum that dwarfed the relatively large amount committed to Laos.

In reaction to the growing appeal of Diem's opponents, the United States pressed him to adopt political reforms in order to become more popular with (i.e., "win the hearts and minds of") the people. But Diem refused to redistribute lands he had taken from the Viet Minh back to the 85 percent of the population of peasants who tilled them. Instead, he sold them off to wealthy capitalists who lived in the cities, and pocketed the proceeds for his government. In addition, Diem, a Roman Catholic from an authoritarian Confucian tradition (Warner, 1963), was unsophisticated in his understanding of the theory of counter-insurgency political-warfare advanced by his American advisors. In short, "America's Mandarin" (Karnow, 1997: 222) was ill-suited to quasi-democratic pursuits. Instead, Diem responded to the growing NLF presence in the South with a policy of repression and strategic hamlets.

The repression took the form of jailing the leaders of the Buddhists and other religious sects that opposed his narrowly based regime (Diem's Catholics represented less than 5 percent of the population). The "hamlets" program moved entire villages behind barbed-wire fences to "protect them" from creeping Viet Cong (i.e., Vietnamese Communist) presence. Although this was part of the counter-insurgency policy recommended by the United States, it had no chance of winning the political loyalty of the inhabitants without accompanying social services. In the absence of such, the hamlets resembled little more than concentration camps (Fall, 1963: 378; Halberstam, 1965: 188). Buddhists and others who practiced ancestor worship resented being moved from the sites of historic family graves. The policy, arguably in violation of the Geneva convention against forced removal of peoples, was so unpopular that by 1963 the number of NLF supporters under arms had grown to 100,000.

In response, the number of US military advisors also rose, from fewer than 1,000 (the maximum number of "outside forces" under Eisenhower) to more than 16,000 by the time of Kennedy's death. About half of these were combat troops initially disguised as flood relief specialists because of the desire to cloud the degree of dependency of Diem upon American military support (Schulzinger, 1997: 110; Karnow, 1997: 267–69). But the Americans had limited impact because the government in Saigon would not embrace a reform program for land ownership, and persisted in an exclusively military response to the political threats against it. When anti-Diem protests became too provocative to ignore—for example, after the self-immolation of several Buddhist leaders in the spring of 1963—the United States decided the remote, unresponsive Diem had to go. This judgment became even more urgent after it was discovered that Diem's brother and head of secret police, Ngo Dinh Nhu, was putting out feelers for talks with the Viet Cong (Buzzanco, 1999: 68–69).

Gathering political cover, in August 1963 President Kennedy dispatched as his new Ambassador to South Vietnam the 1960 Republican candidate for Vice President Henry Cabot Lodge. His mission: replace the Diem government with one more amenable to American advice as to how to fight a counter-insurgency war (Lodge, 1965: 209–12). Unfortunately for the United States, the "removal" of the Diem government resulted in his assassination on November 1, 1963. The 1975 Church Committee whitewashes the US complicity in this affair, spending only seven pages of its 349-page report on this incident (as compared with an average of 55 pages each for the other four assassinations analyzed) and weaselly summarizing that America was "not . . . irrevocably against" and "not . . . actively condoning" the assassination (US Senate, 1975: 217). Nevertheless, the presence of Col. Lucien Conein, chief liaison of the CIA with the South Vietnamese military in Saigon, in the preparation of the coup is persistent, including his providing of $42,000 to the chief plotter for "food for his troops" and "death benefits to those killed in the coup" (US Senate, 1975: 222). When the widow, Madame Nhu, opined after Kennedy himself was assassinated 22 days later that "chickens were coming home to roost," most Americans did not know what she was talking about.

The destruction of the Diem government marked the beginning of the American take-over of the country and its war against the communists. The United States had removed a government without having a competent successor to replace it. In the 20-month period between November 1963 and June 1965, more than a dozen administrations were created and toppled in Saigon (Buzzanco, 1999: 69) before the United States settled upon Generals Nguyen Cao Ky and Nguyen van Thieu as the reliable clients who would run South Vietnam for the duration of the war. During the interregnum between stable regimes, the United States rushed in thousands of civilian advisors to staff the government agencies of the South and, more significantly, changed the mission of American soldiers there from advice to combat. In short, the United States took over the running of the government, the war, and the country itself (Logevall, 1999: 375, 387–88; Vandemark, 1991: 14–15).

In January 1964, the first of these post-Diem coups—engineered by the US Military Advisory Command in Vietnam (MACV), and often referred to as the "Pentagon coup"—replaced Duong Van (Big) Minh, leader of the junta that ousted Diem, with General Nguyen Khanh. Big Minh, so-called because of his relatively tall (for Vietnamese) 5'11" height, proved to be a more independent actor that the United States anticipated. As a Buddhist, he quickly moved to free from jail many of the religious leaders imprisoned by Diem in the spring of 1963. He also attempted to attract support from some noncommunist groups that had joined the NLF and he set up a rural welfare system whose objective was to co-opt, not repress, the NLF. On the diplomatic front, he expressed interest in plans for the neutralization of Indochina being floated by President Charles de Gaulle of France (Sullivan, 1978: 70). Finally, like Nhu before him, Big Minh tried to work out a compromise with Viet Cong (VC) intermediaries (Hess, 1998: 75–77). To the new US president, Johnson, such political flexibility, at a time when the American military was hell bent on mounting a bigger offensive, was out of the question: Big Minh had to go.

But Khanh, a pro-American general committed to a military solution to the political conflict in South Vietnam, lasted only a few months before he too was removed in the spring of 1964. This pattern of revolving-door governments persisted for more than a year, frustrating President Johnson to the point where he was once quoted as saying he wanted "no more of this coup shit" (Halberstam, 1972: 430). Finally, in June 1965, MACV—by this time with 100,000 American troops in country—came up with the team of Ky and Thieu, although no legitimizing election for their administration was even attempted until 1967 (Herman and Brodhead, 1984: 55–92). Democracy was not the goal here, but rather the survival of this vital outpost for global capitalism, and the replacement of France with the United States as hegemon of the region.

The change of American leadership from Kennedy to Johnson was critical in the evolution of US policy. While it can never be known for sure what Kennedy would have done in Vietnam, his previous about-face in Laos, plus his seemingly deeper understanding of the complexity of the political situation in South Vietnam, lead many to believe he would have avoided the escalation that Johnson embarked upon in 1964–65 (Freedman, 2000: 413). Kennedy probably would not have moved so quickly to overthrow Big Minh in January 1964; after that change of government, it was all downhill for America. On the other hand, Kennedy left Johnson with a weak hand to play; it was Kennedy's administration that overthrew Diem without adequately preparing the way for a successor, and it was JFK's foreign policy team that was still advising LBJ during this period.

But 1964 was a presidential election year for Lyndon Johnson, and he was determined that Vietnam would not be "lost" on his watch. Throughout the ten campaign months, as governments came and went in Saigon, Johnson increased the number of military advisors there from 17,000 to 24,000, and rushed in civilian bureaucrats as the United States virtually took over the administration of the government of the South Vietnam. He also greatly intensified clandestine operations against North Vietnam, which was increasingly supporting the insurgency of the VC/NLF in the south. In mid-January 1964, OPLAN34A—a program of more than 1,000 separate raids, acts of sabotage, harassment, and psychological warfare waged by South Vietnamese and Laotian irregular forces in cooperation with the CIA and American Special Forces—was launched against North Vietnam (Shultz, 2000: 40).

In this context, the Gulf of Tonkin incident(s) of August 2–4, 1964, became a critical turning point in gaining domestic political legitimacy for a more aggressive foreign policy. Though running for president as the "peaceful" alternative to the Republican Barry Goldwater, Johnson seized upon an incident of North Vietnamese torpedo boats' firing upon two US destroyers in the vicinity of South Vietnamese commandos infiltrating North Vietnam as part of OPLAN 34A. Claiming the American ships were attacked unprovoked on the high seas (they were actually only 10 miles offshore), the president extracted from Congress a resolution giving him the power to respond "with all necessary measures to repel any armed attack against the forces of the United States" (Goulden, 1969). This Congressional resolution, passed with only two dissenting votes out of 535, became the infamous "blank check" that enabled Johnson to escalate the war after winning the 1964 election as the candidate promising not to "send American boys . . . to do what Asian boys ought to be doing for themselves" (Schulzinger, 1997: 155).

It is beyond the scope of this book to get in to the details of the US war in Vietnam after 1965, during which 2 million people died and more than 3 million Americans were sent to fight in numbers reaching more than 500,000 annually during the four peak years of 1967–70. Suffice to say, for the United States the error was in allowing intervention in a foreign civil war to get transformed from a counter-insurgency operation in which America played an advisory role, into a full-blown conventional war involving the US saturation bombing of one country (North Vietnam, 1965–68), the overt ground invasion of another (Cambodia, in 1970; see CASE 15), and the expansion of a "secret" war in a third (Laos; see CASE 10). In short, it was a political blunder to allow a "Truman Doctrine" operation of military assistance to anti-communist forces in a civil war (as in Greece), to escalate into something bigger than the conventional war in Korea.

There were many differences between the American wars in Korea and Vietnam. In Korea, there was open aggression across an international boundary, when North Korea attacked South Korea on June 25, 1950. The repulsion of the North Korean Army was for three years a conflict involving conventional armies taking and exchanging land. Vietnam in contrast was a political insurgency in which southern VC/NLF partisans were trained and supplied and infiltrated back from the north through the "Ho Chi Minh Trail" in Laos and Cambodia. They rarely stood and fought battles against American forces, but rather engaged in hit-and-run military maneuvers against symbolic government outposts, while winning the allegiance of village peasants through political and military persuasion. The Americans and their South Vietnamese allies were reduced to "search and destroy" operations, with most of the time spent "searching" for the enemy.

The vast American conventional army deployed after 1965 was not up to waging such a political war. Whether the United States would have been more successful if it had kept fighting at the counter-insurgency level of 1961–63 will never be known (Summers, 1981: 48–58). Probably not; because after the removal of Diem, certainly after the ouster of Big Minh, South Vietnam did not have a government that was representative of, or acceptable to, its people. In fact, it hardly had a government at all in 1964 and 1965. The communist-led National Liberation Front had probably won the political war for the hearts and minds of the Vietnamese people in the south by that time. By destroying the countryside of the south with its bombing in support of ground operations there, and by overwhelming its culture and economy with the infusion of three million free-spending American troops, the United States in 1965–73 probably made the situation worse as far as winning the political support of the Vietnamese peasant.

## CASE 12. BRAZIL, 1964

The US involvement in the overthrow of the government of President Joao Goulart in Brazil on April 1, 1964, is not as well known as the American links to the regime changes in Iran, Guatemala, and South Vietnam (CASEs 4, 5, and 11). Indeed, there seems to be an almost inverse relationship between the size and importance of the country, and the attention drawn to the adventures of America in them; see CASE 14, Indonesia). Brazil is the most significant state in South America, its land mass occupying roughly half of that continent, and with a population greater than the next seven states combined. Its coup, and the US reaction to it, started a trend that engulfed the region for the next generation. Although the circumstances of CIA activity in Brazil are similar to those of the more notorious coup in Chile in 1973 (CASE 17), the case is not one that figures prominently in the investigations by the Senate Committee on Intelligence in 1975 or in the diplomatic histories of the times. Nevertheless, American animosity toward Brazil under Goulart is amply substantiated in much secondary literature (Leacock, 1990: 134–48, 161–70; Weiss, 1993) and in the sources noted below from which the following account is drawn.

The Brazilian military had been fearful of Goulart's leftist sympathies as early as 1954, when it pressured President Getulio Vargas's government to fire him as Labor Minister (Skidmore,1967: 130). When, in January 1961, Goulart was elected vice president—on a ticket with right-wing populist Janio Qadros—the military and its backers in the US Army's military aid program became quite concerned. This anxiety intensified when Quadros resigned from office after only seven months. The circumstances are murky, but in this short time it seems that Qadros had refused $300 million in US military aid (he regarded it a bribe) in return for his support of the Bay of Pigs invasion (Bell, 1972: 81; Black, 1977: 39). He also gave an award to Ché Guevara, took anti-colonial positions in the United Nations, and became the first Brazilian president to attend a meeting of non-aligned nations. For such efforts, he was criticized within the Kennedy administration for being an "impulsive neurotic," for his "peculiar temperament," and for "being vulnerable to communist influence" (Black, 1977: 40; Leacock, 1990: 37, 47).

Unlike the 1964 coup to be described below, however, this 1961 change of government was legitimate in that the military did not take over and

Qadros was succeeded by his vice president, although the constitutional transition was not a sure thing. A near civil war broke out between various branches of the military over whether Goulart should be allowed to succeed as president (Gerassi, 1965: 84–88). Constitutionalist military officers prevailed, but it was only a matter of time before their opponents, in Brazil and in the United States, began to organize the counterstrike. In 1962, about $15 million in CIA money was funneled to anti-Goulart candidates in Brazil's state-gubernatorial elections (Agee, 1975: 321). In a preview of what would happen in Chile ten years later, all *new* American economic aid was cut off to the central government, and the only aid that was continued was to military programs, and to selected state governors within Brazil's federal system (Parker, 1979: 87–97). Of the $600 million in loans approved by the A.I.D. during the Qadros/Goulart years, disbursement of 75 percent of it was withheld until after the 1964 coup (Black, 1977: 41).

The new American Institute for Free Labor Development (see CASE 9) also became a source of suspicious funding of Goulart's political enemies (Poelchau, 1981: 47–51). Although technically under the direction of the Agency for International Development, CIA involvement in the money conduit ensured that more than 7,000 labor leaders and union members were trained to support the military, particularly in areas of communications, during times of "national emergency" (Black, 1977: 117; Blum, 1995: 168). CIA moneys also funded propaganda criticisms in books and in the right-wing newspaper chain *Diarias Associades* against Goulart's "neutralist" foreign policy and against specific "socialist" members of his cabinet (Langguth, 1978: 89; Blum, 1995: 166). The (relatively mild) measures being protested were Goulart's nationalization of one International Telephone and Telegraph subsidiary, and the passage of a law limiting the profits foreign corporations could repatriate out of Brazil to 10 percent of their registered capital investment (Black, 1997: 39; Blum, 1995: 164).

In addition to these ideological crimes, Goulart took steps that were particularly threatening to the institutional military. Wary of US ties with the officer class that he felt had led to the earlier removal of Qadros, Goulart attempted to build up a following among noncommissioned officers (Skidmore, 1967: 296–97). When in September 1963, 600 enlisted men rebelled, the president refused to condemn them. After 2,000 sailors mutinied in March 1964, Goulart granted them an amnesty. For many high-ranking officers, this was the last straw. As the army prepared to move against Goulart, its chief of staff General Humberto Castello Branco drew upon a 20-year-old friendship formed with the US Embassy's Defense Attaché, Col. Vernon Walters, a military man with long-standing links to the intelligence community who later was to become Deputy Director of the CIA. Extra petroleum and ammunition was promised for upcoming "military maneuvers." Most critically, a US Navy show of force (including an aircraft carrier and guided missile destroyers) was dispatched into Bra-

zil's territorial waters (Parker, 1979: 68–69; Poelchau, 1981: 51). Like Arbenz in Guatemala in 1954 (CASE 5), Goulart chose to flee rather than risk
the blood of his countrymen in a futile fight to survive.

General Castello Branco assumed power and began 20 years of dictatorial military rule under himself and four uniformed successors. The representative assembly and the state legislatures were closed down, political
parties were outlawed, habeas corpus was abolished, unions were purged
of "leftist" leaders, and several thousand "suspected communists" were
jailed. Fifty thousand persons were arbitrarily arrested and detained in
the first few months after the takeover. Human rights groups estimate
that more than 2,000 persons were subjected to torture (Lernoux, 1982:
170–75, 320–32). About 350 people were killed by the government, and
about half that many simply "disappeared," beginning a phenomenon
that became widely copied throughout Latin America over the next decade as virtually every other country followed the Brazilian example.

One reason for this "domino" effect of Latin American coups was the
reaction of the United States to the new Brazilian regime. Instead of keeping its distance from, and its "deniability" in, the events of April 1, 1964,
the Johnson administration enthusiastically embraced the military dictatorship, sending a telegram congratulating the new government even
before Goulart went into exile. In violation of the spirit of Kennedy's Alliance for Progress, the US A.I.D.'s Office of Public Safety rushed in moneys to train 100,000 new policemen to support the military regime; these
new forces would also provide insurance against any future pro-Goulart
mutinies from within the traditional military (Huggins, 1998: 122–26;
Langguth, 1978: 131). In gratitude for this support, the following year
Brazil volunteered 1,100 troops to the US-"OAS" invasion of Dominican
Republic (CASE 13), the only Latin American country to send more than
a token force.

Over the next 20 years, Brazil became America's leading trading partner
and investment destination in Latin America, and the recipient of increasing amounts of US economic and military aid. Under the "Nixon Doctrine," Brazil was one of the particularly favored regional "policemen" in
the new American foreign policy of that time (see Introduction to Chapter
4). Pursuant to this plan, Brazil in 1969 began training the police of other
Latin American dictatorships, a practice that grew into the infamous
"Operation Condor" later in the decade (see CASE 17: Chile). There is
even some evidence that the Brazilian military was implicated in the early
death (at age 58) of Goulart in exile in Argentina in December 1976
(Rohter, 2000: 10). Democracy, thus, was snuffed out in Brazil, and much
of the rest of South America, for a generation. The US intervention did,
however, bring 20 years of virtually unregulated capitalism to Brazil, resulting in an "economic miracle" of GNP growth. The redistribution of

profits back to the wider society, however, was negligible and the gap between rich and poor widened.

Finally, the case of Brazil presents a good opportunity to ponder the role of the military in Third World countries (Black, 1986). Many of these states have no external enemies; certainly Brazil has never been in a war with any of its neighbors. The role of the military, not to put too fine a point on it, is to protect the government, and certain narrow sectors of society, from the great mass of the country's people who might be moved to change the distribution of wealth and power in the state. In Brazil, where the social stratification is the worst (i.e., most highly skewed) in the world, the gap grew.

As a result, US military aid to the traditional armed forces in countries such as Brazil provides an entree into the state's politics and governing structures. The aid provides the uniformed services in these countries with the modern weapons systems that define their raison d'être. The threat to cut it off—or to continue it flowing while economic aid to the government is cut off—provides a powerful incentive for the military to move against any regime that might pursue policies displeasing to the United States. This tactic was seen in the context of civil wars in the Congo and South Vietnam. In Brazil, and later Chile, it is more domestic politics than war that determines the pattern of selective US military aid flows.

## CASE 13. DOMINICAN REPUBLIC, 1961–66

The American intervention in the Dominican Republic, 1961–66, was a classic blend of traditional Roosevelt Corollary "big stick" methods combined with the new rhetoric of anti-communism. The tactics included a CIA-supported assassination in 1961 (a link kept secret until revealed by the Church Committee (US Senate, 1975: 191) and an outright invasion by 23,000 US troops in 1965. In the four years between the two events, the United States was involved in three other changes of government on this tiny (population 5 million) Caribbean island (see also CASE 29: Haiti, which also occupies the same island).

These events in the Dominican Republic were related to American policy in Cuba, and were part of the "unfinished business" (along with Congo and Laos) left by Eisenhower for the Kennedy administration. As the revolution in Cuba gained in popularity, the United States saw the reactionary regime of Generalissimo Rafael "The Goat" Trujillo in the Dominican Republic as presenting a target similar to that of pre-Castro Cuba; as early as 1958 the CIA started planning his removal (Diederich, 1978: 43–48).

Trujillo had been installed as head of the Dominican Republic's army by American marines in 1924 following an eight-year US military occupation. As military power-behind-the-throne of various puppet presidents since 1930, he had been protecting US economic interests on the island for more than a generation during which his family had come to control three-fifths of the Dominican economy (Zepezauer, 1994: 26; Crassweller, 1996). However, he had become a worry to Eisenhower fearful of the Cuban precedent, and when Trujillo was implicated in a plot to assassinate Venezuela's president, the United States got the Organization of American States to impose economic sanctions on the Dominican Republic in mid-1960 (Atkins and Wilson, 1972: 110–15; Slater, 1967: 192).

Trujillo also was an embarrassment to Kennedy who, as part of his Alliance for Progress, was looking for "third way" reformers to forestall future Castros. In the wake of the failed Bay of Pigs invasion in April 1961, getting rid of Trujillo assumed a higher priority. This was taken care of in short order as elements within the Dominican military, with weapons provided by local CIA operatives, shot to death the aged, now expendable, dictator on a highway outside the capital city on May 30, 1961 (Gleijeses, 1978: 303–7; Blum, 1995: 175; US Senate, 1975: 200–201). But, as in South Vietnam, a larger problem for the United States arose when it came to finding a suitable successor; for this, it would take another five years.

The first choice was Trujillo's playboy son, Rafael Jr. (Ramfis), but he lasted only six months as army chief before his unsuitability became obvious. He was dismissed in November, 1961, by his father's longtime aide, Joaquin Balaguer, who in fact had been the puppet-president at the time of Trujillo's assassination. But Balaguer was too much a part of the old guard and within two months was ousted by a reformist junta under General Pedro Rodriguez Echeverria that hoped to prepare the way for the country's first genuinely free election in 38 years.

Three political parties dominated the campaign. On the right was the National Civic Union, which represented Dominican businessmen and was conservative, but anti-Trujillista; it represented the forces of the transitional government that had exiled Balaguer, Ramfis, and two of the "old Goat's" brothers who still had supporters in the military and desired power. On the left was the June 14 Political Movement, which had some armed and Castroite elements, although the number of actual card-carrying communists in the country (after years of political repression) was less than 100. In the center was the Revolutionary Dominican Party (PRD), which despite its name was only moderately left of center and had a reformist agenda in which private property was respected (Gleijeses, 1978: 39). All three parties were united in their desire to rid the country of the Trujillos and their collaborators.

The PRD was led by Juan Bosch, a social-democratic writer who had spent many of the Trujillo years in exile. He easily won, with 59 percent of the vote in a three-way race on December 20, 1962, the first fair vote for president since 1924. After his inauguration in February 1963, Bosch adopted a program of modest land reform (transferring some private lands to the public sector) and nationalizations of a few business, balanced off with incentives to private enterprise and openness to foreign investment. He seemed to epitomize the first alternative of which Kennedy spoke when the American president uttered his famous "three possibilities . . . a decent democratic regime, a continuation of the Trujillo regime, or a Castro regime. We ought to aim at the first, but we really can't renounce the second until we are sure that we can avoid the third" (Schlesinger, 1965: 769). Unfortunately, when Kennedy made that comparison, he was putting Bosch in the third, not the first, category.

What was most threatening to Kennedy, and to right-wing circles in the United States, was Bosch's tolerance of communists and leftists in labor unions, even though none had been brought into government. Most specifically, Bosch refused to deport from the country 30 to 50 "known Marxists" in the June 14 movement. When in July 1963 a group of Dominican military officers, encouraged by Pentagon aid attachés in the American Embassy, pressed for such a sign of his anti-communist bona fides, Bosch went on television to argue that the protections of the Dominican constitution extended to all citizens, regardless of their political views. After this, his days were numbered. In September 1963—after only seven months in office—Bosch was ousted in a coup fronted by businessman Donald Reid Cabral as head of a three-man junta. Three months later, the new Johnson administration extended American diplomatic recognition. Once again, the United States had chosen capitalism (and a compliant military's complicity in confirming this choice) over democracy (Draper, 1968: 29; Martin, 1966: 477–78).

A year and a half later, on April 24, 1965, this thinly veiled military dictatorship was challenged by a countercoup, led by young "constitutionalist" officers under Col. Francisco Caamano. Its avowed intention was to return the duly elected president (Bosch) to office. Initially, the rebels scored some impressive victories, including the resignation of Reid Cabral and the naming of a former Bosch supporter as provisional president. The move seemed to have been quite popular; thousands of cheering supporters took to the streets. But government "loyalist" forces under General Elias Wessin y Wessin regrouped to fight back.

When, three days later, US Ambassador W. Tapley Bennett claimed that Americans were being caught in a "crossfire," and that some 1,500 "communists" were overrunning the capital (Barnet, 1968: 171), the first of some 23,000 American troops came storming ashore to save the military regime. Although President Johnson later claimed to have not believed the specifics of Bennett's report, he felt the ambassador's alarm could not be ignored (Yates, 1988: 64; Thomas and Thomas, 1967), and so dispatched a 35-ship task force to back up the mission.

The cover story was that the troops were sent to "protect US lives," and to evacuate Americans from neighborhoods under siege in the capital, Santo Domingo. But in surrounding the inner city area with a belt of troops, the United States blocked off Caamano's "constitutionalist" forces from attacking the "loyalist" army in its San Isidro base just outside of town. This action effectively eliminated any prospect for a rebel victory (Yates, 1988: 75; Blum, 1995: 181). When, in mid-May, the Wessin y Wessin forces regained the upper hand (in fighting in which 3,000 died), the US troops assumed a more neutral position as part of a hastily assembled, ex post facto OAS "peace-keeping" force fronted by (see previous case) a Brazilian General and 1,100 of his troops (Slater, 1970: 98–103). This "neutrality" essentially froze the two contending factions of the Dominican army in place for three months while the United States brokered a compromise (Slater, 1970: 126–35; Lowenthal, 1972: 130–31). On September 3, 1965, an agreement was reached that provided for a provisional government under a former Bosch official, in return for which Colonel Caamano went into gilded exile (i.e., a diplomatic posting). A new election was scheduled for June 1, 1966.

Two old foes, the Trujillista Balaguer and the 1962 election winner Bosch, returned from their respective exiles to face one another on the ballot. But Bosch was so fearful for his personal safety that he never left his home during the "campaign." Under the watchful presence of the American troops and helpful US civilian "advisors in civic education," (Herman and Brodhead, 1984: 17–53), familiar "retro" candidate Balaguer easily prevailed among a populace weary from five years of American-inspired political turmoil and instability. After US troops were withdrawn later in 1966, Balaguer adopted some of the strong-armed ways of his military mentor, along with a more adroit sophistication at rigging elections, to rule for the next 12 years (Hartlyn, 1998). He won two more dubious electoral exercises against token opposition in 1970 and 1974 (Black, 1986).

In 1978, when he was finally defeated at the polls, Balaguer refused to step down until President Jimmy Carter threatened to withhold aid and dispatched another US Navy show of force. But eight years later, under President Reagan in 1986, Balaguer, now in his 80s, came back to win again. He served another 10 years before the Clinton administration forced him to cut short his tainted 1994 election mandate to two years. This 20-year history of electoral see-saw reveals a suspicious correlation between the ideological coloration of the administration in Washington and the success of the old Trujillista, Balaguer being allowed to win under Republicans Reagan and Bush, but being forced to cede power under Democrats Carter and Clinton.

From the perspective of Kennedy-Johnson foreign policy at the height of the Cold War, the American adventure in the Dominican Republic, 1961–66, was illustrative of a number of points. As with Guatemala and Brazil before 1965, and with Chile and central America in later decades, various instruments of US intervention were deployed: from the original CIA-planned assassination of Trujillo in 1961, to the toppling of four governments (including one elected) between 1961 and 1965, the "OAS-covered" invasion of 1965, and the "demonstration election" of 1966.

Given the context of the year 1965, a noteworthy comparison to similar US efforts in a more ominous, distant theater—Vietnam—can be made (see CASE 11). First, there was the assassination of embarrassing right-wing leaders (Trujillo, Diem) who would not reform under Kennedy. Then, there was Johnson's sending of combat military troops to salvage a tottering coup-regime against a popular uprising. The same 1965 spring that LBJ sent in 23,000 troops for a two-month war followed by a one-year occupation and "supervised" elections, he dispatched more than 100,000 soldiers to South Vietnam with a similar mission. The target to be rescued was more strategically significant and farther away, but with a proportionate increase in the forces committed and the time spent, the hope was that a comparable victory could be won in Southeast Asia before Johnson stood for reelection in 1968. Unfortunately the "success" in the tiny, nearby Dominican Republic was not that easy to replicate in distant, larger (population 60 million) Vietnam.

## CASE 14. INDONESIA, 1965–66

The war that occurred in Indonesia during *The Year of Living Danger-ously*—to cite the name of a popular movie about the times—is not well known to most Americans, but it was arguably of greater historic signif-icance than the eight-year US war in nearby Indochina (1965–73). For one thing, Indonesia is the world's fourth largest country, with about 220 mil-lion people today, almost three times as many as in Vietnam. Whether it "went communist" or not was obviously of greater intrinsic significance than the fate of Vietnam. Yet the tumultuous events that occurred in the year after October 1965—during which communism was turned back on the Southeast Asian island nation at the cost of some 500,000 lives—were hardly noticed in a United States preoccupied with the escalating war in Vietnam. To the extent that America was involved in the bloody, "creep-ing" coup d'etat that replaced President Sukarno with Army General Su-harto, Indonesia was the ultimate "domino" that was propped up and saved from communism (Scott, 1985: 263–64).

Sukarno had been Indonesia's president since leading its independence war against the Netherlands, 1945–48. In his first decade in office, he be-came a particular thorn in the side of the United States, proclaiming a defiant brand of non-alignment (more bumptious than that of the more diplomatic Tito and Nehru in Yugoslavia and India, respectively). He con-vened the Bandung Conference of neutral nations in 1955 as a specific counterpoint to the SEATO alliance the United States was building in that part of the world. He welcomed Soviet Prime Minister Nikita Khrushchev in one of his first visits to noncommunist Asia. Most threatening to the

United States, he tolerated as part of his country's robust political scene the 1-million-member Indonesian Communist Party (PKI), the largest communist party in the world outside the Soviet Union and China. Although Sukarno was politically to the right of the local communists, he was definitely to the left of center, and he nationalized some American and Dutch rubber plantations and oil interests during his early years (Mortimer, 1974).

For such efforts at independence in foreign and domestic politics, Sukarno became a target of CIA attempts at "destabilization" reminiscent of those used against Castro in the 1950s. He was vilified by the strait-laced Secretary of State John Foster Dulles as an immoral womanizer. Among the more humorous efforts at embarrassment was a CIA production of a pornographic movie that starred a man with an uncanny resemblance to Sukarno (Smith, 1976: 238–40). More seriously, the United States supported rebellion-and-secession movements on the islands of West Sumatra and Sulawesi for seven months in 1957–58. In pursuit of this state-sponsored terrorism, the United States used not only the CIA, but large supplies of US military equipment, and support from the Seventh Fleet and American planes and pilots. Even US bases in (still) occupied Okinawa were used as an assembly point for what has been described as the "CIA's most ambitious military operation to date, tens of thousands of rebels armed, equipped and trained by the US army" (Blum,1995: 102; Prouty, 1974: 363).

But Sukarno beat back this challenge with a brutal counter-insurgency that clamped down on all normal political life in the country. And, as happened at the Bay of Pigs (CASE 8), the local population did not rally to the cause of the rebels. Finally, there was one embarrassing incident that cooled the ardor of Eisenhower to continue any further support for subversion. On May 15, 1958, a plane flown by Allen Lawrence Pope, a decorated Air Force pilot working under cover for the CIA, was shot down while on a bombing mission in support of rebels on the island of Ambon (Smith, 1976: 246–48; Prouty, 1974: 364–66). Despite the end of hostile American activity, relations between the United States and Indonesia were pretty much frozen for the last two years of the Eisenhower administration.

Within Indonesia, the most significant long-term effect of the brief civil war was the destruction of parliamentary government and the end of any prospects of devolution of power to the various regions of the 3,600-miles-long archipelago of 3,000 islands. There were, however, three institutions that emerged stronger from the experience: the communist party, the president, and the army (listed from left to right, politically). But the previous fragile balance of power among them, which had been modulated by the presence of several smaller political parties and various civic groups, had been severely skewed and the country was left with a "brittle tripolarization" of these three major political forces. Sukarno, as the father of his country's independence, tried to bridge the gap by embracing them both under his mantle of nationalism, but the "ingredients for a major political explosion" were just waiting to break out (Kahin and Kahin, 1997: 216, 220).

After 1961, Kennedy attempted to woo Indonesia back into some relationship with the United States with the resumption of foreign aid, particularly aid to the military, which by this time had become wary of both Sukarno and the PKI. Sukarno's health was deteriorating, and the military saw the party as its rival to run a successor government (Crouch, 1978). Under the guidance of Assistant Secretary of State for Far Eastern Affairs Roger Hilsman, a man with roots in the CIA, a program was established so that by 1963, one-third of the Indonesian general staff and about half of the officer corps had some sort of training from the United States (Hilsman, 1967: 377). Among these was the head of the Army's Strategic Reserve Corps, General Suharto, and a number of other officers with a history of collaboration with the Dutch and the Japanese governments during the 1940s (Caldwell, 1974: 47–48, note 50).

As in other cases in this chapter, the transition from Kennedy to Johnson resulted in a simplification, and hardening, of US relations with a Third World country. This also coincided with a time of new British policies in Malaysia that antagonized Indonesia, and Johnson's desire to get UK support for the escalation of the American war in Vietnam. In early 1964, Sukarno was pressing for a plebiscite on whether the peoples of British Borneo should become independent or part of Malaysia. When the United States failed to back "self-determination," and actually proposed membership in the UN Security Council for the expanded Malayan Federation (including Borneo), Sukarno angrily renounced all American aid in March 1964. In August, he extended full diplomatic recognition to North Vietnam and gave rhetorical support to the National Liberation Front in the south (Jones, 2002: 277–78).

In early 1965, after the offices of some US oil companies in Indonesia were seized, the US Ambassador Howard Jones tried to persuade the army to take matters into its own hands. In March 1965, he wrote, "an unsuccessful coup attempt by the PKI might be the most effective development to start a reversal of political trends" if only a "clear-cut kind of challenge" could be found to "galvanize effective reaction" (Kahin and Kahin, 1997: 225, note 11). By mid-1965, Sukarno had become the target of no less than seven assassination attempts, but it was unclear as to whether the perpetrators were linked to the US, the UK, the army, or the PKI, or some subset of those four actors.

The critical events in Indonesia's epochal upheaval began on September 30, 1965, when Lt. Col. Untung, commander of a battalion of Sukarno's palace guard, led a group of junior officers in killing six right-wing generals who were suspected of being associated with the CIA in planning a coup. It is unclear whether these junior officers were trying to protect Sukarno, attempting change within the military, or were engaged in a coup of their own. When they broadcast the names of the members of their Revolutionary Council's presidium, Sukarno was not mentioned. They also alienated much of the army high command by announcing that all noncommissioned officers would be promoted one level and that all ranks above lieutenant colonel would be abolished (Kahin and Kahin, 1997: 227).

The Army's Strategic Reserves under General Suharto struck back, claiming to be defending the existing government. Within 24 hours, its troops had defeated the three battalions that were supporting Col. Untung. But Suharto then went on to eliminate other "suspected leftists" from the military. His justification was that the junior officers had been incited by the PKI, a charge for which there was very little evidence. Although this purge of the armed forces was accomplished in about a week, Suharto did not stop there. Over the next year, his soldiers went on a rampage, killing some 500,000 "enemies of the state," most of them from the PKI, and from the many trade unions, peasant and other mass organizations they controlled.

A particular target of the army's wrath was the ethnic minority community of Chinese who made up about 4 percent of Indonesia's population. The Chinese owned many businesses and were in general richer than, and resented by, the 96 percent of the population that was Muslim. The Chinese were also the dominant group within the PKI, which thus was regarded with great suspicion by the military on both ethnic and ideological grounds (Emmerson, 1976). In many instances, the army turned over weapons to members of local Muslim youth organizations who carried out the killings. In 2001, the US State Department inadvertently revealed that the United States had made payments to "one of the key civilian advisors and promoters" of one of these organizations, known as *Kap-Gestapu* (Risen, 2001: 3).

What caused the massacre to spread beyond a purge of the army was Suharto's anticipation of a power struggle between the army and the PKI after the death of Sukarno. The allegation that the junior officers' coup had been instigated by the PKI presented Suharto the opportunity to move as suggested by Ambassador Jones in March. To gain support for his action, Suharto played the race card, claiming the PKI was supported by China. The massacre he unleashed over the next year has been described as one of the most savage mass slaughters of modern political history (Cribb, 1990: 3; Crouch, 1978: 155; US CIA, 1968: 71n). When President Sukarno tried to halt the massacres, General Suharto charged him with involvement in the original coup and forced him to step down as president in April 1966. Finally, in May 1967, when he had no more political allies and was in poor health, Sukarno was placed under house arrest. The 20-month "creeping coup" was completed.

What was the US involvement in these events? Probably less than in many of the other cases described in this book. But, in addition to the precedents of 1957–58, and the military-aid ties developed in 1961–64, there were two suspicious connections in 1965. First, in a rare CIA "official history" of a coup, mention is made of one Kamarusaman bin Ahmed Mubaidah, also known as "Sjam," who provided the leftist junior officers with the original tip about the right wing generals' coup (US CIA, 1968: 112–17; Mortimer, 1974: 418–40; Wertheim, 1970: 53–54). It is unclear, however, whether Sjam was working for the PKI—as alleged in the CIA study and the official Suharto government version of events (Notosusanto and Saleh, 1968)—or was an agent provocateur for the Indonesian army whose testimony could be used to provide the justification for the subsequent massacre of the left in Indonesia (Blum, 1995: 195; Southwood and Flanagan, 1983; Wertheim, 1970: 55–56).

The second suspicious American activity in 1965 was providing to the army in support of its purge the names of 5,000 leading communists. According to Ambassador Marshall Green, the United States had more, and better, intelligence on the PKI membership than the Indonesian government itself. Over the years, the US Embassy in Jakarta had systematically compiled comprehensive counts of communist operatives, from the top levels down to village cadres. Joseph Lazarsky, Edward Masters, and Robert Martens were among the diplomats with CIA ties in the embassy who produced the virtual "death lists" that enabled the Indonesian army to methodically eliminate the leadership infrastructure of the party (Kadane, 1990: 59). In addition, the United States quickly fulfilled the army's request, on November 6, 1965, for weapons "to arm Muslim and nationalist youth in Central Java for use against the PKI" (Bunnell, 1990: 59–60).

Although there is no clear evidence that the United States was involved in the original failed coup, after Suharto's counter-coup, the deputy chief of the embassy, Francis Galbraith, made it clear to the generals that the United States was "generally sympathetic with and admiring of what the army was doing" (Kahin and Kahin, 1997: 230). In later years, Ambassador Green boasted, "We did what we had to do, and . . . if we hadn't Asia would be a different place today" (Britton, 1975: 14).

In subsequent years, the floodgates of American aid opened up to sustain Suharto's regime, and its particular brand of crony capitalism. From an initial trickle of military supplies that began in 1966 shortly after Suharto removed Sukarno from the presidency, and for 32 years until he lost power in 1998, Suharto received more than $600 million in military assistance, about half of which went to finance more than $700 million in weapons purchases from American companies. "Communism" had been expunged from the largest nation in offshore Asia, and the United States, replacing the Netherlands, had become the hegemon in yet another region of the world. After 9-11-01, the "war on terror" was being used to build up an even greater US presence in the "world's largest Muslim nation."

## POSTSCRIPT: GREECE, 1967–74

In CASE 1, it was noted that the US involvement in the Greek civil war, 1947–49, established a close relationship between American military and intelligence forces and significant sectors of Greek political society, not to mention most of its governments for the next generation. This coziness reached its height during the activist years of Kennedy and, especially, Johnson.

In 1963, an assassination of a leftist member of parliament, Gregoris Lambrakis—memorialized in the Costa-Gavras movie Z—was generally attributed to a right-wing paramilitary gang with close ties to the government, and the CIA. In July 1965, President Johnson was deeply involved in the parliamentary ouster of the center-left coalition government of George Papandreou who was attempting to purge the Greek army of its CIA links (Blum, 1995: 216). Finally, the coup of April 1967, two days before an election that probably would have brought Papandreou back to power, resulted in the government of General George Papadopoulos, a CIA "asset" who had been on the CIA payroll since 1952 (Blum, 1995: 218).

The dictatorship was overthrown in July 1974, when the junta overreached and attempted to take over the island of Cyprus by sponsoring a coup there. This not only provoked Turkey to seize the northern third of the island (which it holds to this day), but also a reaction by more centrist and civilian forces in Greece to remove the dictatorship (Stern, 1977: 123–24). The generals had been weakened several months earlier by a student uprising on November 17, 1973. The revolt, part of a seven-year popular struggle against the dictatorship, also gave birth to a terrorist cell named "November 17," which over the next three decades killed 23 people carefully selected for their political symbolism, including a British General and the US CIA chief in Athens. It was not until 2002, when the leaders of this group were captured, that the *New York Times* could write that Greece could finally "take its place in modern Europe and turn away from an obsession with Washington" (Erlanger, 2002: 1). This distortion of Greek politics began with America's embrace of the Greek right during the 1947–74 period.

## CHAPTER 3 BIBLIOGRAPHY

### Kennedy/Johnson Foreign Policies

Brands, H. W. 1995. *The Wages of Globalism: LBJ and the Limits of American Power.* NY: Oxford University Press.

Cohen, Warren I., and Nancy Bernkopf Tucker (eds.). 1995. *Lyndon Johnson Confronts the World: American Foreign Policy, 1963–1968*. NY: Cambridge University Press.

Halberstam, David. 1972. *The Best and the Brightest: America and Vietnam during the Kennedy Era*. NY: Random House.

Hilsman, Roger. 1967. *To Move a Nation: The Politics of Foreign Policy in the Administration of John F. Kennedy*. NY: Doubleday.

Paterson, Thomas G. (ed.) 1989. *Kennedy's Quest for Victory: American Foreign Policy, 1961–63*. NY: Oxford University Press.

Rostow, Walt Whitman. 1972. *The Diffusion of Power: An Essay in Recent History*. NY: Macmillan.

Taylor, Maxwell. 1959. *The Uncertain Trumpet*. NY: Harper and Row.

"Text of Kennedy's Inaugural Outlining Policies on World Peace and Freedom," *New York Times*, January 21, 1961: 8.

Walton, Richard J. 1973. *Cold War and Counterrevolution: The Foreign Policy of John F. Kennedy*. Baltimore: Penguin Books.

White, Theodore H. 1961. *The Making of the President, 1960*. NY: Atheneum Publishers.

## CASE 7. Congo, 1961–65

Atwood, William. 1967. *The Reds and the Blacks*. NY: Harper and Row.

Borstelmann, Thomas. 1997. "Mobutu, Sese Seko," vol. 3: 156, in Bruce W. Jentleson and Thomas G. Paterson (eds.), *Encyclopedia of U.S. Foreign Relations*. NY: Oxford University Press.

DeWitte, Ludo. 2001. *The Assassination of Lumumba*. NY: Verso Books.

Gibbs, David N. 1991. *The Political Economy of Third World Intervention: Mines, Money and US Policy in the Congo Crisis*. IL: University of Chicago Press.

Jackson, Henry F. 1982. *From the Congo to Soweto: US Foreign Policy toward Africa 1960–80*. NY: W. W. Morrow.

Kalb, Madeleine G. 1982. *The Congo Cables: The Cold War in Africa—From Eisenhower to Kennedy*. NY: Macmillan.

Kelly, Sean. 1993. *America's Tyrant: The CIA and Mobutu of Zaire*. Washington, DC: American University Press.

Kwitny, Jonathan. 1984. *Endless Enemies: The Making of an Unfriendly World*. NY: Penguin. Books.

Mahoney, Richard D. 1983. *JFK: Ordeal in Africa*. NY: Oxford University Press.

Merriam, Alan. 1961. *Congo: Background to Conflict*. Evanston, IL: Northwestern University Press.

Namikas, Lise. 2000. "Intervention in the Congo: The US and Soviet Experiences, 1960," Paper delivered at annual conference of Society for Historians of American Foreign Relations. Toronto, Canada: June 23.

Prouty, L. Fletcher. 1974. *The Secret Team: The CIA and Its Allies in Control of the United States and the World*. NY: Ballantine Books.

Schatzberg, Michael G. 1991. *Mobutu or Chaos? The United States and Zaire, 1960–90*. Lanham, MD: University Press of America.

Smith, Stewart. 1974. *US Neocolonialism in Africa*. NY: International Publishers.

Stockwell, John. 1978. *In Search of Enemies: A CIA Story*. NY: W. W. Norton.

U.S. Senate. Church Committee (Select Committee to Study Governmental Operations with Respect to Intelligence Activities). 1975 (November 20). "The Congo," Part III. A: 13–70, *Interim Report: Alleged Assassination Plots Involving Foreign Leaders*. Washington, DC: US Government Printing Office.

Weissman, Stephen R. 1974. *American Foreign Policy in the Congo, 1960–64*. Ithaca, NY: Cornell University Press.

Weissman, Stephen R. 1979. "CIA Covert Action in Zaire and Angola: Patterns and Consequences," *Political Science Quarterly*, 24(2), Summer: 263–86.

Wrong, Michela. 2000. *In the Footsteps of Mr. Kurtz: Living on the Brink of Disaster in the Congo*. NY: HarperCollins.

## CASE 8. Cuba, 1961

Blum, William. 2000. *Rogue State: A Guide to the World's Only Superpower*. Monroe, ME: Common Courage Press.

Branch, Taylor and George Crile III. 1975. "The Kennedy Vendetta: How the CIA Waged a Silent War against Cuba," *Harper's*, August: 49–63.

Fursenko, Aleksandr, and Timothy Naftali. 1997. *"One Hell of a Gamble": Khrushchev, Castro, and Kennedy, 1958–1964*. NY: W. W. Norton.

Hinckle, Warren, and William W. Turner. 1981. *The Fish Is Red: The Story of the Secret War against Castro*. NY: Harper and Row.

Higgins, Trumbull. 1987. *The Perfect Failure: Kennedy, Eisenhower, and the CIA at the Bay of Pigs*. NY: Norton.

Kaplowitz, Donna Rich. 1988. *Anatomy of a Failed Embargo: US Sanctions against Cuba*. Boulder, CO: Lynne Rienner Publisher.

Karabell, Zachary. 1999. "Cuba: Flying Solo," Chapter 9: 173–205, *Architects of Intervention: The United States and the Cold War, 1946–1962*. Baton Rouge: Louisiana State University Press.

Morley, Morris H. 1988. *Imperial State and Revolution: The United States and Cuba 1952–86*. NY: Cambridge University Press.

Nathan, James A. 2000. *Anatomy of the Cuban Missile Crisis*. NY: Greenwood Press.

*Operation Zapata: The "Ultrasensitive" Report and Testimony of the Board of Inquiry on the Bay of Pigs*. 1981. Frederick, MD: Aletheia Books/University Publications of America.

Paterson, Thomas. 1994. *Contesting Castro: The United States and The Triumph of Cuba*. NY: Oxford University Press.

Prados, John. 1996. *Presidents' Secret Wars: CIA and Pentagon Covert Operations from World War II through the Persian Gulf*. Chicago: Ivan R. Dee Elephant Paperback.

Sullivan, Michael J., III. 1991. *Measuring Global Values: The Ranking of 162 Countries*. NY: Greenwood Press.

U.S. Senate. Church Committee. 1975. "Cuba," Part III.B: 71–190, *Assassination Plots* (see CASE 7).

Vanderbroucke, Lucien S. 1984. "Anatomy of a Failure: The Decision to Land at the Bay of Pigs," *Political Science Quarterly*, 99(3), Fall: 471–91.

Walton, Richard J. 1973. *Cold War and Counterreveolution* (see Kennedy/Johnson Foreign Policies).

Weiner, Tim. 1998. "A Blast at Secrecy in Kennedy Killing: Panel on Assassination Wraps Up Its Six-Year Task," *New York Times*, September 29.

Welch, Richard. 1985. *Response to Revolution: The United States and the Cuban Revolution, 1959–61.* Chapel Hill: University of North Carolina Press.

Zepezauer, Mark. 1994. "Hit #9: John F. Kennedy," pp. 22–23, *The CIA's Greatest Hits.* Tucson, AZ: Odonian Press.

## CASE 9. British Guiana, 1961–66

Blum, William. 1995. "British Guiana 1953–1964: The CIA's International Labor Mafia," Chapter 16: 108–14, *Killing Hope: US Military and CIA Interventions since World War II.* Monroe, ME: Common Courage Press.

Fraser, Cary. 1994. *Ambivalent Anti-Colonialism: The United States and the Genesis of West Indian Independence, 1940–64.* Westport, CT: Greenwood Press.

Fraser, Cary. 2000. "The 'New Frontier' of Empire in the Caribbean: The Transfer of Power in British Guiana, 1961–1964," *International History Review,* 22: 583–610.

"Guyana: Hello, Again," *Economist,* December 13, 1997.

Jagan, Cheddi. 1966. *The West on Trial: My Fight for Guyana's Freedom.* NY: International Publishers.

Kibbe, Jennifer D. 2002. "Kennedy's Decision Making in British Guiana," Paper presented at International Studies Association Convention, New Orleans, LA: March 24–27.

Kwitny, Jonathan. 1984. *Endless Enemies: The Making of an Unfriendly World.* NY: Penguin Books.

Parekh, Hector J. 1999. "Subversion in British Guiana: Why and How the Kennedy Administration Got Rid of a Democratic Government," *Monthly Review,* 51: 50–58.

Rabe, Stephen G. 1999. *The Most Dangerous Area in the World: John F. Kennedy Confronts Communist Revolution in Latin America.* Chapel Hill: University of North Carolina Press.

Romualdi, Serafino. 1967. *Presidents and Peons: Recollections of a Labor Ambassador in Latin America.* NY: Funk and Wagnalls.

Singh, Chaitram. 1988. *Guyana: Politics in a Plantation Society.* New York: Praeger.

Spinner, Thomas J., Jr. 1984. *A Political and Social History of Guyana, 1945–83.* Boulder, CO: Westview Press.

Sullivan, Michael J., III. 1996. *Comparing State Polities: A Framework for Analyzing 100 Governments.* NY: Greenwood Press.

Sullivan, Michael J., III. 1991. *Measuring Global Values* (see CASE 8).

## Indochina-II

Toye, Hugh. 1968. *Laos: Buffer State or Battleground.* NY: Oxford University Press.

Warner, Roger. 1995. *Backfire: The CIA's Secret War in Laos and Its Link to the War in Vietnam.* NY: Simon and Schuster.

## CASE 10. Laos, 1961–73

Blum, William. 1995. "Laos 1957–1973: *L'Armée Clandestine,*" Chapter 21: 140–45, *Killing Hope* (see CASE 9).

Branfman, Fred. 1976 "The President's Secret Army: A Case Study—The CIA in Laos, 1962–1972," in Robert Borosage and John Marks (eds.), *The CIA File.* NY: Grossman.

Branfman, Fred. 1972. *Voices from the Plain of Jars: Life Under an Air War.* NY: Harper and Row.

Castle, Timothy. 1993. *At War in the Shadow of Vietnam: US Military Aid to the Royal Lao Government, 1955–75.* NY: Columbia University Press.

Dommen, Arthur. 1964. *Conflict in Laos: The Politics of Neutralization.* NY: Praeger.

Fall, Bernard B. 1969. *Anatomy of a Crisis: The Laotian Crisis of 1960–1961.* NY: Doubleday.

Goldstein, Martin E. 1975. *American Policy toward Laos.* Rutherford, NJ: Fairleigh-Dickinson University Press.

Hamilton-Merritt, Jane. 1993. *Tragic Mountains: the Hmong, the Americans, and the Secret Wars for Laos, 1942–1992.* Bloomington: Indiana University Press.

Hess, Gary R. 1998. *Vietnam and the United States: Origins and Legacy of War.* NY: Twayne Publishers.

Karabell, Zachary. 1999. "Laos: Into the Jungles," Chapter 10: 206–24, *Architects of Intervention* (see CASE 8).

Langer, Paul F., and Joseph J. Zasloff. 1970. *North Vietnam and the Pathet Lao: Partners in the Struggle for Laos.* Cambridge, MA: Harvard University Press.

McCoy, Alfred W., Cathleen Read, and Leonard P. Adams II. 1972. *The Politics of Heroin in South East Asia.* NY: Harper and Row.

Moore, Robin. 1965. *The Green Berets.* NY: Crown Publishers.

Nashel, Jonathan. 1997. "Laos," vol. 3: 40–41, in Jentleson, *Encyclopedia* (see CASE 7, Borstelmann).

Pace, Eric. 1998. "Charles Pierce Gabeler, 76; Ran Airline for CIA in Laos" (Obituary), *New York Times,* June 24.

Prados, John. 1996. *Presidents' Secret Wars* (see CASE 8).

Prouty, L. Fletcher. 1974. *The Secret Team* (see CASE 7).

Robbins, Christopher. 1985. *Air America.* NY: Avon.

Schlesinger, Arthur M., Jr. 1965. *A Thousand Days: John F. Kennedy in the White House.* Boston: Houghton-Mifflin.

Stevenson, Charles A. 1972. *The End of Nowhere: American Policy toward Laos since 1954.* Boston: Beacon Press.

## CASE 11. South Vietnam, 1961–65

Buzzanco, Robert. 1999. *Vietnam and the Transformation of American Life.* Malden, MA: Blackwell Publishers.

Fall, Bernard B. 1963. *The Two Vietnams: A Political and Military Analysis.* NY: Praeger.

Freedman, Lawrence. 2000. *Kennedy's Wars: Berlin, Cuba, Laos, and Vietnam.* NY: Oxford University Press.

Goulden, Joseph C. 1969. *Truth is the First Casualty: The Gulf of Tonkin Affair: Illusion and Reality.* Chicago: Rand-McNally.

Halberstam, David. 1972. *The Best and the Brightest* (see Kennedy/Johnson Foreign Policies).

Halberstam, David. 1965. *The Making of a Quagmire: America and Vietnam during the Kennedy Era.* NY: Random House.

Herman, Edward, and Frank Brodhead. 1984. *Demonstration Elections: US-Staged Elections in the Dominican Republic, Vietnam, and El Salvador.* Boston: South End Press.

Hess, Gary R. 1998. *Vietnam and the United States* (see CASE 10).

Karnow, Stanley. 1997. *Vietnam: A History.* NY: Penguin Books.

Lodge, Henry Cabot. 1965. *The Storm Has Many Eyes: A Personal Narrative.* NY: W. W. Norton.

Logevall, Frederick. 1999. *Choosing War: The Lost Chance for Peace and the Escalation of the War in Vietnam.* Berkeley: University of California Press.

O'Ballance, Edgar. 1981. *The Wars in Vietnam, 1954–1980.* NY: Hippocrene.

Schulzinger, Robert D. 1997. *A Time for War: The United States and Vietnam, 1941–75.* NY: Oxford University Press.

Shultz, Richard H., Jr. 1999. *The Secret War against Hanoi: Kennedy's and Johnson's Use of Spies, Saboteurs, and Covert Warriors in North Vietnam.* NY: HarperCollins.

Sullivan, Marianna P. 1978. *France's Vietnam Policy: A Study in French-American Relations.* Westport, CT: Greenwood Press.

Summers, Col. Harry G. 1981. *On Strategy: The Vietnam War in Context.* Carlisle Barracks, PA: US Army War College Strategic Studies Institute.

U.S. Senate. Church Committee. 1975. "Diem," Part III.E: 217–24, *Assassination Plots* (see CASE 7).

Vandemark, Brian. 1991. *Into the Quagmire: Lyndon Johnson and the Escalation of the Vietnam War.* NY: Oxford University Press.

Warner, Denis. 1964. *The Last Confucian: Vietnam, Southeast Asia, and The West.* NY: Penguin Books.

## CASE 12. Brazil, 1964

Agee, Philip. 1975. *Inside the Company: CIA Diary.* NY: Ballantine.

Bell, Peter D. 1972. "Brazilian-American Relations," Chapter 3: 77–102 in Riordan Roett (ed.), *Brazil in the Sixties.* Nashville, TN: Vanderbilt University Press.

Black, Jan Knippers. 1986. *Sentinels of Empire: The US and Latin American Militarism.* NY: Greenwood Press.

Black, Jan Knippers. 1977. *United States Penetration of Brazil.* Philadelphia: University of Pennsylvania Press.

Blum, William. 1995. "Brazil, 1961–1964: Introducing the Marvelous New World of Death Squads," Chapter 27: 163–72, *Killing Hope* (see CASE 9).

Gerassi, John. 1965. *The Great Fear in Latin America.* NY: Collier Books.

Huggins, Martha K. 1998. *Political Policing: The United States and Latin America.* Durham, NC: Duke University Press.

Langguth, A. J. 1978. *Hidden Terrors.* NY: Pantheon Books.

Leacock, Ruth. 1990. *Requiem for Revolution: The United States and Brazil, 1961–1969.* Ohio: Kent State University Press.

Lernoux, Penny. 1982. *Cry of the People: The Struggle for Human Rights in Latin America.* Garden City, NY: Doubleday.

Parker, Phyllis R. 1979. *Brazil and the Quiet Intervention, 1964.* Austin: University of Texas Press.

Poelchau, Warner (ed.). 1981. *White Paper, Whitewash: Interviews with Philip Agee on the CIA and El Salvador.* NY: Institute for Media Studies/Deep Cover Books.

Rohter, Larry. 2000. "Brazil Opens Files on Region's Abuses in Age of Dictators," *New York Times,* June 9.

Skidmore, Thomas E. 1967. *Politics in Brazil, 1930–1964: An Experiment in Democracy.* NY: Oxford University Press.

Weiss, W. Michael. 1993. *Cold Warriors and Coups d'Etat: Brazilian-American Relations, 1945–1964.* Albuquerque: University of New Mexico Press.

## CASE 13. Dominican Republic, 1961–66

Atkins, G. Pope, and Larman C. Wilson. 1972. *The United States and the Trujillo Regime.* New Brunswick, NJ: Rutgers University Press.

Barnet, Richard. 1968. *Intervention and Revolution: The United States in the Third World.* NY: New American Library.

Black, Jan Knippers. 1986. *The Dominican Republic: Politics and Development in an Unsovereign State.* Boston: Allen and Unwin.

Blum, William. 1995. "Dominican Republic 1960–1966: Saving Democracy from Communism by Getting Rid of Democracy," Chapter 29: 175–84, *Killing Hope* (see CASE 9).

Crassweller, Robert D. 1966. *Trujillo: The Life and Times of a Caribbean Dictator.* NY: Macmillan.

Diederich, Bernard. 1978. *Trujillo: The Death of the Goat.* Boston: Little, Brown.

Draper, Theodore. 1968. *The Dominican Revolt: A Case Study in American Policy.* NY: Commentary Report.

Gleijeses, Piero. 1978. *The Dominican Crisis: The 1965 Constitutionalist Revolt and American Intervention.* Baltimore: Johns Hopkins University Press.

Hartlyn, Jonathan. 1998. *The Struggle for Democratic Politics in the Dominican Republic.* Chapel Hill: University of North Carolina Press.

Herman, Edward S., and Frank Brodhead. 1984. *Demonstration Elections* (see CASE 11).

Lowenthal, Abraham F. 1972. *The Dominican Intervention.* Cambridge, MA: Harvard University Press.

Martin, John Bartlow (Ambassador). 1966. *Overtaken by Events: The Dominican Crisis from the Fall of Trujillo to the Civil War.* NY: Doubleday.

Schlesinger, Arthur M., Jr. 1965. *A Thousand Days* (see CASE 10).

Slater, Jerome. 1970. *Intervention and Negotiation: The United States and the Dominican Revolution.* NY: Harper and Row.

Slater, Jerome. 1967. *The OAS and United States Foreign Policy.* Columbus: Ohio State University Press.

Thomas, A. J., Jr., and Ann Van Wynen Thomas. 1967. *The Dominican Republic Crisis of 1965.* Dobbs Ferry, NY: Oceana Publications.

U.S. Senate. Church Committee. 1975. "Trujillo," Part III.D: 191–216, *Assassination Plots* (see CASE 7).

Yates, Lawrence A. 1988. *Power Pack: US Intervention in the Dominican Republic, 1965–1966.* Washington, DC: US Government Printing Office, Leavenworth Papers #15.

Zepezauer, Mark. 1994. "Hit #11: Dominican Republic," pp. 26–27, *The CIA's Greatest Hits* (see CASE 8).

## CASE 14. Indonesia, 1965–66

Blum, William. 1995. "Indonesia 1957–58: War and Pornography," and "Indonesia 1965: Liquidating President Sukarno . . . and 500,000 Others," Chapter 14: 99–104 and Chapter 31: 193–98, *Killing Hope* (see CASE 9).

Britton, Peter. 1975. "Indonesia's Neo-Colonial Armed Forces," *Bulletin of Concerned Asian Scholars* (July–September): 14–21.

Bunnell, Frederick P. 1990. "American 'Low Posture' toward Indonesia in the Months Leading up to the 1965 'Coup,' " *Indonesia*, 50 (October): 29–60.

Caldwell, Malcolm. 1974. "Oil Imperialism in Southeast Asia," pp. 21–49 in Mark Selden (ed.), *Remaking Asia: Essays on the American Uses of Power*. NY: Pantheon Books.

Cribb, Robert (ed.). 1990. *The Indonesian Killings of 1965–66*. Melbourne, Australia: Center of Southeast Asian Studies.

Crouch, Harold A. 1978. *The Army and Politics in Indonesia*. Ithaca, NY: Cornell University Press.

Emmerson, D. K. 1976. *Indonesia's Elite: Political Culture and Cultural Politics*. Ithaca, NY: Cornell University Press.

Hilsman, Roger. 1967. *To Move a Nation* (see Kennedy/Johnson Foreign Policies).

Jones, Matthew. 2002. "US Relations with Indonesia, the Kennedy-Johnson Transition, and the Vietnam Connection, 1963–65," *Diplomatic History*, 26(2), Spring: 249–81.

Kadane, Kathy. 1990. "The Indonesia Transcripts," *Covert Action Information Bulletin*, No. 35 (Fall): 59.

Kahin, Audrey R., and George McT. Kahin. 1997. *Subversion as Foreign Policy: The Secret Eisenhower and Dulles Debacle in Indonesia*. Seattle: University of Washington Press

Mortimer, Rex. 1974. *Indonesian Communism under Sukarno: Ideology and Politics, 1959–1965*. Ithaca, NY: Cornell University Press.

Notosusanto, Col. Nugroho, and Col. Ismail Saleh. 1968. *The Coup Attempt of the "September 30 Movement" in Indonesia*. Jakarta: Pembiming Masa.

Prouty, L. Fletcher. 1974. *The Secret Team* (see CASE 7).

Risen, James. 2001. "Official History Describes US Policy in Indonesia in the 60's," *New York Times*, July 27.

Scott, Peter Dale. 1985. "The US and the Overthrow of Sukarno, 1965–1967," *Pacific Affairs*, 58: 239–64.

Smith, Joseph Burkholder. 1976. *Portrait of a Cold Warrior*. NY: G. P. Putnam's Sons.

Southwood, Julie, and Patrick Flanagan. 1983. *Indonesia: Law, Propaganda, and Terror*. London: Zed Books.

U.S. Central Intelligence Agency. 1968 (December). *Indonesia—1965: The Coup that Backfired*. Washington, DC: CIA Research Study.

Wertheim, W. F. 1970. "Suharto and the Untung Coup—The Missing Link," *Journal of Contemporary Asia*. London, Winter: 50–56.

## Postscript. Greece, 1967–74

Blum, William. 1995. " 'Fuck Your Parliament and Your Constitution,' Said the President of the United States," Chapter 35: 215–21, *Killing Hope* (see CASE 9).

Erlanger, Steven. 2002. "Greece Hopes Arrests Earn It Europe's Embrace," *New York Times*, August 5.

Stern, Lawrence. 1977. *The Wrong Horse: The Politics of Intervention and the Failure of American Diplomacy*. NY: Times Books.

# CHAPTER 4

# The Nixon-Ford Realist Consolidations, 1969–76

## INTRODUCTION

Richard Nixon won the presidency in a three-way race (only 43.2% of the popular vote) with the promise that he "had a plan" to end the war in Vietnam. It emerged during his first year in office that his plan was nothing quick or dramatic (like a pull-out or an escalation), but rather involved a redefinition of America's role in the world and a shift from its historic idealist advancing of American values to an embrace of realist balance of power politics. In this recasting of the US place in international politics, Nixon reflected the *realpolitik* mindset of his national security advisor, Henry Kissinger, someone who was not born in the United States and who did not embrace its optimistic, moralist ethos. An immigrant from Nazi Germany, Kissinger insinuated a dour, European perspective into the foreign policy vision he crafted for Nixon (and his successor Gerald Ford) (Thornton, 1989). This meant a de-emphasis of the ideology of anti-communism that had resonated so deeply with both American political parties for 20 years before taken to its unfortunate logical conclusion in Vietnam. Accordingly, it provoked a criticism not only from the opposition Democrats (as might be expected) but also from within the Republican party.

A key aspect of the Kissinger-Nixon global view was the recognition of the USSR and China as legitimate major players in international politics. This *detente* (i.e., relaxation, of anti-communism as an ideology guiding policy) culminated in Nixon's election-year visits to China and the Soviet Union in 1972 (Gardner, 1973). In these trips Nixon practiced a politics of triangulation, playing off the two great communist powers against one another based upon their respective national interests. The trip to China (in February), was the first time an American president shook the hand of a Chinese leader since that country went communist in 1949, and it symbolically repudiated Dulles's snub of Chou en-Lai at Geneva, 1954. The visit to the USSR (in May), to sign strategic arms control and economic trade and investment agreements, occurred while the United States was bombing Hanoi and mining Haiphong in one of the most militaristic weeks of its waning war in Vietnam. (The counterpoising of these two events provided striking evidence of the role of realism in *both* Super Powers' diplomacy [Litwak, 1976].)

But before he got to his reelection victory, Nixon had to wind up the messy business in Vietnam (Nelson, 1995). For this, a second aspect of the Kissinger-Nixon worldview, also based upon calculations of balance of power, required the United States ridding itself of combat military operations in the Third World. Starting in Vietnam, the United States would revert to its Truman-in-Greece role as provider of military *assistance* only. In so doing, the United States would become more dependent upon strong regional allies to fulfill its former combat role (Szulc, 1978; Jones, 1973).

With respect to such policy on the periphery of what Kissinger considered to be the main focus of foreign policy (the USSR and China), the *"Nixon Doctrine"* was developed for the Third World. It envisioned replacing direct American military intervention against communist-inspired revolutions with a system of US aid to surrogates who would police its global interests in their respective regions. In Indochina, the "Nixon Doctrine" meant that South Vietnam would become the local regional ally, with the war becoming "Vietnamized." This meant increased military aid to South Vietnam while the United States *slowly* (not before the 1972 reelection campaign) worked itself out of its combat role; in the words of cynics, "changing the color of the bodies" while allowing the war to continue.

There was a disconnect, however, between the two aspects of Nixon's Grand Design (Schurmann, 1987). The promise to defend South Vietnam was undermined by the *detente* with China and the Soviet Union that virtually removed the rationale for the original commitment. If Americans could play ping pong with China and sell Pepsi to Russia—the two giants of world communism—then what was the point of *fighting a war* to keep one-half of a much smaller country from "going communist"? In the short run, however, the arming of the South Vietnamese—indeed the continued US fighting of their war until after Nixon's reelection in 1972—kept faith with those to whom previous presidents had given the country's word (both in Southeast Asia and in US domestic politics). But in the long run, something had to give, and after the election, geostrategic dynamics proved to be more powerful than domestic politics.

An agreement was signed on January 27, 1973, ending the war between the United States and North Vietnam. To cover America's exit from its generation-long commitment to South Vietnam, Nixon unleashed 12 days of bombing during Christmastime 1972. It was the most devastating air campaign of the entire war and included the dropping of 40,000 tons of bombs upon Hanoi and Haiphong. During this onslaught, virtually everything of any military value in North Vietnam was laid waste. The goal was to provide South Vietnam a significant interval of time during which it could prepare for the North's rebuilding, and during which the United States could definitively divorce itself from responsibility for its ally's fate (Snepp, 1978).

It was in this context of domestic and global politics—and the place of the US Indochina war in that larger picture—that the first case to be studied in this chapter, Cambodia, 1970, must be viewed. In the other cases, implementation of Nixon's "doctrine" involved working with some of the world's most notorious dictators and human rights abusers: the autocratic Shah of Iran in Kurdistan, General Agusto Pinochet in Chile, the racist apartheid South African government in Angola, and the Indonesian military dictatorship in Portuguese East Timor.

The latter two cases occurred under President Gerald Ford, after Nixon's resignation in disgrace in 1974. Ford retained Kissinger as his chief foreign policy advisor, albeit down-grading his influence by shifting his role from the White House National Security Advisor to Secretary of State. But the policy of realism and regional surrogates remained (Greene, 1992). A final case under Ford, related to Indonesia and Vietnam policy, was the pressure on Australia to remove its government in an unusual parliamentary manner.

## CASE 15. CAMBODIA, 1970

The US invasion of neutral Cambodia on April 30, 1970, is probably this book's most notorious foreign policy adventure, both in execution and result. Intended initially as a minor "sideshow" to the main American military operation in South Vietnam (Shawcross, 1979), the sending of 15,000 American troops over the border from South Vietnam into Cambodia led to the virtual destruction of this country and the literal killing of about 25 percent of its people, one of the largest genocides in history. At home in the United States, where the public had been led to believe that the war was winding down, the invasion provoked student protests that closed nearly 1,000 colleges (and caused six deaths at Kent State and Jackson State universities). It also led to the use of a Nixonian neologism, "incursion," to reassure domestic public opinion that the troops were not permanently occupying invaders, but would only be in disputed lands for a temporary period (soon specified as 60 days, until July 1). That is, the US military would be "in and out."

The American military intervention into Cambodia was related to the "Nixon Doctrine" and its Vietnamization program under which the United States, during the four-year period between Nixon's inauguration and his reelection campaign, would turn over the ground, combat fighting of the war against communism in Southeast Asia to the Army of the Republic of (South) Vietnam. But this ARVN was nowhere near ready in the spring of 1970 when a coup in neighboring Cambodia replaced the popular head of state Prince Norodom Sihanouk with his treacherous prime minister, General Lon Nol. When the General asked for American help in attacking North Vietnamese sanctuaries in the eastern part of his country, the Nixon administration was happy to respond. The move was seen as strategically protective of America's quiet, slow (and still unacknowledged) planned withdrawal from South Vietnam.

Ever since the 1954 Geneva Accords, the United States had chafed under the restrictions Cambodia's Prince Sihanouk imposed upon the way the United States fought its war in his corner of Southeast Asia. The mercurial prince had created an island of tranquility in the western three-quarters of his country as war raged around him in Laos and Vietnam (CASEs 10 and 11) and spilt over into his eastern provinces. Neutral Cambodia criticized equally not only the North Vietnamese for sending support for the war down the "Ho Chi Minh Trail" in this part of his country but also the American attempts to bomb this supply route and its occasional forays in hot pursuit of Vietnamese communists seeking sanctuary across this frontier (Osborne, 1974).

Aside from some low-level intelligence contact with (largely marginal) political groups opposed to Sihanouk, Presidents Eisenhower, Kennedy, and Johnson generally respected his neutrality. But this all changed with the accession to power of Nixon and Kissinger. Alternately desirous of signaling a change in style in Washington, and of covering the eventual withdrawal of US ground combat troops from the theater of war, Nixon strove to project the image of a strong leader, one even reckless enough to take chances Johnson had eschewed. He referred to it as his "madman" approach, keeping the enemy off balance and unsure as to "what he might do" (Hersh, 1983: 53, 185).

Pursuant to this strategy, in March 1969 Nixon launched "Operation Menu," a secret bombing campaign against North Vietnamese sanctuaries in Cambodia. The secrecy (from the American people, not from those upon whom the bombs rained) was necessary because it broke the previous year's understanding on suspension of such attacks in which President Johnson enticed the communists to begin talks in Paris on ending the war. Now, and for the next year, the United States carried out more than 3,000 B-52 bombing missions, dropping more than 100,000 tons of bombs on Cambodian territory (Hersh, 1983: 61–65). To maintain the secrecy, pilots were ordered to falsify the geographic coordinates of their targets so as to make them appear to be in South Vietnam, a lie that later became one of the articles of impeachment brought against Nixon in 1974.

It was in this context of American "signaling" for a more aggressive approach to the North Vietnamese presence in Cambodia that General Lon Nol's coup occurred. There is much evidence of American encouragement of his move (Hersh, 1983: Chapter 15). For years, the CIA had cultivated ties with some of Lon Nol's confederates such as Son Ngoc Thanh (who was soon named prime minister) and Sirik Matak, a leader of the heretofore ineffective *Khmer Serei* party that quickly threw its support behind the new government (Shawcross, 1979: 119–22; Morris, 1977: 173; Sihanouk, 1974: 37).

In any event, as expected, as soon as he took over, Lon Nol invoked the long-ignored SEATO Treaty to appeal for help from the United States in moving against the North Vietnamese presence in his country. SEATO had not been taken too seriously by most of its signatories after 1954. The United Kingdom, France, Pakistan, and New Zealand never responded to its terms at all; Australia sent only a token number of troops to help the Americans in South Vietnam. Closer neighbors Thailand and the Philippines provided important rear staging areas for US aircraft, but they sent no troops. But the Nixon administration was only too eager to reward the Cambodian coupster with a military alliance. American arms and advisors (and, for the two months of the "incursion," actual combat troops) began to flow into Cambodia.

The 15,000 US troops were accompanied by 5,000 South Vietnamese, and together they decimated some 1,500 acres of thick jungle forests along the borderlands in which the communists had been hiding for years. Some 800 bunkers were destroyed and many abandoned weapons captured. Yet the incursion failed to "defeat" the North Vietnamese; instead, it only drove them deeper in to the more populated areas of central Cambodia and motivated them, for the first time, to make common cause with the Khmer Workers Party (a 1960 offshoot of the Indochinese Communist Party that had opposed France in the 1940s). Also known as the *Khmer Rouge*, the Workers Party was, before 1970, a fringe group in Cambodian politics with fewer than 3,000 followers (Vickery, 1984: 201). It had no support from North Vietnam, which was satisfied with Sihanouk's turning a blind eye to its transit through the eastern part of the country.

The coup and the incursion also drove Sihanouk himself, the constitutional head of state, into the arms of the *Khmer Rouge*. From his exile in Beijing, China, the prince allowed his name to be used as titular head of the Cambodian resistance to the South Vietnam–allied Lon Nol government. Over the next five years, the United States gave more than $400 million in military aid to Lon Nol . But by bringing this counter-insurgency war into his previously spared country, he became increasingly unpopular among the masses of ordinary Cambodians who pined for the "good old days" under their popular prince.

By April 1975, when the *Khmer Rouge* ousted the "pro-Vietnamese, US-puppet" government of Lon Nol, it had grown to more than 70,000 armed cadre and had the full support of Hanoi (Kiernan, 1985). However, its leader Pol Pot had a utopian vision of a socialist agricultural society and his group murdered almost 2 million of Cambodia's 8 million people in trying to implement it during the years 1975–79 (Kiernan, 1996: 456–60). They emptied the cities of hundreds of thousands of people who, it was said, should never have been there in the first place but had only left the countryside fleeing from American bombs ("forced urbanization" it was called by Pentagon bureaucrats in the 1960s) (Moss and Shalizi, 1971: 185–95). Thousands of women, children, and the aged died in these bayonet-enforced expulsions.

The Pol Pot regime also eliminated the entire class of educated people, specifically targeting any Cambodians who had studied abroad, and even people whose only crime was that they wore eyeglasses (indicative of literacy and/or wealth). The bloodbath was finally ended in 1979 after the Vietnam army entered in a humanitarian intervention applauded by most of the world. But so deep was American opposition to Vietnam in this era, that throughout the 1980s the United States continued to back the genocidal Pol Pot government (still allied with Sihanouk) as the rightful holder of Cambodia's seat at the United Nations while a low-level civil war between the communists, the royalists, and the Vietnam-installed government continued for another 10 years (Brady, 1999; Kiernan, 1993). Stability and nonviolent politics did not return to Cambodia until after the election of 1998.

Even before the *Khmer Rouge* genocide, however, the United States was responsible for some 155,000 deaths by bringing its war for South Vietnam into Cambodia in the years 1970–75. Johnson's "Operation Rolling Thunder" (1965–68) and Nixon's bombing of Cambodia (secretly in 1969 and in support of America's wider war there in 1970–73) dropped 540,000 tons of bombs on this unfortunate land. Paradoxically, the US bombing proved to be a key factor in the ultimate *Khmer Rouge* victory. A US Army study reported that the civilian population feared US air attacks more than they did the communists' scorched earth tactics (Kiernan, 1997: 210). Thus, the long-term result of the 1970 US military intervention in Cambodia was a disaster for Cambodia (Chandler, 1991).

But besides 28 years of disrupted normal politics, Cambodia also represented a significant long-term foreign policy loss for America. The United States did not succeed in replacing France as the capitalist hegemon in Indochina; indeed, the area was lost to capitalism for a generation. And, when the civil war in Cambodia finally ended, it was Japan that was the preferred mediator and first investor of choice for the new coalition regime that emerged in the 1990s.

## CASE 16. KURDISTAN, 1971–75

Kurdistan, a conceivable country the size of Poland with some 24 million people, embraces within it the largest nationality in the world today that does not have its own nation-state. Unfortunately for these Kurds, although located in the contiguous territories that comprise the possible Kurdistan, they are geographically divided among three larger existing states: Turkey, where some 14 million of them live; Iran, where there are about 6 million; and Iraq, where there are 4 million. Whatever other differences may exist between these three countries (and they are legion, especially in the case of Iraq versus Iran), they all agree that the Kurds must never be allowed to unite to promote any common aspiration for Kurdish statehood. Since the demise of the Ottoman Empire and the 1920 Treaty of Sevres, in which the Kurds were promised by the victorious World War I powers a nation-state (similar to that promised to the Zionist Movement at about the same time), Turkey, Iran and Iraq have successfully acted for more than 80 years to prevent this from happening.

In 1972–75, the United States entered into Kurdish politics as part of Kissinger and Nixon's balance of power policies. Responding to pressure from its "Nixon Doctrine" ally, the Shah of Iran, in May 1972 the United States started secretly supporting the Iraqi Kurds in an attempt to undermine the Soviet-supported regime in Baghdad. Some $16 million in covert American aid was channeled over the next few years through Iran to the Kurdish leader, Mustafa Barzani (Blum, 1995: 242; Safire, 1976b: 31). Barzani historically distrusted Iran, but with the United States involved he was encouraged to make a military move against Iraq in an attempt to convert the Kurds' traditional autonomy there into something approaching real sovereignty (Safire, 1976a: 31).

America's aid consisted mostly of small arms and rifles and millions of rounds of ammunition, much of it of Soviet and Chinese origin in order to ensure US "deniability." The covert deliveries were intended for a "destabilization" campaign against Iraq (i.e., "state-sponsored terrorism" in today's language), but the materials provided were never quite enough to carve out an independent state for the Iraqi Kurds. In fact, according to a leaked confidential report from the US House of Representatives Committee on Intelligence, American aid conformed to the limited goals of Iran: a stalemated "Kurd versus Iraq" situation to weaken Baghdad and force it to negotiate with Iran over two issues important to Iran: oil production quotas within the Organization of Petroleum Exporting Countries (OPEC) and a border dispute in the south. Never was enough military aid provided to tip power in the Kurds' favor or to bring about their own sovereign state (*CIA—Pike Report*, 1977: 195–97, 211–17). In the words of William Safire, who was on Nixon's staff at the time the Kurds were first encouraged, and citing a secret CIA memo of March 22, 1974: US policy was to help the Kurds "just enough to keep them bothersome, not enough to win" (Safire, 1976b: 31).

When, in March 1975, Iran finally cut a deal with Iraq on the boundary line in the *Sha'at al-Arab* river delta, the United States abandoned its erstwhile Kurdish allies. Iran would no longer be the conduit for America's weapons to the Kurds. Iraq moved in and executed several hundred Kurdish leaders, and drove 200,000 more out of their villages into Iran. When criticized for this sell-out of these suddenly inconvenient, now expendable, allies, Secretary of State Henry Kissinger coarsely carped, "Covert action should not be confused with missionary work" (*CIA—Pike Report*, 1977: 198; Blum, 1995: 244; Hersh, 1983: 542, note).

The strategic goal of appeasing the preeminent regional power, Iran, and consolidating America's post-1953 influence there, had to be preserved. Links with global capitalism in Iran trumped self-determination for one-tenth as many Kurds in Iraq. This priority even prevailed at a time when the Shah was hurting America by leading OPEC in its first major colluded price increase and boycott in 1973–74. But, despite what Barzani was led to believe, the United States was never a true partisan of Kurdish self-determination. It certainly never supported any moves for autonomy by the Kurds in Turkey or Iran, only those in Iraq, and (until 1991) only during this limited "Nixon Doctrine" period of wooing of Iran to be its regional policeman.

American policy reached the height of hypocrisy in 1988 during the last year of the Iran-Iraq war. The United States was diplomatically tilting toward Iraq in that conflict, and when its leader Saddam Hussein used chemical weapons upon the minority Kurds ("his own people" in later US formulation). More than 182,000 Kurds died during this "Anfall campaign," which included the bulldozing of some 4,000 of the 4,600 Kurdish villages in northern Iraq (Rubin, 2002: 16). But the Kurds were collaborating with Iran (America's enemy) during that war, so the Reagan administration turned its head and uttered not a word of protest or condemnation.

In February 1991, the United States again whetted Iraqi Kurdish aspirations, urging them to rebel during the Gulf War against Iraq (CASE 27). Once again, they were abandoned when that war ended. When, however, Saddam Hussein retaliated against them, and thousands of Kurds fled across the border into Turkey, the United States finally (in April 1991) provided a "safe haven" to protect the Kurds against the Iraqi air force in their northern Iraqi homelands. But even this "no-fly-zone" was designed more for the benefit of Turkey (i.e., to lure the Iraqi Kurds back in to Iraq before they made common cause with the Turkish Kurds in Turkey) than for the poor, expendable Kurds (Farer, 1993).

As this no-fly-zone was patrolled for the next decade, no support for an independent state was forthcoming from either the Bush, Clinton, or second Bush administrations. After 9-11-01, however, the Kurds were again courted to throw their lot in with the United States behind George W. Bush's "war on terrorism" policy of "regime change" in Baghdad. But even in this cause, the most the Kurds can hope for is a modest degree of *autonomy* within a more "democratic and federal" Iraq, not the true sovereignty over their own affairs wielded by every other nationality group of its size in the world.

Such diddling with the hopes of the Kurdish people by the United States over these 30 years has not done any apparent harm to American diplomacy in this Middle Eastern region. It has only been an embarrassment to devotees of human rights and to the Kurds' few sympathizers in the United States, like Safire, today of the *New York Times*.

## CASE 17. CHILE, 1973

9-11-2001 might be a date forever remembered in the United States, but 9-11-*1973* marks a similar date in Chilean history: the day of the coup that assassinated democratically elected President Salvador Allende in one of the most abominable cases of American adventurism in the Third World. One reason this case is so infamous is because US involvement was exposed soon afterwards, in Senator Frank Church's 1975 hearings on covert intelligence operations, and because of the Nixon administration's cavalier defense of its policies. After the coup, National Security Advisor Henry Kissinger quipped that the United States could not "stand by and watch a country go communist due to the irresponsibility of its own people" ("CIA's," 1974: 51–52).

This "irresponsibility" to which Kissinger referred consisted of the Chilean people consistently giving democratic-socialist Salvador Allende about a third of the vote in his electoral pursuits of the presidency in 1958, 1964, and 1970. He lost by 31–29 percent in a close three-way race in 1958, and more heavily (56–39%) in 1964 when centrist and right-wing parties formed a coalition and were rewarded with $2.6 million in CIA campaign financing (Sigmund, 1997: 239; US Senate, 1975, *Covert Action:* 14–17). In 1970, however, it was Allende who broadened his Popular Unity coalition to encompass six parties, making allies of centrists, populists, and communists under the leadership of his Socialist Party, and won a three-way race with some 36.2 percent of the vote, 1.3 percent more than his nearest rival (Sigmund, 1977: 106–7; Israel, 1989).

It was before and after the 1970 presidential election that the hand of the CIA was most in evidence. During the campaign the CIA spent between $800,000 and $1,000,000 on covert action to prevent an Allende victory (US Senate, 1975, *Covert Action:* 20). About $300,000 of this money went in to general anti-Allende propaganda, and some of the rest found its way into the campaigns of his opponents (Sigmund, 1997: 240). Among the corporations that contributed most heavily to the conservative candidate Jorge Alessandri was International Telephone and Telegraph (ITT), whose CEO was a close friend of Nixon (Sergeyev, 1981: 138). After the vote, Chilean law called for the race to be decided by its Congress if no candidate received 50 percent of the popular vote; the tradition was that the representative assembly respected the peoples' choice and elected the leading candidate. It was expected to do so again this time, and it was to prevent this that the American policy became virulent.

The operation consisted of two tracks. In Track I, in the two months between the general election and the assembly ballot, the CIA flooded the Chilean Congress with $500,000 to bribe parliamentarians to vote for the second-place finisher (Treverton, 1990: 2). The plan was that he, after six months in office, would then resign the presidency to allow for a new election in which the previous popular president (barred from running for two *consecutive* terms) would run and presumably defeat Allende handily (as he did in 1964). When the ex-president (Eduardo Frei) refused to go along with that scheme, the United States moved to Track II: pressuring the Chilean military to preempt the political process with a coup d'etat (US Senate, 1975, *Covert Action:* 24–26).

Two high-ranking military officers, General Roberto Viaux and General Camillo Valenzuela, were enlisted in this plot and given about $300,000 for weapons and "life insurance" (Treverton, 1990: 8). But when the head of the army, General Rene Schneider, got word of the conspiracy and refused to go along, he was kidnapped and shot by Viaux two days before the Congress was due to vote (Rojas Sandford, 1976: 75; US Senate, 1975, *Assassination Plots:* 225–27). The result was a backlash among the legislators against both the military and the American interference. Allende was overwhelmingly elected. But, according to Thomas Karamessines, CIA Deputy Director for covert operations at the time, the seeds for the 1973 coup had been sown in the 1970 relationship between US intelligence agents and the Chilean military (Davis, 1985: 360).

As Allende embarked upon a modest economic reform program, nationalizing one (of three) US copper companies (Kennecott, but not Anaconda or Cerro), as well as the nation's telephone network (run by ITT), the United States took retaliatory steps. Nixon and CIA Director Richard Helms set in motion plans to "make the economy scream" and the US Ambassador in Santiago boasted that "not a nut or bolt would be allowed to reach Chile under Allende" (US Senate, 1975, *Covert Action:* 33). US corporations were pressured not to provide spare parts to the nationalized copper company. Loans were blocked from the World Bank and the Inter-

American Development Bank where the United States had predominant voting rights. Loans from private American banks were cut from $219 million in 1970 to $32 million in 1971; government loans from an average of $150 million per year in the 1960s to $40 million in 1971 to $0 in 1972 (Rojas Sandford, 1976: 148). All government economic assistance was cut off; however, aid to the Chilean *military* was continued and even increased, from $6 million to $12 million to $15 million in 1971, 1972, and 1973 (Uribe, 1975: 120).

Despite this outside pressure, in March 1973, Allende's Popular Unity coalition won 44 percent of the vote in nationwide legislative elections, an improvement of 8 percent over its 1970 showing. Its number of seats in the Lower House jumped from 57 to 63 and in the Upper House from 18 to 20. Allende's policies having been shown to be popular, it was time for the United States to take more drastic action. In addition to the continued "aid-signaling" to the military, the CIA began in July 1973 to fund a truck owners' strike that was particularly irksome to middle-class consumers (Petras and Morley, 1975: 134). There is some dispute as to whether the CIA funded these strikers directly or through other groups linked to them; the Church Committee concluded that money was "siphoned off" from "several of the private sector groups that received CIA funds" (US Senate, 1975, *Covert Action:* 31).

Copper miners and physicians also struck, and housewives took to the streets banging pots and pans to protest a 200 percent rise in prices due to the government's deficit spending caused by the lack of international revenues. The US economic stranglehold had begun to take effect (although the judgment from Washington was that Allende had only himself to blame and was merely economically "incompetent" [Sigmund, 1977: 279–83; Rosenstein-Rodan, 1975: 613]). By the time the army moved to overthrow the government on September 11, public opinion had turned against Allende. In a five-hour battle pitting a force of 200 infantrymen, eight tanks, and two fighter jets against a lightly armed presidential entourage of 42 civilians, Allende was murdered and his body riddled with bullets from an infantry patrol led by Captain Roberto Garrido under the command of General Javier Palacios (Rojas Sandford, 1976: 1–5).

The dictatorship of General Agusto Pinochet, which ruled for the next 16 years, was particularly harsh. Three thousand people were killed during its first weeks, including two young American expatriates deemed sympathetic to the former regime: Frank Teruggi and Charles Horman (about whom the Academy Award–winning movie, *Missing,* was made [Hauser, 1988]). In subsequent years, the Pinochet regime became notorious for the torturing and "disappearances" of its political opponents: an estimated 30,000 were jailed, many never to be heard from again. Some 30,000 students were expelled from university, and 200,000 workers were fired from their jobs for political reasons; in response, about 1 million people went into exile (Rojas Sandford, 1976: viii; Amnesty International, 1977: 131–33, 1978: 109–10).

In the mid-1970s, Pinochet's Director of National Intelligence, General Manuel Contreras Sepulveda, organized "Operation Condor," which integrated the intelligence agencies of six other south American countries into secret activities in each other's states against their respective, exiled, political opponents (Kornbluh, 1999: 23). This operation even led to the assassination on the streets of Washington, DC—in a terrorist car-bombing on September 21, 1976—of one of Pinochet's particular nemeses, Allende's Ambassador to Washington Orlando Letelier (Dinges and Landau, 1980).

Finally, Pinochet thwarted normal politics in what had been one of Latin America's oldest democracies (going back to 1895). Even after the political system was returned to civilians in 1989, the military wrote into the constitution a strong role for itself, reserving 20 percent of seats in the Upper House for the armed services and creating a National Security Council in which civilian cabinet members had to share power with the heads of the army, navy, air force, and national police. Most ominously, Pinochet was named Army Commander-in-Chief for another eight years, and Senator-for-Life, thus assuring him amnesty (like his patron in the United States) for any crimes he committed while in office.

For Nixon and Kissinger, the intervention in Chile was one of their finest hours; for the United States in the long-run it represented a significant embarrassment in public opinion, especially throughout Latin America (Valenzuela, 1978). The United States did not have to move so harshly to consolidate its control over capitalism in the Western Hemisphere; even the Senate investigating committee concluded that there was never any real danger of a "loss" of this country to the Soviet Union (US Senate, 1975: *Covert Action:* 127–28). Allende was regarded almost everywhere beyond the White House as a respected social democrat, not a communist (Debray, 1971), having accepted electoral losses back as far as 1958, and continuing to try to implement his socialist vision via the democratic route through the elections of 1973. To replace him with a regime that would become one of the first in the Third World to apply neo-liberal economic policies, the United States was complicit in the death of a democracy and tolerant of a brutal military dictatorship for the next 16 years. In February 2003, in a desperate bid to get Chile's vote in the Security Council for war against Iraq, Secretary of State Colin Powell was forced to admit that US support for the coup was an error and "not part of American history we are proud of" ("Chile," 2003: 10).

## CASE 18. ANGOLA, 1975

In 1975, America embarked upon a new adventure into an area heretofore of little strategic interest to the United States: southern Africa. In

November 1974, Portugal announced plans to leave its 300-year-old colony in Angola within a year, and the United States, fearing Soviet encroachment, moved rapidly to replace the departing European imperialists. From the perspective of President Gerald Ford, having recently succeeded Richard Nixon who resigned that summer, "standing tall" in the Third World against the Soviets was seen as a necessary counterpart to the Nixon-Kissinger policy of *detente* with the USSR in bilateral areas like arms control and trade.

The government of Agostinho Neto, whose Movement for the Popular Liberation of Angola (MPLA) controlled the capital city Luanda, had strong anti-imperialist credentials. It had been battling Portuguese colonialism since 1962, and in this cause had been supported by the USSR (Marcum, 1969: 171; Klinghoffer, 1980: 17). In reply, the Portuguese, taking advantage of its NATO ties with the United States, had used American weapons, including 20 B-26 bombers (Weissman, 1979: 280) during these years to stave off the MPLA independence movement for more than a decade (Bender, 1978a: 156–59).

Neto's party, based in the Mbundu ethnic group with strong support among urban mulattoes in the capital, was by no means a doctrinaire communist group. It was willing to extend the capitalist royalty arrangements Portugal had made with western oil companies operating offshore and in Cabinda province. And it was open to power-sharing with two rival independence movements formed later in the 1960s: the Union for the Total Independence of Angola (UNITA), led by Jonas Savimbi and based in the Ovimbundu tribe in the south; and the National Liberation Front of Angola (FNLA) under Holden Roberto, whose main support was among the Bakongo in the north (Davidson, 1972: 212–14, 241–43). In January 1975, Portugal brought these three parties together and signed the Alvor Accord, which created an interim coalition government and established ground rules for elections leading to independence in November (Sisk, 1987: 80).

But rather than smoothing the transition, this agreement unleashed over the next year a military struggle among the three groups and a torrent of outside intervention in Angola's political affairs. There is much debate over which Great Power intervened first, but it seems that as early as July 7, 1974—before the Alvor Accord and long before any other foreign forces were on the scene (Stockwell, 1978: 67)—the CIA without the approval of the appropriate committee of the National Security Council, had renewed old ties with the FNLA. From its involvement in the Congo (CASE 7), the CIA had had an off-and-on relationship with Holden Roberto as far back as April 1961 (Weissman, 1979: 277). A member of the BaKongo tribe, which has three times as large a presence in Congo as in Angola (Sullivan, 1996: 117), Roberto was a particular favorite of General Mobutu who was instrumental in influencing US policy at this time. To further muddy the waters, China, an ideological rival of the USSR in Africa during this era, was also supporting the FNLA in an effort to stop the Soviet-backed MPLA.

Soon after the Alvor Accord was signed, the United States officially committed $3 million to the CIA's efforts with the FNLA. But when the MPLA was successful that spring in taking over Luanda, the oil-rich enclave of Cabinda in the north, and several southern ports and district capitals, the United States in July committed another $14 million and expanded its support to include UNITA as well. Another $10 million was approved in early September by which time China had become disillusioned and ended its involvement (Harsch, 1977: 97–98). Meanwhile, Portugal was by now convinced that elections could not be held, and that the MPLA had established the most de facto control (especially in the capital). Committed to its departure deadline of November, Portugal prepared to turn over power to this group.

Up to this point only money and military supplies from the outside patrons had poured in to Angola. No external troops were on the scene. Using the precedent of the Congo, the covert American funds were being used by Roberto and Savimbi to hire mercenaries from Portugal, France, Brazil and the white racist regimes of Rhodesia and South Africa. But the Angolan forces led by these soldiers-of-fortune were unsuccessful in seizing any power or territory from the MPLA. In fact, by the time of the November transfer of power, Roberto's FNLA had been effectively eliminated as a serious rival to the MPLA.

But the situation changed dramatically in October 1975, when forces from the regular army of South Africa entered southern Angola in support of Savimbi's UNITA. In November, the new MPLA government appealed to the world community for help. Responding to the anti-colonial message, Cuba committed 50,000 troops to the effort, and embarrassed a surprised Soviet Union into some financing and transport assistance (Gleijeses, 2002: 307). The United States committed another $7 million (making a total of $32 million for the year) (Weissman, 1979: 284) but was left backing a side that never commanded much popular support beyond its base of Ovimbundu tribesmen, and in league with the international racist pariah state, South Africa. The situation was so embarrassing that in December 1975 Congress passed an amendment, authored by Senator Dick Clark (D-IA), forbidding government moneys from going to any more CIA activities in Angola (Bender, 1978b: 26–27).

The Clark Amendment followed a year of hearings by the Select Committee on Intelligence chaired by Senator Frank Church (D-ID) that resulted in the tightening of Congressional scrutiny of the CIA. Brought on by revelations that the Agency had violated its 1947 Charter by spying on anti-Vietnam War protesters in the United States (the CIA was only supposed to operate overseas), the hearings also brought to light for the first time many of the covert operations, including assassination attempts, carried out during the Cold War. Among the operations officially confirmed at this time were the activities described in this book in the cases covering Congo, Cuba, South Vietnam, Dominican Republic, and Chile (CASEs 7, 8, 11, 13, and 17). One result of these hearings was the creation of Intelligence Committees in both the House and the Senate in 1976 and 1977, and passage of the Intelligence Oversight Act of 1980, which mandated *prior* notification to Congress of all future covert activities before they were implemented. This law tightened an earlier 1974 act that only required the president to report approvals of covert operations "in a timely manner."

It was in this context that the Clark Amendment was passed; it was the first (and still, today, the only) time in history that US intelligence forces were enjoined from operating in a specific country. From the perspective of the new Ford administration's policy toward Angola, it wrought significant political and public relations damage. But UNITA's existence had been sustained during the critical July–December 1975 period when power was passed from Portugal to the local MPLA forces. And the continued American-South African *diplomatic* support for UNITA for the next 16 years made it a force to be reckoned with in the southeastern third of the country. Indeed, after the Reagan administration successfully repealed the Clark amendment, more than $250 million in CIA support for Savimbi was provided during the 1986–91 period. As a result, the UNITA forces could not be subdued by the UN-recognized MPLA government in Luanda.

Even after the end of the Cold War in 1991, when the United States finally shifted sides and began supporting the MPLA in a United Nations peace-keeping effort, UNITA survived until the death of Savimbi in November 2001. In short, "normal" politics for the fledgling country of Angola, potentially one of Africa's richest in mineral wealth, was frustrated for more than a generation. By the time a ceasefire agreement was signed in April 2002, the war had become one of the world's longest civil conflicts (27 years). It was also one of the deadliest: close to a million people had died, and about 30 percent of the population (some 3 million people) were driven from their homes (French, 2002: 5). There were so many millions of landmines strewn about the countryside that even apolitical *dilettantes* like Princess Diana of Britain took notice of the situation. Forty years of war were definitely a disaster for the unfortunate Angolans caught up in yet another American "sideshow" to the Cold War with the Soviets (Wright, 1997: 205; Bender, 1987). Nevertheless, there was no foreign policy "loss" for the United States, beyond the embarrassment of being associated with South Africa in the 1970s and 1980s in what might be called state-supported terrorism.

## CASE 19. AUSTRALIA, 1975

In December 1972, E. Gough Whitlam became Australia's first Labor prime minister in 23 years, since before the creation of the ANZUS treaty and the 10 American military bases it brought to that country. As such he was regarded with some suspicion by the Cold War US foreign policy establishment, and in this respect he did not disappoint. Among his first acts as prime minister was to withdraw all Australian military personnel serving under US command in Vietnam. He also ended conscription and released from jail men who had been sentenced for refusing military service. Within a month, he had extended diplomatic recognition to North Vietnam and was criticizing Nixon's Twelve-Days-of-Christmas bombing of Hanoi.

In its brief three years of life, Australia's first left-of-center government since the start of the Cold War also recognized Cuba, North Korea and East Germany; voted against the United States in the United Nations on issues relating to South African racism and Portuguese colonialism; opposed the establishment of a American military base on the Indian Ocean island of Diego Garcia (planned as part of the "Nixon Doctrine" regional surrogates strategy); accepted as political refugees leftists opposed to the military juntas in Greece and Chile; and applied for observer status in the Non-Aligned Movement.

More ominous for America's secret services, Whitlam also cut off Australian overseas intelligence operations in Chile (where it had been cooperating with the United States); fired the head of Australian overseas intelligence for assisting the CIA in East Timor (see CASE 20) (Jose, 1981: 50; Albinski, 1977: 11) and began to question the value of American spy satellite tracking facilities and electronic eavesdropping stations in Australia (Ball, 1980).

The main issue that undermined Whitlam's faith in international interagency cooperation involved Pine Gap, an American intelligence gathering facility near Alice Springs in the remote outback of central Australia. The base could monitor cable traffic throughout Asia and most of the Pacific. Although the facility was supposed to be jointly run by the US and Australian militaries, Whitlam felt that information was being routinely withheld from the Aussie counterparts. American agents also often flew in and out of the center without customs or immigration checks, giving the place virtual extraterritorial status. The agreement to renew America's lease at Pine Gap was due to expire on December 10, 1975, and Whitlam had hinted that he wanted terms of the lease changed (Nathan, 1983: 178–79).

In the fall of 1975, the Australian press reported that the former CIA head of Pine Gap, Richard Lee Stallings, was passing money to the leader of the opposition National Country Party J. Douglas Anthony. It was also widely know that earlier the CIA had funneled funds to the opposition Liberal Party in May 1974, when Labor called, and won, an early election to consolidate its 1972 mandate (Blum, 1995: 246). In fact, the Liberal Party, the main party of government from 1949 to 1972, had regularly received CIA subsidies going back to the days of its support of the American war in Vietnam in the mid-1960s. But, the Australian Labor Party's political distancing of the country from the United States was endorsed by the voters in 1974; in results reminiscent of the Chilean election of 1973 and Guatemala in 1954 (CASEs 17 and 5), the left-wing government was returned to office with an increased majority.

With this added electoral legitimacy as background for the latest allegations of CIA meddling, Whitlam requested a list of all American intelligence operatives in Australia on the eve of a parliamentary debate scheduled for November 11, 1975. On the agenda was the status of Pine Gap's agents and the covert funding of opposition parties. Whitlam and his Labor party claimed to have previously believed that the Pine Gap facility was under the jurisdiction of the US Defense Department. That it was now seen to be probably a CIA facility, with Pentagon cover for CIA officers, allegedly came as a shock (shock!) to Labor politicians.

In addition, it was expected that CIA funding of other operations involving Australia's labor unions using the Nugan-Hand Merchant Bank of Sydney as a money launderer would also be mentioned in this debate. Nugan-Hand had several military intelligence officers on its board, and links to Air America, the CIA airline in Laos (CASE 10). Among its $1 billion in assets were an office in Thailand that acted as conduit for drug money for the CIA's secret army of Hmong tribesmen, and a branch in Switzerland that handled investments for the Shah of Iran (Kwitny, 1987: Chapter 16; Nathan, 1983: 182–83; Blum, 1985: 249).

It was in this context that the United States threatened to cut off all intelligence links with Australia as long as Whitlam governed. It is unclear whether this decision was approved by President Ford, or was simply an act of the Agency having a bureaucratic fit. The entire event goes unmentioned in the memoirs of Gerald Ford and Henry Kissinger, and in most other official, and establishment, accounts of the era. In any event, Australia's Governor General, Sir John Kerr, reflecting concern for "national security" (Coxsedge et al., 1982: 35), fired Whitlam, dismissed the parliament, and called for a general election. In the interim, he appointed Malcolm Fraser, the head of the opposition Liberal Party, as acting prime minister.

The *announced* reason for this action was that the Upper House, controlled by the Liberals, had since mid-October refused to vote on the government's budget appropriation bill, precipitating a political stalemate. This is not an unusual situation in parliamentary government and it would not normally trigger such drastic action by the Head of State. Although the Governor General is constitutionally empowered to dismiss the government (usually, in practice, for failing to keep the confidence of the *Lower* House), this was the first time in Australia's 74-year history that it was ever done at all. Most constitutional lawyers regarded Kerr's action as improper (Jaensch, 1992: 81; Ward, 1978: 398–419). It is also noteworthy that despite his being the Queen's representative in Australia, neither she nor the British Foreign Office were notified of his action until after it had occurred.

A more complete explanation for Governor General Kerr's behavior can be derived from a look at his history of involvement with CIA fronts in Australia, and the actions of CIA officials in the country just before the government's dismissal. Earlier in his career, Kerr had been a high-ranking member of two organizations with CIA ties: the Congress for Cultural Freedom and Law Asia. The first published the anti-communist propaganda magazine *Quadrant;* the second was an organization of lawyers funded by the Asia Foundation (a CIA conduit) who wrote articles in the mainstream media critical of China and North Vietnam (Marchetti and Marks, 1974: 172–73; Barclay, 1985; Freney, 1977: 34). The day before he dismissed Whitlam, Kerr was informed by the Australian Defense Ministry that the CIA had given an ultimatum to its Australian counterpart that it was on the verge of breaking off interagency cooperation (Bell and Bell, 1993: 148).

In any case, Whitlam's Labor Party lost the election of December 13, 1975, and the Liberals returned to power for the next 12 years. Thus, for roughly 35 of 38 years during the height of the Cold War—from 1949 until 1987—the party of ANZUS and in favor of close ties with the United States prevailed in Australia. Unlike many of the other cases in *American Adventurism Abroad,* this change of government did not result in any material damage to the people of Australia, and could even be regarded as an American foreign policy victory. However, it is embarrassing that covert tactics normally reserved for underdeveloped polities in civil turmoil were visited upon a mature democracy over a minor diplomatic (inter-agency) dispute. But the episode consolidated the shift (begun with the ANZUS Treaty of 1951) of Australia away from British hegemony and toward that of the United States.

In closing this shabby episode, it might be noted that the only organization to receive an increase in funding in new Prime Minister Fraser's first budget was Australian Intelligence; the only *person* to receive a salary increase—a whopping 171 percent—was Governor General Kerr (Nathan, 1983: 177).

## CASE 20. EAST TIMOR, 1975

December 7, 1975, is a date that will live in infamy in the history of East Timor. On that day, Indonesia's military invaded and took over the tiny

(half-)island (13,000 square miles) that had recently received its independence from departing colonial power Portugal (Joliffe, 1978; United Nations, 1976). Just 24 hours earlier, US President Gerald Ford and Secretary
of State Henry Kissinger had visited Indonesia and had given the green
light of American approval to the operation (Zunes and Terrall, 2002: 15;
Chomsky, 2001: 127). The only caveat the two Americans issued regarding
the anticipated attack was that it succeed quickly because they would then
"be able to influence the reaction if what ever happens, happens after we
return" home (Hitchens, 2002: 9; McMahon, 2002: 15).

American acquiescence in the assault was needed because 90 percent of
the military equipment being used by the Indonesian army in 1975 was
supplied by the United States under a weapons-export program approved
by Congress only for self-defense (Pinto and Jardine, 2002: 15; US House
of Representatives, 1977: 76–80). At the December 6th meeting with the
Indonesian generals planning the next day's assault, Kissinger mused, "It
depends on how we construe it; whether it is in self defense or is a foreign
operation" (Hitchens, 2002: 9). Later to his staff, he used almost the same
language: "Can't we construe a communist government in the middle of
Asia as self-defense?" (Zunes and Terrall, 2002: 15). Or, as the Australian
ambassador in Jakarta, Richard Wolcott, quoted the American Ambassador
David Newsome: the view of the United States was that "if Indonesia were
to intervene, the United States would hope they would do so 'effectively,
quickly, and not use our equipment'" (Budiardjo and Liong, 1984: 9).

Definitional niceties aside, Indonesia used these American weapons
over the next few years to kill about 100,000 Timorese (US House of Representatives, 1977: 38, 61). Given its small total population of 600,000, this
massacre represented a genocide rivaling in proportion that of the *Khmer
Rouge* in Cambodia (CASE 15) (Jardine, 1999; Chomsky, 2001: 139). During
this time, attempts were made in the United Nations to send missions to
investigate the reported atrocities. But they were always blocked by the
United States, along with Japan, Thailand, Singapore, Australia, and other
nations with significant economic ties with Indonesia (Chomsky and Herman, 1979: 159).

After the departure of Portugal, there was disagreement in East Timor
between those political leaders in the Fretilin Party who wanted independence, those in the Timorese Democratic Union who wanted greater political autonomy but still linked to Portugal, and those in the Apodeti
Party who wanted accession to Indonesia (Leifer, 1976: 348). The United
States refused to accept the middle way (advocated by Portugal and most
of the United Nations) of referendum and negotiation to settle the dispute
("Communique of Portugal," 1980: 8–9). Instead, the Ford administration
justified its backing of Indonesia in terms of realist geopolitical payback
for years of Indonesia's backing the losing American policy in Vietnam
(Chomsky and Herman, 1979: 153–54, 186). With a population of 160 mil-

lion, fifth largest in the world, Indonesia was the ultimate anti-communist "domino" in Southeast Asia, and an important exporter of oil to the capitalist world. Establishing a good relationship with its ruling general also fit the pattern of the US moving into yet another area of previous European (Portuguese) hegemony, this time via the "Nixon Doctrine" of backing regional surrogates to do its global policing against communism and "instability" (Lewis, 1999: 19).

Although there was no evidence that the Timorese independence leaders were in any respect "communist"—in 1996 two of them (Catholic Bishop Carlos Belo and Foreign-Minister-in-Exile Jose Ramos Horta) received the Nobel peace prize for their non-violent resistance to the Indonesian occupation—1975 was still a critical year in the Cold War. South Vietnam had "fallen" to the communists in April and the new US president was looking for any opportunity to display American power and commitment (see also CASE 18: Angola). Over time, American support for the occupation of East Timor for the next 24 years showed a clear preference for the crony capitalism of Indonesia's military dictator Suharto (CASE 14), and for Indonesian colonialism, over democracy and self-determination for the people of East Timor (Nairn, 1998: 6). It is also no coincidence that US has sold more than $1 billion in weapons to Indonesia since 1975 (Chomsky, 2001: 135).

The damage to the people of Timor, in addition to the initial genocide, was a generation of repression before a government came to power in Indonesia that would even talk about the possibility of some form of autonomy (Taylor, 1991). The beleaguered nation finally got its freedom after the Suharto regime fell in 1999, although it took another 2,000 deaths and a United Nations peace-keeping force to ensure it. By this time, there was also a more sympathetic administration in Washington (Clinton's); the Cold War, and Kissinger's *realpolitik* approach to it, were long past (Lewis, 1998: 15). Complicity in genocide did not, however, result in much of a loss for American foreign policy. The Timorese were another of those hapless, expendable peoples (like the Guyanese, Laotians, and Kurds—Cases 9, 10, and 16) whose significance was too small for most of the world, or even many Americans, to notice.

## CHAPTER 4 BIBLIOGRAPHY

### Nixon/Ford Foreign Policies

Gardner, Lloyd. 1973. *The Great Nixon Turnabout: America's New Foreign Policy in the Post-Liberal Era*. NY: New Viewpoints.
Greene, John Robert. 1992. *The Limits of Power: The Nixon and Ford Administrations*. Bloomington: Indiana University Press.
Jones, Alan M. (ed.). 1973. *US Foreign Policy in a Changing World: The Nixon Administration, 1969–73*. NY: David McKay.

Litwak, Robert. 1984. *Detente and the Nixon Doctrine: American Foreign Policy and the Pursuit of Stability 1969–76*. NY: Cambridge University Press

Nelson, Keith L. 1995. *The Making of Detente: Soviet-American Relations in the Shadow of Vietnam*. Baltimore: Johns Hopkins University Press.

Schurmann, Frank. 1987. *The Foreign Politics of Richard Nixon: The Grand Design*. Berkeley: University of California Institute of International Studies, No. 65.

Snepp, Frank. 1978. *Decent Interval: An Insider's Account of Saigon's Indecent End Told by the CIA's Chief Strategy Analyst in Vietnam*. NY: Vintage Books.

Szulc, Tad. 1978. *Illusion of Peace: Foreign Policy in the Nixon Years*. NY: Viking Press.

Thornton, Richard C. 1989. *The Nixon-Kissinger Years: The Reshaping of American Foreign Policy*. NY: Paragon House.

## CASE 15. Cambodia, 1970

Brady, Christopher. 1999. *United States Foreign Policy towards Cambodia, 1977–1992: A Question of Realities*. NY: St. Martin's Press.

Chandler, David P. 1991. *The Tragedy of Cambodian History: Politics, War, and Revolution since 1945*. New Haven: Yale University Press.

Hersh, Seymour. 1983. *Price of Power: Kissinger in the Nixon White House*. NY: Simon and Schuster.

Kiernan, Ben. 1997. "Cambodia," vol. 1: 210–11, in Bruce W. Jentleson and Thomas G. Paterson (eds.), *Encyclopedia of United States Foreign Relations*. NY: Oxford University Press.

Kiernan, Ben (ed.). 1993. *Genocide and Democracy in Cambodia: The Khmer Rouge, the United Nations, and the International Community*. New Haven: Yale University Press.

Kiernan, Ben. 1985. *How Pol Pot Came to Power: A History of Communism in Kampuchea, 1930–1975*. London: Verso Books.

Kiernan, Ben. 1996. *The Pol Pot Regime: Race, Power, and Genocide in Cambodia under the Khmer Rouge, 1975–1979*. New Haven: Yale University Press.

Morris, Roger. 1977. *Uncertain Greatness: Henry Kissinger and American Foreign Policy*. NY: Harper and Row.

Moss, Laurence A. G., and Zamarack M. Shalizi. 1971. "War and Urbanization in Indochina," Chapter 14: 175–200, in Jonathan Grant, Laurence A. G. Moss, and Jonathan Unger (eds.), *Cambodia: The Widening-War in Indochina*. NY: Simon and Schuster.

Osborne, Milton. 1974. *Politics and Power in Cambodia: The Sihanouk Years*. NY: Longman

Shawcross, William. 1979. *Side-Show: Kissinger, Nixon and the Destruction of Cambodia*. NY: Simon and Schuster.

Sihanouk, Prince Norodom. 1974. *My War with the CIA: The Memoirs of Prince Sihanouk*. NY: Pantheon Books.

Vickery, Michael. 1984. *Cambodia, 1975–82*. Boston: South End Press.

## CASE 16. Kurdistan, 1971–75

Blum, William. 1995. "Iraq 1972–1975: Covert Action Should Not Be Confused with Missionary Work," Chapter 39: 242–44, *Killing Hope: US Military and CIA Interventions since World War II*. Monroe, ME: Common Courage Press.

*CIA—The Pike Report.* 1977. Nottingham, UK: Spokesman Books. Reprints of leaks from confidential *Staff Report* of US House of Representatives, Select Committee on Intelligence (Pike Committee), first printed in *The Village Voice,* February 16 and 23, 1976.

Farer, Tom. 1993. *Human Rights and Foreign Policy: What the Kurds Learned (A Drama in One Act).* Washington, DC: Georgetown University Institute for Diplomacy, Case Study 515.

Hersh, Seymour. 1983. *The Price of Power: Kissinger in the Nixon White House.* NY: Simon and Schuster.

Rubin, Michael. 2002. "Kurdistan Dispatch: Bomb Shelter," *New Republic,* June 17: 16–17.

Safire, William. 1976. "Mr. Ford's Secret Sellout," *New York Times,* February 5.

Safire, William. 1976. "Son of Secret Sellout," *New York Times,* February 12.

## CASE 17. Chile, 1973

Amnesty International. 1977, 1978. *Reports.* London: Amnesty International Publications.

"Chile: Powell Comment on Coup Welcomed," *New York Times,* February 25, 2003.

"(The) CIA's New Bay of Bucks," *Newsweek,* September 23, 1974: 51–52.

Davis, Nathaniel (Ambassador). 1985. *The Last Two Years of Salvador Allende.* Ithaca, NY: Cornell University Press.

Debray, Regis. 1971. *Conversations with Allende: Socialism in Chile.* London: New Left Books.

Dinges, John, and Saul Landau. 1980. *Assassination on Embassy Row.* NY: Pantheon.

Hauser, Thomas. 1988. *Missing: The Execution of Charles Horman: An American Sacrifice.* NY: Simon and Schuster.

Israel, Ricardo. 1989. *Politics and Ideology in Allende's Chile.* Tempe: Arizona State University, Center for Latin American Studies Press.

Kornbluh, Peter. 1999. "Chile Declassified," *Nation,* August 9/16: 21–24.

Petras, James, and Morris H. Morley. 1975. *United States and Chile: Imperialism and the Overthrow of Allende.* NY: Monthly Review Press.

Rojas Sandford, Robinson. 1976. *The Murder of Allende and the End of the Chilean Way to Socialism.* NY: Harper and Row.

Rosentein-Rodan, Paul N. 1975. "Why Allende Failed," pp. 613–17 in US House of Representatives. Committee on Foreign Affairs. Subcommittee on Inter-American Affairs. *Hearings: US and Chile during the Allende Years, 1970–73.* Washington, DC: US Government Printing Office.

Sergeyev, F. F. 1981. *Chile: CIA Big Business.* Moscow: Progress Publishers.

Sigmund, Paul E. 1997. "Chile," vol. 1: 239–41, in Jentleson, *Encyclopedia* (see CASE 15, Kiernan).

Sigmund, Paul E. 1977. *The Overthrow of Allende and the Politics of Chile, 1964–1976.* Pittsburgh: University of Pittsburgh Press.

Treverton, Gregory F. 1990. *Covert Intervention in Chile, 1970–73.* Washington, DC: Georgetown University Institute for the Study of Diplomacy, Case 503.

Uribe, Armando. 1975. *The Black Book of American Intervention in Chile.* Boston: Beacon Press.

U.S. Senate. Church Committee (Select Committee to Study Governmental Operations with Respect to Intelligence Activities). 1975 (November 20). "Schneider," Part III.F: 225–54, *Interim Report: Alleged Assassination Plots Involving Foreign Leaders*. Washington, DC: US Government Printing Office.

U.S. Senate. Church Committee (Select Committee to Study Governmental Operations with Respect to Intelligence Activities). 1975 (December 18). *Staff Report: Covert Action in Chile, 1963–1973*. Washington, DC: US Government Printing Office.

Valenzuela, Arturo. 1978. *The Breakdown of Democratic Regimes: Chile*. Baltimore: Johns Hopkins University Press.

## CASE 18. Angola, 1975

Bender, Gerald. 1978. *Africa and the Portuguese: The Myth and the Reality*. Berkeley: University of California Press.

Bender, Gerald. 1987. "The Eagle and the Bear in Angola," *Annals of the American Academy of Political and Social Science*, vol. 489: 123–32.

Bender, Gerald. 1978. "Kissinger and Angola: Anatomy of a Failure," pp. 65–143 in Rene Lemarchand, *American Policy in Southern Africa: The Stakes and the Stance*. Washington, DC: University Press of America.

Davidson, Basil. 1972. *In the Eye of the Storm: Angola's People*. Garden City, NY: Anchor Books.

French, Howard. 2002. "Exit Savimbi, and the Cold War in Africa," *New York Times, Week in Review*, March 3.

Gleijeses, Piero. 2002. *Conflicting Missions: Havana, Washington, and Africa, 1959–1976*. Chapel Hill: University of North Carolina Press.

Harsch, Ernst, and Tony Thomas. 1977. *Angola: The Hidden History of Washington's War*. NY: Pathfinder Press.

Klinghoffer, Arthur Jay. 1980. *The Angolan War: A Study in Soviet Politics in the Third World*. Boulder, CO: Westview Press.

Marcum, John A. 1978. *The Angolan Revolution: vol. 2: Exile Politics and Guerilla Warfare, 1962–1976*. Cambridge: Massachusetts Institute of Technology Press.

Sisk, Timothy D. 1997. "Angola," vol. 1: 79–81, in Jentleson, *Encyclopedia* (see CASE 15, Kiernan).

Stockwell, John. 1978. *In Search of Enemies: A CIA Story*. NY: W. W. Norton.

Sullivan, Michael J., III. 1996. *Comparing State Polities: A Framework for Analyzing 100 Governments*. Westport, CT: Greenwood Press.

Weissman, Stephen R. 1979. "CIA Covert Action in Zaire and Angola: Patterns and Consequences," *Political Science Quarterly*, 24(2), Summer: 263–86.

Wright, George. 1997. *The Destruction of a Nation: United States' Policy toward Angola since 1945*. Chicago: Pluto Press.

## CASE 19. Australia, 1975

Albinski, Henry S. 1977. *Australian External Policy under Labor*. Australia: Queensland University Press.

Ball, Desmond. 1980. *A Suitable Piece of Real Estate: American Installations in Australia*. Sydney, Australia: Hale and Iremongers.

Barclay, Glen St. John. 1985. *Friends in High Places: The Australian-American Security Relationship since 1945*. NY: Oxford University Press.

Bell, Phillip, and Roger Bell. 1993. *Implicated: The United States in Australia*. NY: Oxford University Press.

Blum, William. 1995. "Australia 1973–1975: Another Free Election Bites the Dust," Chapter 40: 244–49, *Killing Hope* (see CASE 16).

Coxsedge, Joan, Ken Coldicutt, and Gerry Harrant. 1982. *Rooted in Secrecy: The Clandestine Element in Australian Politics*. Balwyn North, Victoria, Australia: Committee for the Abolition of Political Police.

Freney, Denis. 1977. *The CIA's Australian Connection*. South Sydney, Australia: D. Freney Publisher.

Jaensch, D. 1992. *The Politics of Australia*. South Melbourne, Australia: Macmillan.

Jose, Jim. 1981. "The Whitlam Years: Illusion and Reality ," pp. 45–55 in Pat Flanagan (ed.), *Big Brother or Democracy? The Case of Abolition of ASIO*. Australia: University of Adelaide, Department of Continuing Education.

Kwitny, Jonathan. 1987. *The Crimes of Patriots: A True Tale of Dope, Dirty Money, and the CIA*. NY: W. W. Norton.

Marchetti, Victor, and John D. Marks. 1974. *The CIA and the Cult of Intelligence*. NY: Alfred A. Knopf.

Nathan, James A. 1983. "Dateline Australia: America's Foreign Watergate?" *Foreign Policy*, no. 49 (Winter): 168–85.

Ward, Russell. 1978. *The History of Australia: The Twentieth Century, 1901–1975*. London: Heinemann.

## CASE 20. East Timor, 1975

Budiardjo, Carmel, and Liem Soei Leong. 1984. *The War against East Timor*. London: Zed Books.

Chomsky, Noam. 2001. "East Timor, the United States, and International Responsibility: Green Light for War Crimes," Chapter 9: 127–48, in Richard Tanter, Mark Selden, and Stephen R. Shalom (eds.), *Bitter Flowers, Sweet Flowers: East Timor, Indonesia, and the World Community*. Lanham, MD: Rowman and Littlefield.

Chomsky, Noam, and Edward S. Herman. 1979. *The Political Economy of Human Rights, Volume 1: The Washington Connection and Third World Fascism*. Boston: South End Press.

"Communique of the Council of Ministers of Portugal," in Michael Chamberlain (ed.), *East Timor International Conference Report*. NY: Clergy and Laity Concerned, and East Timor Human Rights Committee, 1980.

Hitchens, Christopher. 2002. "Kissinger's Green Light to Suharto," *Nation*, February 18.

Jardine, Matthew. 1999. *East Timor: Genocide in Paradise*. Monroe, ME: Common Courage Press.

Jolliffe, Jill. 1978. *East Timor: Nationalism and Colonialism*. Englewood Cliffs, NJ: Prentice-Hall.

Leifer, Michael. 1976. "Indonesia and the Incorporation of East Timor," *The World Today*, September: 347–54.

Lewis, Anthony. 1998. "Their Suharto and Ours," *New York Times*, May 25.

Lewis, Anthony. 1999. "The Fruits of Realism," *New York Times*, September 7.

McMahon Robert J. 2002. "Guilty!" *Nonviolent Activist*, January–February.

Nairn, Allan. 1998. "Indonesia's Killers," *Nation*, March 30: 6–7.

Pinto, Constancio, and Matthew Jardine. 1997. *East Timor's Unfinished Struggle.* Boston: South End Press.

Taylor, John G. 1991. *Indonesia's Forgotten War: The Hidden History of East Timor.* London: Zed Books.

United Nations. 1976. *Decolonization: East Timor.* NY: United Nations, Department of Political Affairs, Trusteeship, and Decolonization, Publication No. 7.

U.S. House of Representatives. 1977 (March 23). Committee on International Relations. Subcommittees on International Organizations and on Asian and Pacific Affairs. *Human Rights in East Timor and the Question of the Use of U.S. Equipment by the Indonesian Armed Forces.*

Zunes, Stephen, and Ben Terrall. 2002. "East Timor: Reluctant Support for Self-Determination," Chapter 1: 11–30, in Ralph G. Carter, *Contemporary Cases in U.S. Foreign Policy: From Terrorism to Trade.* Washington, DC: CQ Press.

# PART III

# The Four-Year Aberration, 1977–80

Part III of *American Adventurism Abroad* consists of one chapter, which treats the four-year presidency of Jimmy Carter as a transition between the excesses of the first 30 years of the Cold War and its denouement (after a brief revival) in the 1980s. There are no formal case studies as in the chapters covering the other nine post–World War II presidents, although there were at least five occasions—Congo, Nicaragua, El Salvador, Iran, Afghanistan—when Carter might have been tempted to intervene more forcefully than he did. That he did not is testimony to his commitment to break from the pattern of global power projection in pursuit of hegemony in the wake of America's disastrous experience in Vietnam. That Carter went as far as he did on a few of these occasions shows how difficult it was to buck the tradition of attempting to control the capitalist world under the guise of containing communism.

Part III thus contains only this one chapter covering this one president whose four years in office proved to be so exceptional compared to his six predecessors and three successors studied in this book. The specifics of the five "nonexamples" of *restrained* military intervention are discussed only briefly in Chapter 5 as a more general attempt is made to explain the unusual Carter interlude between the presidents who preceded and followed him.

# Jimmy Carter's Human Rights Pause, 1977–80

The four years of Jimmy Carter's presidency represent an aberration to this book's theses regarding American intervention in the Third World. Reacting to the diplomatic debacle in Vietnam—in particular the definitive defeat of the South Vietnamese ally in May 1975—Carter ran for president in 1976 with a distinctly different foreign policy voice from that of any other post–World War II candidate. He said he would never lie to the American people, and he often expressed the wish that no Americans would die in combat during his presidency; he pledged a government that was "honest, decent, open, fair, and compassionate" and a foreign policy that reflected "the decency and generosity and common sense of our own people" (Carter, 1975: 9; Smith, 1986: 28).

More than other recent presidential candidates, he explicitly embraced moralism and religion in his campaign, saying he loved Jesus Christ above all else, anticipating (and provoking) the rise of the religious *right* in electoral politics in subsequent years. In particular, he hoped that displays of his faith in mankind's goodness would help to bind the wounds inflicted upon the American psyche as a result of the Vietnam War. Symbolically, in his first week in office he appointed two heroes from different sides of that experience to high-profile subcabinet positions: Max Cleland, a triple-amputee war veteran, to head the Veterans Administration; and Sam Brown, a leader of the Mobilization against the War, to head VISTA (Volunteers in Service to America), the domestic peace corps.

Among the foreign policy lessons Carter had learned from the extremist years of 1961–76 and the Vietnam fiasco were: (1) America should not overextend its ground combat troops in its foreign policy commitments; (2) the United States should not militarily intervene into other nations' civil wars; (3) US public opinion would not back overt, conventional wars that drag on without prospect of victory; and (4) the American public disapproved of embarrassing covert operations employing tactics that went against American values.

This last lesson reflected the year of hearings by the Senate Special Committee on Intelligence under Senator Frank Church discussed in CASE 18. In openly aligning US foreign policy with lofty ideals and moral values, particularly the promotion of peace and human rights, Carter consciously presented a contrast, and a corrective, to the "value-less" balance-of-power realism of Nixon, Ford, and Kissinger (Skidmore, 1996: 29–30). But, just as Nixon's realist correctives to the Kennedy-Johnson excesses spawned an ideological backlash within the Republican right, so too did Carter's moralism provoke a reaction among traditionalists in his party.

In his first major foreign policy speech, at Notre Dame University's commencement on May 22, 1977, President Carter asserted that the United States need have no "inordinate fear of communism" (Melanson, 2000: 102). During his first two and one-half years as president, Carter negotiated the return of the Panama Canal and ended military aid to allied Third World dictators with poor human rights records in "secondary strategic" locales (like central America)—two actions that marked a distinct break from previous American Cold War foreign policies (Vance, 1983: 28–29). He also presided over the Middle East peace process in which Israel and Egypt exchanged diplomatic recognitions in March, 1979 (and for which he finally received the Nobel Peace Prize in 2002.)

But this new, more moralist foreign policy lasted only until the middle of 1979. And even during this period, Carter was torn between the idealist inclinations of his Secretary of State Cyrus Vance, which emphasized human rights and avoided military interventions, and the more traditional anti-communist themes of his National Security Advisor Zbigniew Brzezinski, which stressed military activism as well as moral disapproval of Marxism-Leninism (Brzezinski, 1983: 48–57; Skidmore, 1996: 95–97).

From early 1977 to mid-1979, Vance's worldview seemed to prevail. During this time, there were a few opportunities for Carter to intervene in Third World crises, and most of his predecessors probably would have. But during this first phase of his presidency, Carter studiously kept American military might out of events in Congo, Nicaragua, El Salvador, and Iran (Rosati, 1991: 127–47; Strong, 2000: 268–70).

In 1977 and again in 1978, Carter refrained from injecting US force into a crisis in Congo's Shaba (formerly Katanga) province. (Since Congo was discussed in Chapter 3, its name had been changed to Zaire, and that of its leader to Mobutu Sese Seko). President Mobutu, "America's man" in the Congo since 1960 (CASE 7) and its ally in the 1975 secret war against

Angola's MPLA Government (CASE 18), asked for help. Even though the instability in Shaba was linked to the war in Angola, Carter kept American operatives out, strictly adhering to the 1975 Clark amendment, which forbade any intelligence appropriations from being expended in that conflict (Bender, 1977: VII.7).

Nicaragua was one of the Third World dictatorships with human rights problems and insignificant security implications that Carter had decided to stop supporting with American military aid, a beneficence which had been flowing to the ruling Somoza family (father, son, and brother, respectively) for the previous 40 years. In 1978–79 the opposition Sandinista National Liberation Front took advantage of Anastasio Somoza's unaccustomed estrangement from his America patron to oust him in a revolution that drew the support from most sectors of Nicaraguan society (Steinmetz, 1994: 82–88, 128–29). After briefly trying to find some "third way" leadership within Somoza's National Guard, Carter decided the search was hopeless and instead opted to try to work with the Sandinistas' socialist reform government and even to offer some conditional economic aid.

In Iran, the aging, ailing Shah (CASE 4) was ousted in January 1979, in a revolution led by Ayatollah Ruhollah Khomeini and other Islamic religious fundamentalists. Unlike Eisenhower in 1953, Carter did not move to restore America's client. Instead, Carter attempted to get the old autocrat medical care in Egypt, Panama, and other places around the world before making the ill-fated judgment to admit him to the United States in October 1979. This decision led to the seizure of the American embassy in Tehran and, over the next year, the military mission to rescue the hostages being held there (Kegley, 1994: 4–8). The failure of this mission, it could be argued, led the end of the Carter presidency.

The "loss" of Iran and Nicaragua, along with the "give-away" of the Panama Canal, were particularly upsetting to the right-wing of the Republican Party led by Ronald Reagan, the former governor of California who was during this period regularly criticizing the president on his syndicated radio talk show. This group had never reconciled itself to the loss in Vietnam; indeed, it denied the US "lost," and preferred to say America merely "left" Southeast Asia and could have won had it stayed and fought harder. These "Reagan Republicans" criticized Nixon for signing the 1973 Paris Peace Accords with North Vietnam and, as will be described in the next paragraph, also faulted Ford for signing the 1975 Helsinki agreement with the USSR. (They also could never forgive Kissinger for his advice in these matters and froze him out of executive branch positions he desired when they came to power in the 1980s.)

As the 1980 campaign loomed, Carter was also being criticized by "neoconservatives" in the right-wing of the Democratic Party who had flocked to the Committee on the Present Danger, an anti-communist pressure group formed at the time of the 1975 Helsinki Accords. These were agreements that were signed by the US and USSR at the height of *detente* under President Ford and that recognized the territorial boundaries that emerged from World War II in Europe (and hence gains by the Soviet Union at the expense of Poland and Germany). In return, the USSR agreed to increased economic, social, and cultural contacts between peoples on either side of the Iron Curtain. Although this led to the breakdown of barriers and the end of the Cold War in the next decade, right-wing ideologues in both major parties saw Helsinki as a sell-out to communism. Within the Republican Party, these forces lobbied unsuccessfully on behalf of Reagan in the 1976 Republican presidential primary against Ford. By 1980, the Committee on the Present Danger was drawing Democrats disenchanted with Carter's "no inordinate fear of communism" position, the Panama Canal Treaty, and the evolving events in Nicaragua and Iran (Kirkpatrick, 1979: 34; Sanders, 1983: 263–70).

In this context Carter moved to the right in anticipation of his 1980 reelection campaign. To preempt being threatened from the left in the Democratic Party, he had earlier (in July 1979) dismissed from his Cabinet those members sympathetic to the presidential aspirations of Senator Edward M. Kennedy (Califano, 1981: 429–42). Anticipating a more formidable threat from the right by Republican Reagan in the general election, Carter next adopted a series of policies to shore up his support among society's more conservative sectors.

In August 1979, a presidential directive (PD-15) was issued retargeting American nuclear weapons from those sites consistent with a nuclear deterrence strategy to those more in line with nuclear "war-fighting." In September 1979, in a sop to the Miami Cuban exile community, a Soviet brigade that had been on that island since 1963 was "discovered" and tensions were heightened. Also that fall, Carter backed a coup in El Salvador that brought to power some "progressive" military officers perceived as better at staving off a Nicaragua-style leftist insurgency than the more reactionary militarists the United States had supported there since 1971 (see CASE 21).

On October 22, 1979, Carter bowed to pressure from his friend David Rockefeller and his critic Henry Kissinger—representing, respectively, the views of the Democrat-oriented Trilateral Commission and the Republican-leaning Council on Foreign Relations—and admitted the deposed Shah of Iran to the United States for humanitarian medical treatment (Bill, 1988: 49; Sick, 1985: 180). Providing such sanctuary to the despised, discredited leader, who was regarded as a common criminal by the new regime in Iran, triggered the seizure of the American embassy in Tehran by incensed student leaders on November 4. The new revolutionary government, wishing to live up to its own rhetoric, refused to move against them (Steigman, 1993: 6–7, 13).

The holding of 52 Americans hostage in the embassy for the next 444 days—until the end of the Carter presidency—would have sufficed to keep the foreign policy agenda militarized for the rest of the election campaign. But the Soviet Union provided the coup de grace for the original Carter foreign policy, with its invasion of Afghanistan on December 27, 1979. In response, Carter announced a new "doctrine" to defend Middle Eastern oil (actually quite remote from Afghanistan)—with, if needed, nuclear weapons. (This *"Carter Doctrine"* was later invoked in defense of the war on Iraq in 1991; see CASE 27). In a further bow to the Pentagon, he approved long-deferred plans for a Rapid Deployment Force, an expansion of American capabilities for Third World interventions specifically targeted now at the Persian Gulf region (Bradsher, 1985: 192–93). On a more symbolic and political level, he suspended the sale to the USSR of US grain and high-technology items agreed to during the 1972 *detente*, cut off all post-1975 Helsinki-type cultural and scientific exchanges, and prohibited American athletes from participating in the 1980 Olympic Games held in Moscow the following summer. For his part, Brzezinski proclaimed an "arc of crisis" from Afghanistan to Somalia and traveled to Pakistan to brandish a rifle at the Soviet enemy at the Khyber pass.

But despite all this campaign year militarism, Carter (unlike all other presidents in this study) never did send any American combat troops into any new Third World interventions. And he kept his promise about not losing a man in combat for more than three years—until April 24, 1980, when he made the election-influenced decision to try to liberate the Iranian hostages and eight members of the Delta Force rescue team died. But no new combat commitments were made under Carter, and his emphasis on human rights survived not only the 1980 campaign but became a more prominent part of American foreign policy even under his Republican successors.

Apart from human rights, however, the Carter aberration in American foreign policy did not survive his four-year term. He was succeeded by Republicans who, as mentioned, had no desire to bind up the wounds of Vietnam, but rather were looking for opportunities (even if they had to be artificially stimulated) to prove that the Vietnam experience was the exception and that the United States could fight and win wars in pursuit of its global hegemony. The five cases to be studied from the Reagan administration, and the three under Bush, all show this tendency; even the three under the Democrat Bill Clinton do not repudiate it although they are given different justifications. By the time of the presidency of George W. Bush in 2001, the impulse was unmistakable: in response to the terrorist attacks by 15 Saudis and 4 Egyptians, the United States launched wars on Afghanistan and Iraq. This is a long way from Jimmy Carter's world.

The next chapter shows how Ronald Reagan significantly escalated the

American response to three of the situations begun under Carter: El Salvador, Nicaragua, and Afghanistan. Meanwhile, the war in Congo resolved itself, and Iran was lost to US influence for a generation, a legacy more of the 1953–79 policies of installing and supporting the Shah than of Carter's penchant for restraint.

## CHAPTER 5 BIBLIOGRAPHY

### Carter Foreign Policy

Bender, Gerald. 1977. "Zaire: Is There Any Rationale for US Intervention?" *Los Angeles Times*, March 27.

Bill, James. 1988. *The Shah, the Ayatollah, and the US*. NY: Foreign Policy Association.

Bradsher, Henry S. 1985. *Afghanistan and the Soviet Union*. Durham, NC: Duke University Press.

Brzezinski, Zbigniew. 1983. *Power and Principle: Memoirs of the National Security Advisor, 1977–1981*. NY: Farrar, Straus, Giroux.

Califano, Joseph. 1981. *Governing America: An Insider's Report of the Carter Years*. NY: Simon and Schuster.

Carter, Jimmy. 1975. *Why Not the Best?* Nashville, TN: Broadman Press.

Kegley, Charles W. 1994. *Hard Choices: The Carter Administration's Hostage Rescue Mission in Iran*. Washington, DC: Georgetown University Institute for the Study of Diplomacy, Case 360.

Kirkpatrick, Jeane. 1979. "Dictatorships and Double Standards," *Commentary*, 68(5), November: 34–45.

Melanson, Richard A. 2000. *American Foreign Policy since the Vietnam War: The Search for Consensus from Nixon to Clinton*. Armonk, NY: M. E. Sharpe.

Rosati, Jerel. 1991. *The Carter Administration's Quest for Global Community: Beliefs and Their Impact on Behavior*. Columbus: University of South Carolina Press.

Sanders, Jerry. 1983. *Peddlers of Crisis: The Committee on the Present Danger and the Politics of Containment*. Boston: South End Press.

Sick, Gary. 1985. *All Fall Down: America's Tragic Encounter with Iran*. NY: Random House.

Skidmore, David. 1996. *Reversing Course: Carter's Foreign Policy, Domestic Politics, and the Failure of Reform*. Nashville, TN: Vanderbilt University Press.

Smith, Gaddis. 1986. *Morality, Reason and Power: American Diplomacy in the Carter Years*. NY: Hill and Wang.

Steigman, Andrew. 1993. *The Iran Hostage Negotiations, November 1979–January 1981*. Washington, DC: Georgetown University Institute for the Study of Diplomacy, Case 348.

Steinmetz, Sara. 1994. *Democratic Transition and Human Rights: Perspectives on US Foreign Policy*. Albany: State University of New York Press.

Strong, Robert A. 2000. *Working in the World: Jimmy Carter and the Making of American Foreign Policy*. Baton Rouge: Louisiana State University Press.

Vance, Cyrus. 1983. *Hard Choices: Critical Years in American Foreign Policy*. NY: Simon and Schuster.

# PART IV

# Transition to the Contemporary Era, 1981–2000

Part IV of *American Adventurism Abroad* moves in to this book's final era, which begins with the administration of President Ronald Reagan (1981–89) who, it will be argued, was a transitional figure. He entered office determined to reverse the attempted changes in foreign policy of the early Carter years, and succeeded in temporarily reviving the Cold War. But, as will be shown in Chapter 6, Reagan's militarism operated mainly on a rhetorical and symbolic level. The five cases studied during these years— El Salvador, Nicaragua, Grenada, Libya, and Afghanistan—all represented limited uses of American force compared to previous standards. The lessons of the "extremist years" had been well learned even if a "Vietnam Syndrome" was never admitted by the political establishment in either party. And, by the time of his last two years in office, Reagan was moving to end the rivalry with the Russians that had defined American foreign policy for the previous 40 years.

Chapter 7 links George H. W. Bush and Bill Clinton as the first two post–Cold War presidents, 1989–2001. Their interventions—in Panama, Iraq, Somalia, Haiti, and Yugoslavia—in some respects represented a return to traditional Great Power behavior. But in their strategic and economic objectives, as well as in the methods they employed and the results that ensued, the policies of both Bush and Clinton confirm this book's theses of dubious long-term foreign policy achievements in the Third World and disastrous short-term losses for the local societies affected. The goal of promotion of international capitalism and replacing Europe as hegemon in the periphery of the global capitalist system was again dominant, now being justified not by anti-communism but as the natural behavior of the "world's only remaining Super Power."

Part IV, Chapters 6 and 7, covers 20 years, three presidencies, and 10 cases, and finishes the survey of American intervention in the Third World before the start of the post 9-11-01 "war on terrorism."

## CHAPTER 6

# Ronald Reagan: The Last Cold Warrior, 1981–88

## INTRODUCTION

In many respects Ronald Reagan was lucky. The ex–movie star president entered the world scene just about the time the rival Soviet leaders of his era (Brezhnev, Andropov, Chernenko) were exiting the stage. When asked in 1984 why he had never met with any of his Soviet counterparts, he replied, "They keep dying on me" ("Transcript," 1984).

As a result Reagan had a relatively empty slate on which to make significant revisions to the idealist policies of Carter's first two and one-half years, and even to the 30 years of Cold War containment that preceded Carter. Reagan was a member of the 1940's "rollback" wing of the Republican Party, which criticized Truman's "mere containment" of the Soviet Union as "cowardly" and urged a more confrontational policy of turning back communism from the areas where it had spread during World War II (see CASE 4). Not one Cold War president in the next 30 years had embraced such an extreme worldview. Reagan now had the opportunity to put this ideology into practice, which he proceeded to do . . . but skillfully and with the use of symbolism and illusion evocative of his Hollywood melodramas (Halliday, 1983).

Reagan's rhetoric about the Soviets' "evil empire" was never backed with any serious American military interventions to turn back the tide (Bell, 1989). His *"Reagan Doctrine"* for rolling back communism in places where it already existed—not even announced until his second term— was limited in Ethiopia, Cambodia, and Angola to diplomacy and low levels of military aid (Scott, 1998). The countries about which the most attention was generated and interventions actually made—Nicaragua, Grenada, and Libya—were pygmy states representing no real security threat to the United States (McMahon, 1985). But Reagan seemed to have a virtual obsession with the "communist" government in Nicaragua, the "Cuban airstrip" in Grenada, and the "mad dog" Muammar Qaddaffi in Libya, issues that resonated with the American public (DeMause, 1984). The other two cases covered in this chapter—El Salvador and Afghanistan—were more important in size and political significance, but intervention in the first built upon Carter's policy, and involvement in the second was comparatively discreet considering its era-ending impact.

The Salvadoran intervention illustrates one other difference between Carter and Reagan, two idealists who used different conceptual rubrics to organize their policies. For Carter, it was human rights; for Reagan, democracy. Although Reagan spoke tough and thereby gained the support of many "hard-liners" who considered themselves "realists," he had opposed the Kissinger-Nixon brand of balance-of-power realism since the 1972–75 era of *detente,* and based much of his challenge to President Ford in 1976 Republican Party primary on this issue. Reagan's invocation of democracy—most compellingly advanced during his speech to the British parliament on June 8, 1982—enabled him both to embrace the idea and to throw down the gauntlet to the Soviets and other leftist *betes noires.* Right-wing autocrats, on the other hand, were treated somewhat more gently as being not totalitarian, but "merely authoritarian" and subject to change (Kirkpatrick, 1982; Sklar, 1986).

Reagan was able to square the circle between robust rhetoric and relatively restrained action by a gigantic increase in military spending. The Carter era $140 billion "Defense" Department budget was doubled in Reagan's first four years. And a series of relatively easy Third World targets were singled out to make good on his promises of a bolder foreign policy. This chapter analyzes five of them.

## CASE 21. EL SALVADOR, 1979–91

American policy in El Salvador, 1979–91, varied as the presidency shifted from Jimmy Carter to Ronald Reagan to George H. W. Bush. Under Carter and in the early Reagan years, the United States opted for what might be considered a centrist policy in the Salvadorean context: a civilian president brought to power by a (reformist) military coup under Carter in 1979–80, followed by rigged (demonstration) elections under Reagan in 1982 and 1984. By the end of Reagan's term, and up through today (2004), however, power had been returned to the most extreme (albeit civilian) right-wing forces in Salvadorean society (Diskin and Sharpe, 1986).

Under neither Carter nor Reagan was the Farabundo Marti National

Liberation Front (FMNLF), the most left political party driven into underground armed belligerency by the late 1970s, accepted as a genuine alternative. Carter, in campaign mode by fall of 1979, supported the removal of the reactionary military regime the United States had backed since 1971, and its replacement by one committed to some social reform along with a reinvigorated counter-insurgency war (White, 1982: 24). This "creeping coup" actually took some six months and a series of three changes of personnel (minicoups within the ruling juntas) in September 1979, January 1980, and March 1980, during which the progressive military officers who engineered the first coup and who were aligned with El Salvador's socialist Movement for National Revolution (MNR), were gradually replaced by more conservative military officers interested in some cosmetic political reform, but no real threat to the 14 families who made up the Salvadorean economic elite (Keogh, 1984: 173–76).

In any case, the losing civilian candidate of the rigged 1971 election, Jose Napoleon Duarte of the centrist Christian Democratic Party (PDC), was brought in as the relatively benign face of the coup regime after the third coup in 1980 (Armstrong and Shenk, 1982: 177–79; Webre, 1979). With a middle name befitting one born to rule, and a diploma from Notre Dame University, Duarte was potentially the "third way" leader the United States often sought, but seldom found, in the Latin American Cold War context. But, as Reagan ushered in a more militaristic American involvement in next-door Nicaragua (CASE 22), politics in El Salvador became increasingly polarized (LaFeber, 1983: 290). For example, $25 million in new military aid was channeled to the government, more than all American aid to El Salvador since 1946, and more than the rest of US aid to the entire hemisphere in 1981 (Leogrande, 1998: 89–90). This resulted in increased activity by paramilitary forces ("death squads") linked to the government and only too happy, for a price, to help "pacify" villages suspected of sympathizing with the rebels.

In this context, Oscar Romero, a prominent archbishop sympathetic to the rebels' cause of redistribution of wealth and greater sharing of power, was assassinated (Brockman, 1982). There were also infamous incidents such as: the massacre at El Mozote, an entire village of more than 700 people (Danner, 1994); the summary executions of four American churchwomen (claimed by Secretary of State Alexander Haig to have been caught in an "exchange" of gunfire while running a roadblock); and in later years the murders of a half-dozen Jesuit priests and their housekeeper. The result was to intimidate from participation in politics all but the most militarized and center-right forces. In particular, the two most-left of El Salvador's five political parties (FMNLF and MNR) were driven out of the picture.

In these conditions, the Reagan administration was able to sponsor two rigged elections, in 1982 and 1984, in which Duarte's leadership of the junta, and America's commitment to "democracy," were endorsed (Herman and Brodhead, 1984: 93–152). After Duarte's death from cancer, however, the winners of subsequent elections were from the political party (ARENA) associated with the right-wing death squad led by Roberto d'Aubuisson, a man described by the US Ambassador in San Salvador as a "psychopathic killer" (White, 1982: 24; Nairn, 1984: 20). ARENA scored easy victories in 1987 and 1990 over the leaderless Christian Democrats and the 1970s old-guard Party of National Conciliation (PCN). The use of US military aid and technical expertise in support of these dubious electoral exercises showed the shrewdness of Reagan's shift from human rights to democracy as the lodestone of American foreign policy (Bonner, 1984: 299; Carothers, 1991: 3–9). Elections were easier to control than the human rights violations of El Salvador's military and paramilitary forces (McClintock, 1985: 293–95, 329–40).

US involvement in the mayhem of such groups was not direct. It was limited to money and training for the official military, which merely turned a blind eye to their death squad adjuncts. The aid was considerable, averaging more than $700 million per year under Reagan and, unlike the Nicaragua *contra* funding, above board (Keith, 1997: 82). It was, after all, aid to a legally established government, however tainted. But the price for the peasants of El Salvador was high. More than 75,000—85 percent of them civilian supporters of the FMNLF according to 1990s UN Truth Commission (Clifford, 1997: 458)—were killed in this "sideshow" to Reagan's central effort in Nicaragua where only half as many perished (see CASE 22).

It was also not as disruptive to American politics. Reagan, after all, was only continuing Carter's policy, so Democratic congressmen throughout the 1980s were less apt to criticize this venture. In January, 1989, newly inaugurated President Bush moved to get those Reagan-era wars in central America off of the top of the foreign policy agenda (and off of the front pages of American newspapers) (Leogrande, 1990: 620). Aid was cut to the El Salvador Government as well as to the Nicaraguan *contras*. And just as the latter moved in to the political arena and won a share of the government in the 1990 Nicaraguan elections, the Salvadoreans entered into a 1991 peace process run by the United Nations (with enthusiastic backing from the new, more internationalist, American president). By 1992 the formerly outlawed (i.e., "terrorist") FMNLF was participating in elections and winning a healthy, though minority, share (about 25–33%) of seats in the representative assembly.

All told, American policy in El Salvador, from 1979–91—across one Democratic and two Republican administrations—must be counted as a foreign policy success. Capitalism was never seriously threatened, and even democracy was strengthened from the perspective of the 1990s. But, tied as it was to Reagan's expanded (and arguably unnecessary) rollback assault upon Nicaragua next door, the more traditional containment policy in El Salvador probably lasted longer and cost more (in terms of lives as well as money) than was necessary. In particular, the high civilian death toll, and the continued rule to this day of the most right-wing political party, was a high price for the local population to pay.

## CASE 22. NICARAGUA, 1981–88

Ronald Reagan's first foreign policy target, and the one that obsessed him for the next eight years, was Nicaragua. This tiny nation of some 2 million people probably represented the kind of place that Carter had in mind when he professed "no inordinate fear of communism"; his administration certainly did not move strongly against the Sandinista revolution of 1978–79 (Lake, 1989: 260). In fact, by 1980 the United States was still providing about $15 million in economic aid (Ambrose and Brinkley, 1997: 317) to its leader Daniel Ortega who, it was argued with some reason, could be seen as a progressive improvement over the 43-year Somoza family dictatorship it replaced. By 1980, a crash education campaign had reduced illiteracy among the peasantry from 50 to 10 percent, and capital investment in agriculture had increased by 149 percent. The Sandinistas tolerated a mixed economy and planned for elections in which opposition parties would be allowed to participate. Mexico, not Moscow, was the more obvious model for Nicaragua's political and economic development (Pastor, 1987: 193–97).

Reagan, on the other hand, saw an easy bogeyman for his goal of a fresh restart from the "defeatist" policies of the previous president (Burns, 1987: 22–23; Gutman, 1988: 19–26). While Nicaragua was not seriously strategically significant, Reagan claimed that the Soviet Union (through its Cuban proxy) was the main influence behind Nicaragua's revolutionary regime. In order for the United States to restore Somoza-style capitalism, a civil war would be supported, with $20 million per year in secret CIA funding being channeled to counter-revolutionaries (*contras*) drawn from the previous regime's National Guard (Chomsky, 1985: 133). This amount of money paled in comparison to the $700 million per year Reagan committed to the war in El Salvador. But, even relatively moderate, potentially "third-way," political forces like the Sandinistas could not be allowed to survive as an example of what might be tolerated in the "backyard" of the capitalist world's reigning hegemon (Melrose, 1985).

Reagan's formidable communications skills were employed to portray the *contras* as "freedom fighters" and to defame Ortega as a "dictator in designer glasses" and the "malignancy in Managua" (Gutman, 1988: 322). On the economic front, the United States engineered a boycott of loans and investments from capitalist financial institutions, slashed sugar imports from Nicaragua by 90 percent, and unleashed a propaganda campaign to spread fear and alienate citizens from the government. Politically, the United States pressured opposition party candidates to withdraw from the 1984 presidential election to make the popular Sandinistas' victory at that poll appear tainted (Sklar, 1984: 192–200). But as in the cases of Guatemala, Guyana, and Chile where leftist governments increased their electoral popularity after being targeted by the United States, Sandinista candidates were overwhelmingly endorsed in the 1984 general election, which was widely regarded as free and fair. Six opposition parties representing a broad range of opinion won 35 of 96 seats in the representative assembly. Public debates and opposition rallies were tolerated by the government, no candidates were barred from participation (unusual in central America), and public campaign financing was provided even for pro-US candidates (Morley and Petras, 1987: 81–82).

Despite, possibly because of, this high level of popular participation in politics, the CIA began its program of support for counter-revolutionary forces—"state-supported terrorists" by any objective standard (Brody, 1985; Chamorro, 1987: 57–58)—who (with their families) were housed, trained and supplied in neighboring Honduras and Costa Rica. At their height they numbered some 20,000 men under arms, and the fingerprints of their American handlers were frequently in evidence. This was most evident in the cases of the blowing up of the fuel depot in the port of Corinto in 1983, and the mining of the harbor at Managua in 1984, for which action the World Court condemned the United States in 1985 (Blum, 1995: 292; Chamorro, 1987: 54–55).

Another embarrassment to the Reagan administration occurred when a manual prepared by the CIA entitled *Psychological Operations in Guerrilla Warfare* came to light. In it were detailed instructions that encouraged the use of violence against civilians, and gave advice on such tactics as political assassination, mob violence, kidnapping, and blowing up public buildings. The manual suggested "professional criminals" be hired for "selective jobs" and recommended confronting authorities to provoke shootings to "cause the death of one or more people to create a martyr for the cause." It also said "it is possible to *neutralize* carefully selected and planned targets such as court judges, police and state security officials" (Blum, 1995: 293–94, italics added, word commonly interpreted to mean "remove by assassination").

Over time, the Democratic-controlled House of Representatives became disaffected not only with the goal of this policy—obviously "regime change," despite Reagan's claim that he was only trying to put pressure on the Sandinistas to stop aiding the rebels in El Salvaldor—but also with some of the means being employed to carry it out. In a series of "Boland amendments" (named for the author, the Chair of the House Intelligence Committee), Congress first restricted and then totally cut off CIA funding for *contra* operations in the military appropriations bills of 1982–86. Thus were planted the seeds for Reagan's comeuppance.

In 1985 and 1986, the *contras*, and their supporters in the administration, had to get creative to sustain financial support for continued military activities. One idea was to increase their already notorious drug trafficking to a level that became so extensive that they are often blamed for the crack cocaine epidemic that spilled into the United States in the mid-1980s (Scott and Marshall, 1991: 4; Webb, 1998). Another fount of funds came from the basement of the White House where Marine Col. Oliver North, and assorted agents from the office of CIA Director William Casey (Miami Cubans, ex-Generals John Singlaub and Richard Secord) schemed to sell weapons to Iran, and funnel the proceeds to the *contras*, an illegal operation that blew up into the embarrassing "Iran/*contra* affair" in October, 1996 (Woodward, 1987: 399, 430–31, 465–69; Draper, 1991: 86–92).

This potentially impeachment-scale imbroglio, however, had some fortunate fall-out for Reagan. The Republicans lost their majority in the Senate, and while at first this might not seem favorable to the president, it provided him the cover to move more to the center of the political spectrum in his final two years. Combined with rapidly evolving events in the USSR under its new leader, Mikhail Gorbachev, Reagan was able to sign the arms control agreements (on Intermediate-range Nuclear Forces and Strategic Arms Reduction) that soon led to the end of the Cold War. But he continued, with restored Congressional funding, to attempt to overthrow the Sandinista regime until his last day in office (Arnson, 1989: 212, 220).

The result of this eight-year war was devastating to Nicaragua. The dead totaled 30,000, about as many as those who died in the struggle to overthrow forty years of Somoza dictatorships (Sullivan, 1991: 38). The economy, once in the mid-range among Latin American states, shrank by three-quarters, and still hasn't recovered; its GNP/capita today (about $450 per year) is closer to that of Haiti (the worst in the hemisphere) than that of its Central American neighbors. The natural progression of its domestic politics was also thwarted. The example of a left-of-center political regime with a mixed economy was not allowed to succeed.

When the next elections were held in 1990, after the suspension of support for the *contra* war by the new US president, George H. W. Bush, the Sandinistas, hurt by the war-wracked economy, were defeated. They were, however, allowed to keep control of the Defense Ministry in the government of Violeta Chamorro, a centrist coalition that was broad enough to also include many *contra* leaders. The fact that these political rivals were able to work together without fighting in 1978–80, and after 1990, shows the personal nature of Reagan's eight-year war policy in this unfortunate country. But it was of a piece with his policy of picking on small, relatively insignificant targets in an effort to inflate America's sense of purpose and power. In this respect it was a lesson learned by the George W. Bush administration, which selected Afghanistan, and a virtually disarmed Iraq, as the first targets in its "war on terrorism."

## CASE 23. GRENADA, 1983

Political unrest on the tiny Caribbean island of Grenada in October 1983, presented Ronald Reagan with a happy set of circumstances. First, it offered him another minor target of opportunity against which rhetorical broadsides and a cheap ($75 million) military invasion could be launched (Scheinen, 1997: 254). Second, it occurred just as he was experiencing one of his greatest diplomatic embarrassments in the Middle East.

Grenada began to concern some Americans during the Carter years when in 1979 the left-wing New Jewel Movement, led by charismatic leader Maurice Bishop (Searle, 1984), ousted the corrupt capital-friendly government of eccentric, UFO-sighting, Eric Gairy. But as with Nicaragua, Grenada—the smallest of islands in the far southeast reaches of the Caribbean traditionally in the purview of Great Britain—was of little strategic concern to President Carter (Pastor, 1988; Schoenhals and Melanson, 1985). Its main export products were nutmeg and bananas, its GDP barely reached $100 million, and its population was only about 85,000 (Thorndike, 1985).

But for the right-wing in American politics, Bishop's accession to power represented "another Cuba" in the hemisphere. In an early campaign speech, Ronald Reagan likened the Caribbean to "a Communist lake" where "the United States resembles a giant, afraid to move" (Dugger, 1983: 518). During his first year as president, Reagan authorized a military training exercise in the region that simulated an amphibious assault on "Amber and the Amberines," a flimsily disguised reference to Grenada and the Grenadines (its related six-island cluster). In 1982, he pointedly excluded the country from his Caribbean Basin (foreign aid) Initiative. On March 23, 1983, during the debate over Nicaragua, a prime-time presidential address linked Grenada to Cuba and Nicaragua in a "red triangle" and cited intelligence reports that Cuban soldiers were building an 10,000-foot airport runway for its tiny neighbor to be able to accommodate Soviet long-range bombers (Nardin and Pritchard, 1990: 3).

In October 1983, two events conspired to present Reagan the opportunity for action. First, Bishop was killed in a coup by an even more left-wing faction of his movement (led by Bernard Coard and General Hudson Austin). Second, this assassination occurred on October 19th, three days before an American barracks in Beirut, Lebanon, was blown up resulting in the deaths of some 240 marines. The US troops in Lebanon had been inserted in 1982 in the wake of an Israeli invasion of that country. As noted in this book's Introduction, American foreign policy regarding Israel is not within the scope of this study. Suffice to note here, the US military had been sent in as part of a *multilateral* peacekeeping force to provide cover for Israeli forces to withdraw without having Lebanese forces attacking during their retreat (Kennedy and Haas, 1994: 5–6). Sixteen months later, these US troops were still sitting in Lebanon, their basic mission completed and seemingly forgotten by American society and the administration.

Grenada presented an excellent "wag the dog" scenario in which Reagan could distract attention from the disaster in Lebanon. Within hours of news of the barracks blow-up, on October 23, 1983, Reagan gave the approval for "Operation Urgent Fury," an American invasion of Grenada. In addition to the assassination of Bishop (about whom Reagan could have cared less), the new regime in Grenada was asserted to be a "threat to the lives" of some 600 Americans studying at St. George University Medical School in another part of the island. They would have to be "rescued" from "radicals and terrorists." No possible motive for these students being threatened was ever offered by the US government, and in fact the Revolutionary Military Council under General Austin was "extremely solicitous" of their welfare offering to facilitate the departure of any students wishing to leave (Kwitny, 1984: 28). In retrospect, it seems the US invasion "served more to endanger American lives than to protect them" (Black, 1984: 20).

Notwithstanding this murky situation at the site, Reagan, with heavy-handed diplomacy, next extracted from a heretofore obscure Organization of Eastern Caribbean States, a request for intervention to "restore and maintain law and order in the country" and "peace and security in the region" (Treverton, 1994: 205). The OECS was established in 1981, and was comprised of the recently freed British colonies of Grenada (not present during these deliberations), Antigua, Dominica, St. Kitts, St. Lucia, and St. Vincent. Its authority was invoked because the United States could not get legitimation for its intervention from the Organization of American States (whose Secretary General resigned over its failure to *prevent* this operation [Connell-Smith, 1984: 443]), nor from the United Nations Security Council, which actually voted (with only the United States dissenting) to condemn the invasion (Davidson, 1986).

There is some controversy over the circumstances under which the United States extracted the request from the OECS. America's first appeal for a request was made only orally, and secretly, on Friday, October 21. It was only after the invasion was well underway that a written statement was released four days later. In the interim, the leader of the organization, Mrs. Eugenia Charles of Dominica, was flown to Washington for a personal meeting with the president. CIA records show that at one point $100,000 was given to her government for a "secret support operation" (Woodward, 1987: 290), and in 1982 the United States had begun supplying funds to build a $10 million road in her small country. After the invasion, the United States also produced a *retroactive* request from Paul Scoon, the British-appointed Governor General of Grenada and ceremonial head of state, asking for intervention, even though the United States was a "non-participating country" in the OECS (McKean, 1999: 13).

Needless to say, the military operation was deemed a complete success. In a matter of four days, the United States had ousted the Coard government and taken over the island. In actuality, however, the US military performed rather poorly. To defeat a token force of about 800 Grenadians, and some 600 Cubans (all but 43 of whom were aged construction workers), the United States required more than 7,000 military personnel from all four services backed up by an aircraft carrier task force. Intelligence and communications were poor, command structure was inappropriate, and the military operations were slow and inefficient. In the end, the United States suffered 18 dead (versus 25 Cubans and 45 Grenadians), and 113 wounded. Nevertheless, the military issued 1,600 medals for heroism, more than one for every five troops involved (Rosati, 1999: 205–6).

Despite the bureaucratic sloppiness and dubious legality, the US invasion ended 300 years of British hegemony in Grenada, and—in a result reminiscent of Suez in 1956 (CASE 6)—replaced it with that of the United States (Dunn and Watson, 1985). The episode was one of the rare times when UK Prime Minister Margaret Thatcher disagreed with Reagan. No evidence of any Soviet presence was ever discovered, and the Cuban "soldiers" were admitted to be an engineering brigade providing technical assistance in the enlargement of the country's airstrip to make it competitive with other Caribbean islands trying to attract tourism. Within a year, the United States itself had completed work on the runway and presided over an election in which power returned to pre-1979 "center-right" forces, though not to Gairy or his party.

But more than a foreign policy success, "Operation Urgent Fury" was a domestic political coup for Ronald Reagan. In addition to distracting attention away from the debacle in Lebanon, he had created the perfect *leitmotif* for his upcoming "Morning in America" presidential reelection campaign. The United States was back, and standing tall. Gone was the pessimism and malaise of the Carter era. The US could engage in foreign military interventions and prevail (Curry, 1984).

## CASE 24. LIBYA, 1981–86

The American assault upon Libya, 1981–86, is a curious episode in American adventurism in the Third World. Although bigger than Grenada and Nicaragua, Libya (despite its large geographic size on the north African map) is actually another tiny country (population 4 million) about which few Americans cared before Reagan brought it center-stage as part of his practice of inflating symbolic foreign policy dragons—the "Mad Dog of the Middle East" in the president's words (Anderson, 2003: 30)—which he would later slay. But Libya as a target was largely a rhetorical foil providing added justification for Reagan's doubled "Defense" Department budget.

Libya had been under the rule of Col. Muammar Qaddaffi since September 1, 1969, when the 29-year-old career soldier ousted senile King Idris, who was vacationing in Turkey. Despite a lot of revolutionary rhetoric, Qaddaffi was regarded by the USSR as too unstable to court as a satellite; he was also religious and not a devotee of "scientific" anything, let alone socialism (Bearman, 1986; Blundy and Lycett, 1987). Moreover, Qaddaffi was certainly never regarded as a serious threat by the neighbors who knew him best: Mubarak's Egypt (population: 60 million) or Boumedienne's Algeria (population: 25 million). In short, Qaddaffi provided a perfect bogeyman for Reagan and an unsophisticated American audience. He provided a name and a face for America's newest menace as identified by the Reagan's bellicose first Secretary of State, Alexander Haig: international terrorism (*Terrorism*, 1985: i–iii).

Almost from Day 1, Reagan and Haig singled out terrorism (and no longer human rights) as the focus of the new administration's foreign policy. This priority, however, lasted only as long as Haig, who was dismissed after 17 months in office for, among other reasons, being out of step with the more laid-back Californians in Reagan's White House. But during this time, Exhibit Number One as a sponsor of terrorism was Qaddaffi, a somewhat quixotic character who could be ridiculed for his garb (flowing robes, sunglasses, high heels) and pretensions to leadership in the Arab world (Haley, 1997: 68). In 1981, various incidents seemed to have been created by the United States to provoke Libya into some sort of response (Cooley, 1982: 264). They were not taken *too* seriously, however; $10 billion in oil trade continued to flow between the two countries.

The first action involved the Gulf of Sidra, a 120-mile indentation in Libya's 800-mile Mediterranean coastline. Qaddafi claimed the entire Gulf as Libyan territory; the rest of the world recognized only a 12-mile territorial sea along its scooped-out littoral. In August 1981, the United States decided to challenge Libya's claims to sovereignty with a naval sea-air military demonstration during what was labeled a training exercise. When warning shots were fired by Libyan Air Force jets at Navy F-14 fighters more than 30 miles inside the waters claimed by Qaddafi, the American planes retaliated by blowing two of them out of the sky (Woodward, 1987: 166–67).

The second activity in 1981 involved a series of leaks to American news media about the prospects of a Libyan "hit team" trying to get into the United States to assassinate President Reagan. These stories were taken seriously by journalists for several months before they were largely discredited (Campbell and Forbes, 1985: 6; Woodward, 1987: 183–86). They did serve the purpose, however, of putting American public opinion on alert to a new menace beyond international communism.

After 1982, the United States stopped importing Libyan oil and periodic criticisms of Qaddaffi's "support for terrorism" continued for the next few years, despite the departure of Haig and particularly during Reagan's run for reelection in 1984. Also, in 1985, the CIA planted a car bomb in the suburbs of Beirut in an attempt to assassinate Sheikh Muhammad Hussein Fadlallah, religious leader of Lebanon's Shi'ites who were considered responsible for the bombing of the US marine barracks in 1983 (see CASE 23). The sheikh escaped harm, but 85 other innocent civilians died, collateral damage in an early episode of the "war against terrorism" (AbuKhalil, 2002: 83).

The high point of the terror-related staged offensive against Qaddaffi occurred in 1986 (Hersh, 1987: 17). Again, there were two events. The first was "Operation Prairie Fire" in which three aircraft carrier battle groups assembled off the coast of Libya for another "training" exercise, scheduled to begin on March 22. The US force consisted of 45 ships and 200 planes. Again, as in 1981, three ships crossed the 32nd parallel, the line claimed by Qaddafi as Libyan waters. In response, Libya fired six missiles at US reconnaissance planes supporting the exercise. All missed; but over the next two days, the United States struck back destroying Libyan radar sites and two patrol boats. Seventy-two Libyans were reported killed; there were no American casualties, and a great victory was proclaimed (Woodward, 1987: 440–44).

But the precedent had been set for a second incident a month later, which was to have longer-lasting, and tragic, results for America. It came in response to an event that would have resonance with the American public: the bombing at 2 a.m. on April 5th of a *discotheque* in West Berlin popular with US soldiers and in which three were killed (two Americans) and 230 wounded. (The Libyan side to the propaganda offensive launched on behalf of the dead soldiers is that there was "no proof" that any Libyans were involved in the bombing, and that the evidence cited implicated Syrians and Palestinians in East Berlin as well as the Libyan Embassy. The *"discotheque,"* moreover, might have been more properly labeled a brothel in which Westerners were seen to be debauching the morals of immigrant Turkish [i.e., Muslim] women.)

In any case, America's response to the unclear incident was to launch a ferocious air assault (30 bombers with four bombs each), targeted specifically at places where Qaddaffi was known to live. Although he himself survived this arguable assassination attempt, 31 other innocent souls, including his 15-month-old daughter, were killed. Most of the world did not buy America's version of the provocation, and the air attack had to be launched from US bases in the United Kingdom. Neither France, Italy, nor Spain (NATO allies all) allowed any overflight of their lands for this mission. The planes had to travel a circuitous 14-hour, 2,800-mile route, out over the Atlantic Ocean and around the straits of Gibraltar, before reaching their Libyan targets.

Once again, the "forceful action" was applauded by Americans as a success. For some months thereafter Reagan touted an alleged "lapse" in Libyan terrorism; Qaddaffi had been taught a lesson. But on December 28, 1988, one month before Reagan left office, Libyans were implicated in an even more devastating terrorist incident: the blowing up of Pan-Am Flight No. 103, over Lockerbie, Scotland, killing some 259 unsuspecting persons, including 192 US citizens (Emerson and Duffy, 1990: 12, 159). It seems like Qaddaffi got the last word in his tiff with Reagan.

In sum, Libya never represented a target of any strategic significance. The former Italian colony was midwifed to independence by the UN and UK after World War II, and was never assumed to be in the US sphere of influence (Pelt, 1970). Under King Idris, the United States had its largest air base in the Middle East in Libya. But since 1969, the quirky Qaddaffi has not allowed Libya to be anyone's client (Haley, 1984: 229–30). Neither was the five-year American harassment of Libya based on any economic or foreign policy goals. Unlike most of the other cases in this book, the US military assaults were not related to Qaddaffi's domestic political structures or ideology, but to Reagan's domestic political desire for the United States to look strong and stand tall.

After Pan-Am 103, the United States was able to get the United Nations to endorse limited sanctions on flights in and out of Libya. But these affected mainly elites engaged in international travel. By the late-1990s, only the United States was committed to them, whereas Italy, Germany, Britain and Spain were still importing Libyan oil. Thus, the damage to Libya, unlike most of the other targeted states in *American Adventurism Abroad*, was limited. As of 2001, it was more the United States that was isolated from Libya, than Libya from the rest of the world. But because of the domestic political cost of contradicting Reagan's anti-terrorism policy (even though it was only center-stage briefly and applied only to a few states), his successors have chosen to tolerate this comparatively low-cost estrangement from this relatively inconsequential country. After 9-11-01, of course, anti-terrorism has assumed renewed respectability as an organizing principle for diplomacy; perhaps Reagan and Haig, circa 1981–82, were just ahead of their time in adjusting to the end of the Cold War and the need for a new target to replace anti-communism as the rallying point for public support for an aggressive foreign policy.

## CASE 25. AFGHANISTAN, 1981–88

Of all Ronald Reagan's interventions in the Third World, Afghanistan is probably the one about which he spoke the least, but where he accomplished the most. The Soviet Union invaded Afghanistan on December 27, 1979, but even before this time the CIA under Jimmy Carter had been deeply involved in Afghan politics (Anwar, 1988: 152–53, 183). This went back to April 1978, when a leftist political party (Khalq, under Noor Mohammed Taraki) ousted the army general Mohammed Daoud Khan whose family had been ruling Afghanistan since 1747. Taraki was in turn thrown out in September 1979 by a more Western-oriented Hafizullah Amin, a man who had attended colleges in the United States (Columbia, Wisconsin), where he developed ties to the Asia Foundation (see CASE 19) (Bonosky, 1985: 33–34; Cogan, 1993: 76). It was to remove him that the Soviets responded to a request from yet a third Afghan leader, Babrak Karmal, to intervene and restore the country's traditional neutrality between East and West in the Cold War.

The Soviets did so with a vengeance, sending in some 100,000 troops—the first time that the Red Army was dispatched to a country beyond the Eastern European states they liberated at the end of World War II. But Afghanistan bordered the USSR, and was a country where Russia had for centuries vied with Great Britain for influence (Meyer and Brysac, 2000). Although the UK fought three wars (in 1839–42, 1878–80, and 1919) to maintain this buffer state between the Russian and British Empires, the United States had never previously considered it significant (Poullada, 1995). Its economic aid to the backward, remote country was only one-fifth of that given by the neighboring USSR ($500 million vs. $2.5 billion) during the Cold War up to this point (Merrill, 1997: 24).

But Jimmy Carter, at the height of his primary election campaign against Senator Kennedy, reacted as if the Soviet move represented a threat to the United States and to the global balance of power. In addition to the anti-Soviet steps mentioned in Chapter 5, Carter ratcheted up CIA spending in support of whatever anti-Soviet forces might be found in Afghanistan to some $30 million in 1980. By 1983, Reagan was sending in more than $300 million per year in secret aid to the struggle, more than 15 times the annual amount going to the more widely noticed Nicaraguan *contra* operation. At its height, in 1987, the CIA committed $687 million to the cause. It was the second largest operation in the CIA's history, exceeded only by the 10-year secret war in Laos (CASE 10). As in some of the other CIA-supported subversions in this study, the use of drug money was significant in lubricating this war machine. In the Golden Crescent of south-central Asia—source of 50 percent of America's heroin and 75 percent of that in Europe, with a street value of $9 billion in 1983—the profits associated with the trade in opium by CIA-linked warlords were considerable (Marshall, 1991: 47–53; Vornberg, 1987: 11).

By the first year of the Reagan administration, a robust resistance to the Babrak Karmal regime had developed (Kakar, 1995). This was motivated not only by traditional anti-Russian nationalism in Afghan society—

whose ethnic mix is 47 percent Pathans, 27 percent Tajiks, 9 percent Uz-beks—but also, and more significantly, by the common chord of Islam among the three groups. This religious fundamentalism in some respects reflected the return to roots occurring in the revolution next door to the west in Iran. It was also fueled by the fact that the Soviet supported government had embarked upon a modernization campaign based on Marxism (Magnus and Naby, 1998: 129), including equality for women.

Being estranged from Iran at this time, the United States cultivated more congenial conduits for its CIA contributions to these Islam-inspired insurgents who considered themselves holy warriors (jihadi or mujahedeen). Saudi Arabia supplemented the annual CIA subsidies with some $100 million of its own each year, bringing the resistance fighters' total outside financing for the decade of the 1980s close to $5 billion (Cogan, 1993: 77). Pakistan, neighboring state to Afghanistan's east, provided logistical staging and, through its military Inter-Services Intelligence Directorate, manpower, training, and technical aid.

The significant support going to the resistance spurred the creation of more than a dozen Afghan groups who became not only enemies of the government, but also rivals of each other. They vied among themselves for the backing of various outside groups linked to the former monarchy in exile in Rome, to various Persian Gulf kingdoms, and to Tajikistan, Uzbekistan, Pakistan, and Iran. Amidst this jockeying for power, US policy consistently supported the most extreme right-wing (meaning Islamic Fundamentalist) Pathan forces backed by Pakistan and Saudi Arabia. These groups were preferred not only over the leftist-modernizers installed by the Soviet Union, but also over more moderate monarchists, Tajiks (under Burhanuddin Rabbani and Ahmed Shah Massoud), and Uzbeks (under Abdul Rashid Doestam).

Washington could have supported several secular and nationalist Afghan groups, encouraging them to form an alliance with three traditionalist Islamic factions, two of them monarchist. Instead, it financed three fundamentalist factions, most notably the Hezbi-i-Islami under Gulbaddin Hekmatayar. This forced the moderate Islamic groups in 1983 to ally with the fundamentalists in the Islamic Alliance of Afghan Mujahedeen (IAAM). It is this group with which Osama bin Laden became involved. As a major disburser of Saudi (and some CIA) moneys, he was the prime mover of a campaign that enrolled about 30,000 non-Afghan Muslims (roughly divided between Arabs and non-Arabs) in the war. He personally recruited some 4,000 volunteers from Saudi Arabia, and became the nominal leader of the 15,000-strong Arab-Afghan jihadi (Hiro, 1999: 17–18).

After several years of stalemated war, claiming more than 1 million lives including 13,000 Soviets (Cordovez and Harrison, 1995: 373), two things turned the tide in favor of the insurgents: Mikhail Gorbachev's ascension to power in the USSR in 1985, and the addition of Stinger missiles to the military materiel provided by the United States in 1986. As part of his "New Thinking" in foreign policy, Gorbachev put Soviet client-states from Eastern Europe to East Asia on notice that they would have to reform their economies and survive on their own (following the *perestroika* example in the USSR itself). Afghanistan was one of those alerted, shortly after the Politburo decision of October 17, 1985 (Malkin, 2000: 57; Mendelson, 1988: 110–12); and the Soviet-instigated change of leadership in May 1986—from Babrak Karmal to Najibullah—reflected this new policy. Meanwhile, the portable ground-to-air Stinger missiles, introduced in September 1986, provided a significant equalizer to the government's Russian helicopters. Able to be carried on shoulders and small vehicles, these mobile weapons suited the *mujahedeen's* guerrilla war-fighting style (Bearden, 2001: 21–22).

On April 14, 1988, the US and USSR agreed to cease supplying their respective proxies in Afghanistan, and within one year (by February, 15, 1989) all Soviet troops were gone. For the United States this was a significant foreign policy achievement. Some would claim that it was the critical "battle" of the Cold War (Galeotti, 1995), one that the Soviets lost by overextending themselves—"their Vietnam" (Borer, 1999: xiv)—but that the United States significantly abetted by its years of support to the anti-Soviet *jihad*. But, in the long run, American involvement in Afghanistan had significant deleterious "blowback" effects. The fundamentalist Arab Muslims the CIA trained and financed to go fight in Afghanistan returned home to disrupt domestic politics in Sudan, Egypt, Algeria, and Saudi Arabia. More ominously for the United States, they applied the skills learned in Afghanistan to engage in anti-American terrorism during the next decade in places as far afield as Yemen (bombing of the *USS Cole*, 2000: 17 dead); east Africa (Kenya and Tanzania, 1998: 12 Americans among 257 dead); Saudi Arabia (al Khobar barracks, 1996: 19 Americans killed, more than 400 wounded; Riyadh, 1995: 5 American service personnel killed); and New York City (the World Trade Center, 1993: 6 dead, 1,000 wounded) (Rashid, 2000: 130; Cooley, 1999: 215–41).

As far as the local society was concerned, the devastation of Afghanistan was much worse. Between 1979 and 2000, more than 2 million people were killed and some 5 million refugees (20 percent of the population) fled the country because the war never stopped when the USSR departed in 1989 (Rais, 1994). The US, in particular, lost interest in the place after 1989, but with the weapons the Super Powers left behind, the various Afghan parties continued to fight. First, the Soviet-supplied client, Najibullah, defied expectations and stayed in power for three more years, until April 1992. The Uzbek/Tajik-dominated government that succeeded him lasted four years (1992–96), before being ousted by a new force, the Taliban, led by fundamentalist Pathans. This group, the most extreme of all in terms of application of Koranic law and subjugation of women, emerged from the ruins of war in a manner similar to the *Khmer Rouge* (CASE 15), determined to remake their society and the world. As part of their anti-Western vision, they provided training camps for the *al Qaeda* network of Islamic Fundamentalists, descendants of the IAAM, who perpetrated the bombings of 9-11-01.

The site of America's greatest Cold War victory had provided the groundwork for the most devastating attack in history upon its own homeland.

## CHAPTER 6 BIBLIOGRAPHY

### Reagan Foreign Policy

Bell, Coral. 1989. *The Reagan Paradox: US Foreign Policy in the 1980s*. New Brunswick, NJ: Rutgers University Press.

De Mause, Lloyd. 1984. *Reagan's America*. NY: Creative Roots.

Halliday, Fred. 1983. *The Making of the Second Cold War: The Early Reagan Years*. London: Verso Books.

Kirkpatrick, Jeane. 1982. *Dictatorships and Double Standards: Rationalism and Reason in Politics*. NY: Simon and Schuster.

McMahon, Jeff. 1985. *Reagan and the World: Imperial Policy in the New Cold War*. NY: Monthly Review Foundation.

Scott, James M. 1998. *Deciding to Intervene: The Reagan Doctrine and American Foreign Policy*. Durham, NC: Duke University Press.

Sklar, Holly. 1986. *Reagan, Trilateralism, and the Neo-Liberals: Containment and Intervention in the 1980s*. Boston: South End Press.

"Transcript of the Reagan-Mondale Debate on Foreign Policy," *New York Times*, October 22, 1984: B4.

### CASE 21. El Salvador, 1979–91

Armstrong, Robert, and Janet Shenk. 1982. *El Salvador: The Face of Revolution*. Boston: South End Press.

Bonner, Raymond. 1984. *Weakness and Deceit: US Policy and El Salvador*. NY: Times Books.

Brockman, James R. 1982. *Oscar Romero, Bishop and Martyr*. Maryknoll, NY: Orbis Books.

Carothers, Thomas. 1991. *In the Name of Democracy: US Policy toward Latin America in the Reagan Years*. Berkeley: University of California Press.

Clifford, J. Garry. 1997. "Reagan, Ronald Wilson," vol. 3: 454–61, in Bruce W. Jentleson and Thomas G. Paterson (eds.), *Encyclopedia of American Foreign Relations*. NY: Oxford University Press.

Danner, Mark. 1994. *The Massacre at El Mozote*. NY: Vintage Books.

Diskin, Martin, and Kenneth Sharpe. 1986. *The Impact of US Policy in El Salvador, 1979–1986*. Berkeley: University of California Press.

Herman, Edward, and Frank Brodhead. 1984. *Demonstration Elections: U.S.-Staged*

*Elections in the Dominican Republic, Vietnam, and El Salvador.* Boston: South End Press.

Keith, LeeAnna Y. 1997. "El Salvador," vol. 2: 82–83, in Jentleson, *Encyclopedia* (see above, Clifford).

Keogh, Dermot. 1984. "The Myth of the Liberal Coup: The United States and the 15 October 1979 Coup in El Salvador," *Millennium: The Journal of International Studies,* 13(2): 153–83.

LaFeber, Walter. 1983. *Inevitable Revolutions: The United States in Central America.* NY: W. W. Norton.

Leogrande, William M. 1990. "From Reagan to Bush: The Transition in US Policy toward Central America," *Journal of Latin American Studies,* 22: 595–621.

Leogrande, William M. 1998. *Our Own Backyard: The United States in Central America, 1979–1992.* Chapel Hill: University of North Carolina Press.

McClintock, Michael. 1985. *The American Connection, Volume 1: State Terror and Popular Resistance in El Salvador.* London: Zed Books.

Nairn, Allan. 1984. "Behind the Death Squads," *Progressive,* May: 1, 20–29.

Webre, Stephen. 1979. *Jose Napoleon Duarte and the Christian Democratic Party in Salvadoran Politics.* Baton Rouge: Louisiana State University Press.

White, Robert E. (Ambassador). 1982. "Central America: The Problem that Won't Go Away," *New York Times Magazine,* July 18: 21–28ff.

## CASE 22. Nicaragua, 1981–88

Ambrose, Stephen E., and Douglas G. Brinkley. 1997. *Rise to Globalism: American Foreign Policy since 1938.* NY: Penguin Books.

Arnson, Cynthia. 1989. *Crossroads: Congress, the Reagan Administration and Central America.* NY: Pantheon Books.

Blum, William. 1995. "Nicaragua 1981–1990: Destabilization in Slow Motion," Chapter 49: 290–305, *Killing Hope: US Military and CIA Interventions since World War II.* Monroe, ME: Common Courage Press.

Brody, Reed. 1985. *Contra Terror in Nicaragua: A Report of the Fact-Finding Mission, Sept. 1984–Jan. 1985.* Boston: South End Press.

Burns, T. Bradford. 1987. *At War with Nicaragua: The Reagan Doctrine and the Politics of Nostalgia.* NY: Harper and Row.

Chamorro, Edgar. 1987. *Packaging the Contras: A Case of CIA Disinformation.* NY: Institute for Media Analysis, Monograph Series Number 2.

Chomsky, Noam. 1985. *Turning the Tide: U.S. Intervention in Central America and the Struggle for Peace.* Boston: South End Press.

Draper, Theodore. 1991. *A Very Thin Line: The Iran-Contra Affairs.* NY: Hill and Wang.

Gutman, Roy. 1988. *Banana Diplomacy: Making of American Policy in Nicaragua 1981–87.* NY: Simon and Schuster.

Lake, Anthony. 1989. *Somoza Falling.* Amherst: University of Massachusetts Press.

Melrose, Dianna. 1985. *Nicaragua: The Threat of a Good Example.* NY: Oxfam.

Morley, Morris H., and James Petras. 1987. *The Reagan Administration and Nicaragua: How Washington Constructs its Case for Counterrevolution in Central America.* NY: Institute for Media Analysis, Monograph Series Number 1.

Pastor, Robert A. 1987. *Condemned to Repetition: The United States and Nicaragua.* NJ: Princeton University Press.

Scott, Peter Dale, and Jonathan Marshall. 1991. *Cocaine Politics: Drugs, Armies, and the CIA in Central America.* Berkeley: University of California Press.

Sklar, Holly. 1988. *Washington's War on Nicaragua.* Boston: South End Press.

Sullivan, Michael J., III. 1991. *Measuring Global Values: The Ranking of 162 Countries.* NY: Greenwood Press.

Webb, Gary. 1998. *Dark Alliance: The CIA, the Contras, and the Crack Cocaine Explosion.* NY: Seven Stories Press.

Woodward, Bob. 1987. *Veil: The Secret Wars of the CIA 1981–1987.* NY: Simon and Schuster.

## CASE 23. Grenada, 1983

Black, Jan Knippers. 1984. "The Selling of the Invasion of Grenada," *USA Today*, May: 19–21.

Connell-Smith, Gordon. 1984. "The Grenada Invasion in Historical Perspective: from Monroe to Reagan," *Third World Quarterly*, 6(2), April: 432–45.

Curry, W. Frick. 1984. "Grenada: Force as First Resort," *International Policy Report*, January: 1–7. Washington, DC: Center for International Policy.

Davidson, Scott. 1986. *Grenada: A Study in Politics and the Limits of International Law.* Brookfield, VT: Ashgate Publishing.

Dugger, Ronnie. 1983. *On Reagan: The Man and His Presidency.* NY: McGraw-Hill.

Dunn, Peter M., and Bruce W. Watson (eds.). 1985. *American Intervention in Grenada: The Implications of Operation "Urgent Fury."* Boulder, CO: Westview Press.

Kennedy, David M., and Richard N. Haass. 1994. *The Reagan Administration and Lebanon.* Washington, DC: Georgetown University Institute for the Study of Diplomacy, Case 340.

Kwitny, Jonathan. 1984. "Oh, What A Lovely War!" *Mother Jones*, June: 27–33, 46.

McKean, Ashley E. 1999. "The Grenada Intervention: Victory or Deceit?" *International Studies Association, Foreign Policy Section Newsletter*, Spring: 11–17.

Nardin, Terry, and Katheleen D. Pritchard. 1990. *Ethics and Intervention: The United States in Grenada, 1983.* Washington, DC: Georgetown University Institute for Diplomacy, Case 502.

Pastor, Robert. 1988. "The Invasion of Grenada: A Pre- and Post-Mortem," pp. 88–97 in Scott B. MacDonald, Harald M. Sandstom, and Paul B. Goodwin Jr. (eds.), *The Caribbean after Grenada.* NY: Praeger.

Rosati, Jerel A. 1999. *The Politics of United States Foreign Policy.* Fort Worth, TX: Harcourt Brace College Publishers.

Scheinen, David. 1997. "Grenada Invasion," vol. 2: 254, in Jentleson, *Encyclopedia* (see CASE 21, Clifford).

Schoenhals, Kai P., and Richard A. Melanson. 1985. *Revolution and Intervention in Grenada: The New Jewel Movement, the United States, and the Caribbean.* Boulder, CO: Westview Press.

Searle, Chris (ed.). 1984. *In Nobody's Backyard: Maurice Bishop's Speeches 1979–1983.* Totowa, NJ: Bibliographic Distribution Center, 1984.

Thorndike, Tony. 1985. *Grenada, Politics, Economics and Society*. London: Frances Pinter Publishers Marxist Series.

Treverton, Gregory. 1994. "Deciding to Use Force in Grenada: A Successful Intervention?" pp. 194–208, *Making American Foreign Policy*. Englewood Cliffs, NJ: Prentice-Hall.

Woodward, Bob. 1987. *Veil* (see CASE 22).

## CASE 24. Libya, 1981–86

AbuKhalil, As'ad. 2002. *Bin Laden, Islam, and America's New "War on Terrorism."* NY: Seven Stories Press.

Anderson, Scott. 2003. "The Makeover (of Qaddafi)," *New York Times Magazine*, January 19: 28–34ff.

Bearman, Jonathan. 1986. *Qadhafi's Libya*. London: Zed Books.

Blundy, David, and Andrew Lycett. 1987. *Qaddafi and the Libyan Revolution*. Boston: Little, Brown.

Campbell, Duncan, and Patrick Forbes. 1985. "Tale of Anti-Reagan Hit Team Was 'Fraud,' " *New Statesman*, August 16.

Cooley, John K. 1982. *Libyan Sandstorm*. NY: Holt Rinehart, Winston.

Emerson, Steven, and Brian Duffy. 1990. *The Fall of Pan Am 103: Inside the Lockerbie Investigation*. NY: Putnam.

Haley, P. Edward. 1997. "Libya," vol. 3: 67–70, in Jentleson, *Encyclopedia,* (see CASE 21, Clifford).

Haley, P. Edward. 1984. *Qaddafi and the United States since 1969*. NY: Praeger.

Hersh, Seymour. 1987. "Target Qaddafi," *New York Times Magazine*, February 22: 17–26.

Pelt, Adrian. 1970. *Libyan Independence and the United Nations: A Case of Planned Independence*. New Haven, CT: Yale University Press.

*Terrorism, A Closer Look: The Haig Doctrine*. Oakland, CA: Investigative Resource Data Center, 1985.

Woodward, Bob. 1987. *Veil* (see CASE 22).

## CASE 25. Afghanistan, 1981–88

Anwar, Raja. 1988. *The Tragedy of Afghanistan: A Firsthand Account*. NY: Verso Books.

Bearden, Milton. 2001. "Afghanistan, Graveyard of Empires," *Foreign Affairs,* 80(6), November/December: 17–30.

Bonosky, Phillip. 1985. *Washington's Secret War against Afghanistan*. NY: International Publishers.

Borer, Douglas. 1999. *Super Powers Defeated: Vietnam and Afghanistan Compared*. Portland, OR: Frank Cass Publisher.

Cogan, Chares G. 1993. "Partners in Time: The CIA and Afghanistan since 1979," *World Policy Journal*, Summer: 73–82.

Cooley, John K. 1999. *Unholy Wars: Afghanistan, America and International Terrorism*. Sterling, VA: Pluto Press.

Cordovez, Diego, and Selig S. Harrison. 1995. *Out of Afghanistan: The Inside Story of the Soviet Withdrawal*. NY: Oxford University Press.

Galeotti, Mark. 1995. *Afghanistan: The Soviet Union's Last War*. Portland, OR: Frank Cass Publisher.

Hiro, Dilip. 1999. "The Cost of an Afghan 'Victory,' " *Nation*, February 15: 17–20.

Kakar, M. Hassar. 1995. *Afghanistan: The Soviet Invasion and the Afghan Response, 1979–1982*. Berkeley: University of California Press.

Magnus, Ralph H., and Eden Naby. 1998. *Afghanistan: Mullah, Marx, and Mujahid*. Boulder, CO: Westview Press.

Malkin, Lawrence. 2000. "Afghanistan: Reflections in a Distorted Mirror," *World Policy Journal*, Fall: 51–59.

Marshall, Jonathan. 1991. *Drug Wars: Corruption, Counterinsurgency, and Covert Operations in the Third World*. Forestville, CA: Cohan and Cohen Publishers.

Mendelson, Sarah E. 1998. *Changing Course: Ideas, Politics, and the Soviet Withdrawal from Afghanistan*. NJ: Princeton University Press.

Merrill, Dennis. 1997. "Afghanistan," vol. 1: 24, in Jentleson, *Encyclopedia* (see CASE 21, Clifford).

Meyer, Karl E., and Shareen Blair Brysac. 2000. *Tournament of Shadows: The Great Game and the Race for Empire in Central Asia*. Washington, DC: Counterpoint.

Poullada, Leon B. 1995. *The Kingdom of Afghanistan and the United States: 1828–1973*. Lincoln: University of Nebraska Press.

Rais, B. Rasul. 1994. *War without Winners: Afghanistan's Uncertain Transition after the Cold War*. NY: Oxford University Press.

Rashid, Ahmed. 2000. *Taliban: Militant Islam, Oil, and Fundamentalism in Central Asia*. New Haven, CT: Yale University Press.

Vornberg, William. 1987. "Afghan Rebels and Drugs," *Covert Action Information Bulletin*, No. 28 (Summer): 11–12.

# CHAPTER 7

# The Post–Cold War Era: Bush, Clinton, and the Search for New Themes, 1989–2000

## INTRODUCTION

In the first decade after the end of the Cold War, Presidents George H. W. Bush and Bill Clinton struggled to define some overarching public purpose for American foreign policy that could rally public opinion as rabidly as anti-communism had for the previous two generations. In the three cases involving Bush, the rationale varied from "fighting drugs" (Panama) to the creation of a "New World Order" (Iraq), to "feeding the hungry" (Somalia, 1992). Clinton's reasons ranged from "nation-building" (Somalia, 1993) to "enlargement of democracy and markets" (Haiti; Bosnia), to saving NATO and stopping ethnic cleansing (Kosovo). The goal of expanding America's role as hegemon of the global capitalist system was, of course, never articulated.

Precisely when the Cold War ended is subject to some dispute. By the time the USSR gave its 1991 Christmas present to the world—dissolving itself on December 25th—the Cold War was definitely over. Others place the end two years earlier, with the fall of the Berlin wall on November 9, 1989. Between these dates, during the first three years of Bush's administration, 1989–91, there were a few bumpy patches on the transition path: the killings in Lithuania, the Communist Party coup that Russian President Boris Yeltsin stopped from toppling Soviet President Gorbachev, and so forth. Throughout this time, Bush practiced a rather conservative foreign policy reflective of his personality: it wouldn't be prudent to provoke the Soviet Union as it was in the process of destroying itself (Mervin, 1998; Duffy and Goodgame, 1992).

Bush's three military interventions into the periphery of the global capitalist world reflected this caution, as well as a few other aspects of his personality and background. The minor invasion of Panama in December 1989 was a reversion to traditional American pre–Cold War behavior in its home hemisphere. But Bush had issued a statement with Gorbachev in Malta just three weeks earlier proclaiming the Cold War over, and his justification for ousting Panamanian dictator Manuel Noriega had to draw upon a totally new rationale: fighting a drugs war (Halliday, 1990). In the major war against Iraq, January–March 1991, Bush drew upon his previous internationalist credentials (Ambassador to the United Nations and China, Director of the CIA, Vice President, etc.) to assemble a formidable coalition of 33 countries, plus overwhelming UN legitimation of their hostile action. The lame-duck intervention in Somalia, in December 1992, can only be explained as a personal attempt to make one noble humanitarian gesture before departing the historical scene (Rauch, 2000).

Bill Clinton entered the presidency with a relatively blank foreign policy slate on which to make his mark (Miller, 1994; Hyland, 1999). Initially, in Somalia, 1993, Clinton moved aggressively to expand Bush's "end-starvation" mission into one of "nation-building." After suffering a minor but embarrassing setback, Clinton withdrew into a policy more reflective of his, and his party's, ambivalent attitude toward militarism dating from the last years of the Vietnam War. In Haiti, 1994, Clinton engineered an "immaculate intervention," a nonviolent military invasion, with no deaths. In Bosnia, 1995, he waited three years before addressing in a military fashion a problem that could have been dealt with four years earlier (by Bush, even) had not both men been afflicted with a larger, more existential problem: just what would be the guide for American foreign policy in the post–Cold War world, now that Mikhail Gorbachev had robbed the United States of its enemy (Carpenter, 1992).

It was this lack of a lodestone—something to replace fighting communism—which bedeviled the foreign policies of both Bush and Clinton (Cox, 1996), and why they are both treated in this same chapter in *American Adventurism Abroad*. It helps to explain why Bush was unable to translate his 90 percent popularity after winning the war in the Persian Gulf into reelection a year later. In addition to the "stupid economy," candidate Clinton could clobber the incumbent for coddling dictators from China to the Balkans. But the issue also undermined Clinton who grappled with rationales such as enlarging the space for capitalism and democracy, finding a role for an expanded NATO, and reversing ethnic cleansing, as justifications for his later interventions in Haiti, Bosnia, and Kosovo (Brinkley, 1997; Mandelbaum, 1996).

In short, the question of grand national purpose haunted both parties after the end of the Cold War, and was not answered until 9-11-01. In the wake of that tragedy, the United States once again had an organizing concept—fighting terrorism—for its diplomacy, and in particular for its interventions in the periphery of the global capitalist system.

## CASE 26. PANAMA, 1989

Within three weeks of proclaiming the "end of the Cold War" in Malta, President George Bush ordered an American invasion of Panama on December 20, 1989. Since the Cold War was over, a new excuse had to be invented for such an American military expedition (Morton, 1990). Bush had in his inaugural address eleven months earlier enunciated the rationale for a return to a more traditional American role in Latin America: to rid the world of the "scourge" of drugs ("Transcript," 1989: 10). A more important unspoken reason: under the Panama Canal Treaties of 1977, the United States was to hand over the joint operation of the canal to a fully Panamanian Commission on January 1, 1990, and the United States had become distrustful of Panama's military and intelligence chief, Manuel Antonio Noriega.

The American military intervention in Panama, "Operation Just Cause," was one of the most unusual in this story of American adventurism in the Third World. The announced justification for the insertion of 24,000 US troops into an allegedly sovereign state, was to arrest its military leader on a drugs charge issued by a Florida court. Amazingly, the American Army was being used as a posse to execute a warrant on a drug kingpin. In truth, the US show of force echoed an older, more ominous tradition: to remind its smaller neighbors who was still in charge in the hemisphere despite the end of the Cold War. In the absence of the OAS-sanctioned policy of intervening in Panama "to contain communism"—in fact, the OAS condemned this action by a vote of 20–1—the United States would revert to its 1823–1935 behavior of policing order in the banana republics to the south.

Capitalism was not at stake in Panama in 1989 so much as that country's status as a satellite state, and the trustworthiness of Noriega, its de facto leader. A graduate of the notorious School of Americas from its days in Panama City, Noriega was a known drug trafficker and valued CIA informant for the previous 30 years (Kempe, 1990: 26). Since 1968, he had been the power-behind-the-throne of his country's various presidents. There is some suspicion that he plotted the mysterious 1981 airplane death of popular Head of State Omar Torrijos, architect of the 1977 canal treaties (Zepezauer, 1994: 82). After the 1984 election, he had the losing candidate and leader of the opposition, Hugo Spadafora, beheaded (Sanchez Borbon, 1988: 62).

During the Carter years, Noriega's ties to the CIA were temporarily terminated (Strong, 1992: 201), but when Bush became vice president, this valued asset from his days as CIA Director (1975–76) was restored to the

Agency payroll at a salary of some $200,000 per year (Dinges, 1990: 51; McWilliams and Piotrowski, 2001: 349). The reason was that the Panamanian strongman was now being courted as an ally in the US-sponsored *contra* war against Nicaragua's Sandinistas (CASE 22). In short, over the years Noriega was tolerated as a useful tool by the US defense and intelligence establishment. He was especially valued as a source of good information about drug dealing in Colombia and Cuban diplomatic activities in Central America and the Caribbean (Hogan, 1997: 355; Kempe, 1990: 162–65).

But by 1987, Noriega's coziness with the Medellin drug cartel in Colombia made him a major political embarrassment to President Reagan. It was also discovered that he had been trading intelligence secrets with Cuba as well as with the United States (Collie, 1989: 22). Vice President Bush in particular seemed to take it as a personal insult that his former colleague in central American skullduggery was playing both sides of the street in the sharing of sensitive political intelligence. Probably not coincidentally, a series of protests in June and July 1987 led to riots in Panama, which Noriega ruthlessly put down with 1,500 arrests and hundreds of injuries. The unrest was suspiciously similar to the kind of outcry that had (with American involvement) led to the removal of Ferdinand Marcos in the Philippines the previous year (Strong, 1992: 204; and see CASE 3), and in later years Noriega pointed to this period as the start of a "30-month state of war" between Panama and the United States (McConnell, 1991: 281).

In February 1988, two courts in Florida came down with indictments linking Noriega to the Medellin cartel in the trafficking of narcotics and the laundering of drug profits. The American government responded, on April 8, 1988, by imposing economic sanctions and freezing $56 million in Panamanian assets in the United States (Independent Commission, 1991: 23). But the Reagan administration held off any more confrontational activity (including support for a coup) during the presidential election campaign of his vice president throughout the rest of 1988.

Following Bush's inaugural shift of foreign policy priorities to fighting a drugs war (Lapham, 1989: 47), the context for a more overt move against Noriega came in May 1989, when Noriega halted the counting of ballots in Panama's presidential election because his preferred candidate was losing. In July, the commander of US armed forces in Panama, who opposed the use of American force to remove Noriega, was replaced by a more aggressive warrior. In August, the number of US troops in Panama was increased from 10,000 to 12,000 in a not-so-subtle hint to Noriega that it was time to for him to go. In October 1989, Bush gave the green light to a coup attempt, but refused to commit sufficient resources for its success (Rockman, 1997: 202). Plainly, some more definitive action was needed.

In December, Noriega made his "state of war" assertion and began subjecting off-duty American military personnel to a series of arbitrary arrests and searches. Seizing upon an incident in which an American marine was killed at a roadstop on December 16th, Bush made the decision to invade. Responding to JCS Chairman Colin Powell's demand for "overwhelming force" against the 3,000 armed combatants in Panama's 15,000 man "Defense Force" (Stiles, 1995: 322), Bush authorized the largest landing of American paratroopers since World War II and the first-ever combat support missions for the F-117A stealth attack aircraft (Strong, 1992: 209). The "war" lasted 14 days and resulted in the deaths of 23 American soldiers, along with 300 wounded. According to former Attorney General Ramsey Clark's Independent Commission of Inquiry, upwards of 4,000 Panamanian lives were lost, only 700 of them military. Six villages were totally obliterated, and some $1 billion in businesses destroyed as well (Independent Commission, 1991: 39). But Noriega was finally captured and spirited away to a Florida jail, where he rots away today serving a 40-year sentence.

The suspected winner of the May 1989 election (Guillermo Endara) was duly sworn into office on a military base in the US Canal Zone, though only for the "remaining years" of his elected term. Panama was immediately granted $50 million in "reconstruction aid" (Conniff, 1992: 164). Meanwhile, in preparation for the turn-over of the administration of the canal, now back on schedule, the Noriega-dominated Panamanian army was abolished. In its place a new "domestic police force," trained by the United States, was commissioned.

In sum, George Bush's excellent adventure in Panama, can be regarded as quite a success. Unlike most of the other cases in this book, local Panamanian politics was not disrupted, but in fact restored. Despite the OAS condemnation, there was no loss of influence by the United States. In fact traditional control by the Colossus of the North—tenuous at best during the years of the nationalist Torrijos and the uncontrollable loose cannon, Noriega—was reasserted (Scranton, 1991). A more compliant Panamanian government was back in place in plenty of time before the final departure of the US troops from the Canal Zone in 2000. American hegemony in Panama had been restored to its 1903 roots.

## CASE 27. IRAQ, 1991

To most Americans, the Persian Gulf War in which the United States led a UN-sanctioned coalition of 33 states in the expulsion of Iraq from Kuwait was George Bush's finest hour. A closer look, however, reveals serious errors that may have misled Iraq into thinking the United States would not react to the move into its "19th province," significant dissembling as to the real objectives of the war, and methods as nefarious and costs as dear as in any of the other interventions in *American Adventurism Abroad* (Fox, 1991: viii; Hybel, 1993: 8–10).

As in the case of Panama, the ferocity of George Bush's reaction to Iraq's move into Kuwait on August 2, 1990, was that of one subject to a treacherous betrayal by an earlier co-conspirator. During the Iran-Iraq War (1980–88), the Reagan administration quietly favored Iraq. Iran was regarded as the greater strategic enemy; so the United States quietly channeled some low-level technology (Jones, 1994), some valuable intelligence, and some million dollars of aid to Iraq. The secular Ba'athist dictatorship was deemed to be fighting for the cause of America's Saudi and Gulf Arab allies against the onslaught of Islamic fundamentalism and Persian imperialism (Hiro, 1991: 3, 68). Kuwaiti oil tankers were reflagged as American ships to keep them from being targeted by Iran. The United States even turned its head as Saddam gassed "his own people" (see CASE 16). Finally, after the war ended, and in the first year of the Bush administration, $1 billion in agricultural credits granted during the war were extended, in the hopes of wooing Iraq as a continued strategic ally against the ayatollahs' Iran (Jentleson, 1994: 132–37).

When in July 1990 the Iraqi Foreign Minister asked the American Ambassador in Baghdad about the US attitude toward an Iraq-Kuwait border dispute, he was told the United States did not have a position on the matter ("Glaspie Transcript": 130). To resolve this dispute—which dated from the UK's drawing of Iraq's borders in 1932, and which the UK had to defend by force at the time of Kuwait's independence in 1961—was one of the reasons Iraq went to war with Kuwait in 1990. Other *casi belli* included getting some relief from repayments of loans Kuwait had made to Iraq during its "Arab war" against Iran and stopping Kuwait from "slant drilling" in to the Rumailia oil field that lay under the border of the two countries (Draper, 1992: 41).

Bush's extreme reaction to this Arab "border war" must have taken Iraq by surprise. Declaring Saddam a modern-day Hitler out to conquer the entire Arabian peninsula (Sciolino, 1991), Bush asserted that the move in to Kuwait "would not stand" and immediately dispatched 150,000 American soldiers to protect Saudi Arabia in "Operation Desert Shield." He then set about organizing the diplomatic framework for the multinational coalition that six months later, in "Operation Desert Storm," expelled Iraqi forces from Kuwait. The building of this coalition reflected Bush's background in diplomacy, and also his realization that with the end of the Cold War, the United Nations could be called upon to act as was originally planned—that is, to repel clear-cut cases of aggression—without being hampered by Cold War vetoes from the permanent members of the Security Council. Successfully including the USSR and China in the UN's condemnations of Iraq was seen as the beginning of a New World Order (Sklar, 1992: 25).

In this collaborative context, the war's $61 billion cost was to be borne chiefly (78%) by the largest sellers and buyers of oil: Kuwait and Saudi

Arabia, Germany and Japan, respectively. The ground combat fighting (some 700,000 troops) was done mainly by the United States (425,000), Saudi Arabia, Egypt, Britain, and Syria. The air war was waged primarily by the US and the UK. Egypt and Syria and many of the other 25 poorer contributors to what critics called the "checkbook coalition" were compensated with aid and debt forgiveness for their efforts in providing wider international legitimacy to the cause (Graubard, 1992: 120; Smith, 1992: 147, 154).

The real reason for the furious American reaction to Iraq's invasion, however, was not to repel aggression (the official United Nations mandate), and certainly not to bring democracy to Kuwait (what many Americans believed at the time). Rather (and in keeping with the Carter Doctrine (see Chapter 5), it was to ensure that control over Kuwait's oil was kept in hands that would be friendly to Western capital (Pelletier, 2001: ix–xi). In this respect the American action to assure that Persian Gulf oil would remain in the control of Kuwait, Saudi Arabia, and the other sheikdoms on good terms with Western oil corporations, completed the US replacement of the UK, begun at Suez 34 years earlier, as the region's economic hegemon.

The oil of Kuwait could not be allowed to fall to such an "unpredictable"—that is, uncontrollable—state as Iraq. Although that country had a long history of participating in the global capitalist market for its oil—and nowhere else to sell its main export—Iraq under Saddam Hussein was deemed too "unstable"—that is, too independent to trust as a trading partner. If Iraq succeeded in its aggression against Kuwait, it would double its control of the world's oil resources from 10 to 20 percent; if it moved into Saudi Arabia, this percentage would rise to 48. Although there was no evidence of such designs, this was a chance the capitalist world felt it could not take. Other aggressions into foreign territory in the Middle East region—Israel into Jordan and Egypt in 1967, Syria into southern Lebanon in 1976, Israel into Lebanon in 1982, Iran and Iraq into one another's lands in 1980–88—were condemned by the US and UN, but not met with the globally sanctioned armed response as faced Iraq in 1990. But none of those earlier aggressions threatened global capitalist markets in oil (Amin, 1994: 227–29; Salinger and Laurent, 1991: 88–89, 130).

America's allies in this "noble" cause included some of the world's most reactionary monarchies (including Kuwait, which still only allows about 5 percent of its population to vote, and Saudi Arabia, which allows no votes at all [Sullivan, 1996: 176–79]), as well as one member on the State Department's short list of terrorist states: Syria. The methods employed by the US-led coalition involved not only a major war (40 days of bombing, 100 hours of ground battle, 100,000 dead Iraqis), but also (in the bombings of his various residences) the attempted assassination of Saddam himself (Clark, 1992: 206–9). Finally, and with little regard for regional geopolitical instability, American war plans included the stirring up of secessionist movements among the Shiite Arabs of southern Iraq, and the Kurds in the north.

After the war, American support for the insurgencies of the Shiites (55% of Iraq's population) and the Kurds (20%), was abandoned (for the second time in a generation in the case of the Kurds; see CASE 16). Democracy, or majority rule, was never the US goal for these repressed peoples, although they did eventually get delayed allied-patrolled "no-fly-zones" so they could be somewhat protected from Saddam's attempts at reassertion of his minority (i.e., Sunni Arab government) control over their areas. But in terms of becoming independent political entities, these peoples were deemed expendable, and even today, after America's 2003 war against Iraq, are only being protected for "greater autonomy" in some future federal Iraq, not for the independence they were led to believe they might receive.

After the liberation of Kuwait, Saddam was allowed to remain in power because the UN mandate for war did not go beyond the expulsion of Iraq from Kuwait. More to the point, the Great Powers had an interest in allowing Iraq to remain intact as a bulwark against a potentially expansive Islamic Iran (Cordesman, 1994). But Saddam's regime was then subjected to a decade of severe economic sanctions and no-fly-zones as punishment for his refusal to allow UN inspections (agreed to at the end of the war) to ensure it had not re-armed. These sanctions, originally hoped to cause Iraq's military to oust its leader, caused at least another 400,000 of its most vulnerable citizens (mainly children) to die, according to the United Nations (Arnove, 2001: 15).

Thus, it is not clear that the 1991 American war in Iraq was as big of a victory as it seemed at the time. To be sure, it assured Western corporate control over the oil and saved "jobs, jobs, jobs" (as the Secretary of State promised at the time) for another generation (Baker, 1995: 335–37). But the long-term appeal of Saddam Hussein's message of independence from, and defiance of, the global hegemon is still unclear. In explaining its *jihad* against America, Osama bin Laden regularly added the plight of the people of Iraq-under-sanction to his two main causes: "Israel's occupation of Palestine," and "infidel troops in the Land of the Prophet." Those latter were the 5,000 American soldiers in Saudi Arabia dating from the days of "Desert Shield." Rushed out to protect Saudi Arabia from Iraq in August 1990, they did not leave after the end of the "Desert Storm" Gulf War.

By the end of the decade, most members of the "checkbook coalition" in the region had split with the US and UK in the Western powers' continuing punishment of Iraq's people. Even France and Russia on the UN Security Council worked during the 1990s toward treating Iraq, even though still under Saddam Hussein, as a more normal member of the global community, and not the international pariah US domestic politics seemed to require he remain.

As far as Iraq's society is concerned, the war, and especially its aftermath, was an unmitigated disaster. Including the civilian deaths during the war itself (Human Rights Watch, 1991: 17–19), probably half million innocent people (i.e., noncombatants) died, and its economy was decimated—all to restore and preserve the monarchy in Kuwait, and to ensure Western control over the oil economy of the lower Persian Gulf.

## CASE 28. SOMALIA, 1992–94

The US intervention in Somalia, 1992–94, spanned 16 months of two administrations and cost $2 billion. It began under George Bush, who in a truly bizarre moment of American adventurism in the Third World, sent 28,000 US troops on a whimsical "Operation Restore Hope" to feed the hungry in the midst of a civil war on the Horn of Africa.

Somalia was a state that seldom came on America's diplomatic radar screen before the mid-1970s (Lefebvre, 1991). A former colony of the United Kingdom and Italy, it became a Soviet ally soon after its independence in 1960; then, after the Marxist revolution in Ethiopia in 1975, the two neighboring east African states switched patrons: Ethiopia being supported by the USSR, Somalia by the US. From 1977 to 1989, $1 billion in American aid flowed into Somalia, leaving a flood of weapons that have been used ever since to destroy any semblance of centralized rule in this hapless nation of 8 million people.

By late 1989, a multisided civil war based on clan conflict was raging. In January 1991, the government of longtime dictator Siad Barre had been overthrown; the country has been divided into several warring fiefdoms ever since. By mid-1992, rival militias prevented farmers from planting new crops, and control over the distribution of food was being used by all sides as a weapon in the conflict. Soon, famine and malnutrition had engulfed more than 70 percent of the population; 300,000 people had died and more than a million were barely subsisting in relief camps (Cusimano, 1995: 2–3).

In response to this humanitarian disaster, the internationalist President Bush supported the United Nations Operation in Somalia, UNOSOM-I, a relatively small (500-member) UN peacekeeping force sent in April 1992 to protect the distribution of food relief in the camps. During the rest of this presidential campaign year, however, Bush hesitated to do any more, even as the UN assessment of the job to be done grew, and its peacekeeping force similarly—to about 3,000 by mid-summer.

It is difficult to discern Bush's motives for the decision to commit first 3,000 Marines, and then 25,000 soldiers in mid-December 1992. The fact that the Cold War was over and there was no Great Power to protest US intervention was certainly part of the "New World Order" picture to which Bush related (Tucker and Hendrickson, 1992: 29–43). It was also true that by December Bush had become a lame-duck president, serving out the last two months of his term after being defeated in the November election by Bill Clinton. There is some speculation (Coll, 1997: 4; Menkaus, 1995: 8; Wines, 1992: 12) that the man responsible for the deaths of more than 100,000 Iraqis (see CASE 27), desired a more positive balance to his foreign policy legacy. Saving the starving children of Somalia seemed a worthwhile job that could be accomplished in the remaining weeks of his term.

To pull off this unusually large-scale military/humanitarian mission required all of Bush's vaunted diplomatic skills. For the first time in United Nations history, an intervening force was justified under Chapter VII of the UN Charter: not to keep agreeing contestants apart (peace-keeping), but to impose order upon warring parties (peace-making). To accomplish this, a new Unified Task Force (UNITAF) had to be created by the UN—formally a multinational operation, but actually a unilateral military operation of the US authorized by the UN. It was also the first time the UN sent a force into a country without the consent of its government, the reasoning being that there was no government to make such a request (United Nations, 1996).

By the time Bush exited the presidency the following month, most of the humanitarian mission had been accomplished; food was being distributed and famine had been stopped. But Bill Clinton took office with a new diplomatic idea of "aggressive multilateralism": using the United Nations and other international organizations to accomplish great goals in the post–Cold War era (Miller, 1994: 629). Among the objectives, although not enunciated until fall 1993, was the "enlargement" of the space for democracy and markets in the world (Lake, 1993). The use of the word "enlargement" was designed to invoke comparison with "containment"; markets was a less-charged word than capitalism (Brinkley, 1997: 114–16).

Finding itself with 28,000 armed Americans protecting a full contingent of (by now) some 10,000 international soldiers and civil servants in Somalia, the Clinton administration moved to address the root causes of the famine: the civil war that had caused the Somali nation to collapse in the first place. In an ambitious effort at "nation-building," the US/UN would inevitably be drawn in to take sides in this Somali war. But first, most of the troops from the US humanitarian mission were withdrawn, and then, in May 1993, yet another UN force, UNOSOM-II, was created consisting of 14,000 international troops, including 4,200 Americans.

When the troops of one Somali warlord, Mohammed Farah Aideed, were deemed responsible for the death of 24 UN peacekeeping forces from Pakistan on June 5, 1993, he became Public Enemy No. 1 for the international forces. A massive effort was undertaken to find and capture Aideed.

This culminated on October 3, 1993, in the Battle of Mogadishu (Bowden, 1999: 309–12) in which several hundred of Aideed's supporters were killed—but he was not captured or killed despite attempts to assassinate him via "targeted" bombings.

More significantly for future US foreign policy, 18 American soldiers were also killed, and one of the bodies was dragged through the streets, a gruesome act that was captured by CNN television cameras. For the American people, most of whom had forgotten troops were even in Somalia after the completion of their original humanitarian mission, this came as a rude shock. Clinton was forced by public opinion to announce that the operation was virtually completed and that the troops would be coming home within six months (Hirsch and Oakley, 1995; Sloyan, 1994: 29).

This pledge was dutifully accomplished (on March 25, 1994) and for many Americans it seemed the unhappy episode was over. But there were some long-term deleterious consequences for President Clinton and subsequent American policy. One month after the United States pulled out of Somalia, a small UN Assistance Mission operation in Rwanda (UNAMIR) came under assault in the midst of bloody ethnic Hutu-Tutsi fighting. More than 800,000 people were killed as the Hutus committed genocide upon the minority Tutsi population (Prunier, 1997: 265). The UN was virtually paralyzed as the United States refused to commit any troops—or even to allow the UN to commit troops—in response to one of the largest massacres in history. US "national interests" were not involved; there were no markets or democracy (the two main Clinton foreign policy goals) to protect in the ethnic turmoil in this tiny, preindustrial state. Years later, on a trip to Africa in 1998, Clinton apologized for America's inaction (Power, 2001: 84–86; Melvern, 2000).

Many observers point to the Somalia foreign policy "defeat"—or at least its memory as a symbol of a hapless foreign policy—as one of the reasons Clinton's Democrats lost control of the US Congress in 1994, a setback that crippled the president for the rest of his term. Along with the Republican Congress came a virulent distaste for having almost anything to do with the United Nations, including even the regular payment of annual dues for the next six years. The timid response in Rwanda (which predated the Republican Congress), and the long-delayed multinational responses in Yugoslavia (CASE 30), and in Sierra Leone and Congo later in the decade, can all be traced back to Clinton's failure in Somalia in 1993.

## CASE 29. HAITI, 1994

President Bill Clinton's "immaculate invasion" of Haiti (Shacochis, 1998: 114) in September 1994 was unique in the history of US military interventions in the Third World. Although it eventually involved 23,000 troops, the initial "assault" was made by three unarmed diplomats, carefully chosen by Clinton to represent various points of the American political spectrum (Morley and McGullion, 1999: 131): from the left, ex-President Jimmy Carter; from the center, ex-military chief, and newly announced Republican, Colin Powell; from the right, Democratic Senator Sam Nunn. Duly covered politically, Clinton was able to move, two months before the 1994 Congressional election, to redeem a campaign pledge he had made two years earlier: to reverse a Bush policy that had caused serious suffering for the people of Haiti.

Haiti occupies the western third of the island of Hispaniola and has a population of about 7 million, most of whom are descendants of African slaves brought there by the French; it has historically been the poorest country in the Western Hemisphere. In February 1991, Haiti inaugurated the first freely elected president in its history: an ex-priest, Jean-Bertrand Aristide, who had received 70 percent of the vote. Aristide's left-wing platform was popular with the masses: it proposed reducing the power of the country's military establishment and redistributing the economic wealth historically concentrated within an elite sliver of society (Stotzky, 1997). Seven months later, on September 30, 1991, in a reversion to 187 years of Haitian tradition, Aristide was overthrown in a military coup led by General Raoul Cedras.

The reaction of the Bush administration was to deplore (rhetorically) the loss of democracy, and to apply (weakly and spottily) an economic sanctions regime against the upper class's luxury items and financial transactions (Ives, 1995: 73–74). Within Haiti, a reign of terror was unleashed by a junta with visible ties not only to the economic elite but also to the US intelligence establishment. Among those with such connections were more than a dozen men who are today living in protected exile in the United States. These include such swells as General Jean-Claude Duperval, Colonel Carl Dorelein, and the leader of a particularly notorious death squad (the Front for the Advancement of Progress in Haiti, or FRAPH), Emmanuel "Toto" Constant (Blum, 2000: 82; Grann, 2001: 60).

Under this regime, more than 4,500 of Aristide's supporters were killed, and 40,000 others forced to flee in rickety boats across the Caribbean to Florida, 900 miles to the north. In contrast to the welcome given to comparable Cuban political refugees ("boat people"), Bush pronounced these darker-skinned asylum seekers to be "merely economic" in motivation, fleeing from the impact of the sanctions (the average annual per capita income had dropped from $350 to $200). He refused them entry, particularly during the election year 1992, returning some to Haiti and impounding others in Guantanamo Bay, Cuba (Farmer, 1994: 263–97).

Candidate Bill Clinton criticized these policies during the 1992 presidential campaign and promised to "restore democracy to Haiti," a position particularly popular with the African American base of his

Democratic Party. In office, Clinton attempted in July 1993 to negotiate (under UN auspices on Governor's Island, NY), a deal in which Aristide would be returned to office and Cedras and his colleagues given amnesty for crimes committed during the previous two years. The agreement was broken when the *USS Harlan County,* the transport ship with 270 UN peacekeepers and Aristide's transition team, was turned back; a junta-sanctioned armed mob led by FRAPH refused to let it dock in the harbor at Port-au-Prince. Another year would pass before Clinton, reminded of his campaign promises by the Congressional Black Caucus, was moved to more aggressive action. The immaculate reconception of the ex-Rev. Aristide in the fall of 1994 was a surprising reversal not only of Bush's policy, but of years of condescending US history toward Haiti (Montague, 1940; Schmidt, 1971).

Going back to America's 19-year occupation of Haiti, 1915–34, the United States had typically tolerated repression of the economic aspirations of the black masses by a small, largely mulatto, upper class in league with a handful of American investors (Nicholls, 1979: 247). During the Cold War, the policy was carried out by US intelligence personnel via the military aid program (Blum, 1995: 373; Trouillot, 1990). The relationship was especially notable during the times of Francois "Papa Doc" Duvalier, 1957–71, and his son Jean-Claude "Baby Doc" Duvalier, ruler for the next 15 years. Like the Somozas in Nicaragua (CASE 22), the family Duvalier had their own private army, the *Tontons Macoutes,* to enforce their unique brand of crony capitalism (Wilentz, 1989: 34–35). In the course of a 29-year reign, 40,000 of their political opponents were killed, and a million more driven into exile (Sullivan, 1996: 173). Following riots over the lack of food in 1985, and an American threat to withhold aid pending reforms, the younger Duvalier flew to a cushy exile in southern France on February 7, 1986, aboard a plane provided by the United States (Farmer, 1994: 124).

For the next five years, the United States supported a series of military regimes while making weak efforts at introducing the rudiments of at least procedural democracy (i.e., rigged elections, which would give the resulting government a semblance of legitimacy). Bush's willingness to tolerate the overthrow of Aristide in September, 1991, echoed two similar failures in Haitian elections during President Reagan's term. All the while, the US military aid mission and the CIA were cultivating ties with Haitian security forces, both the traditional military and paramilitary successors to the *Macoutes* (Nairn, 1994: 460), in an effort to protect the elite establishment. Even after the arrival of Carter-Powell-and-Nunn in "Operation Uphold Democracy," Cedras and other members of his junta were given a month's time to gather their assets and prepare for a comfortable retirement in exile to which, in the manner of the younger Duvalier, they were transported in American military planes (Morley and McGillion, 1999: 131–32).

Aristide was not totally free from his American "saviors" after his return to power. As part of the 1993 Governor's Island understanding with the Clinton administration, he was being returned only to finish the remaining 16 months of his five-year electoral term. Under the Haitian constitution, two consecutive terms were not allowed and using the Panama precedent (see CASE 26) the United States took advantage of this. Those businesses in the United States that had benefited from the years of dependent capitalism (low wages, no unions, etc.) did not want a genuine social reformer at Haiti's helm for the long term.

Using its leverage over a renewed $1.2 billion aid package, the United States got Aristide to keep to the original election schedule, after which he left office in February 1996. In so doing, he became the first freely elected civilian Haitian leader to finish out his term and turn over power to another. For Clinton, this restoration of democracy—in a military intervention without the loss of a single American life—could only be regarded as a foreign policy success. The fact that Clinton and Carter, two idealist Democrats presided over this most unusual of interventions in a traditional arena of gunboat diplomacy, made for some interesting distinctions from the historic norm (Perusse, 1995: 102–4, 130–34). Citing the need to uphold the Governor's Island agreement, Clinton was able to get the United Nations to endorse for the first time an intervention force for the purpose of restoring democracy. The troops that followed Carter's coercion of the junta's departure were kept in Haiti for another two years, trading upon Aristide's legitimacy to create a "permeable democracy in which restructured state institutions (especially the military and the police) and an economic development model (free markets) would serve long-term US interests" (Morley and McGillion, 1999: 133).

After 1995, however, for those in the Republican-controlled Congress, who preferred Duvalier-style capitalism, the return of democracy to Haiti under a provocative populist (Aristide, 2000: 89) was a disappointment. The threat of a successful example of democratic socialism could not be tolerated even in the weakest of economies. Subsequent US aid, controlled by Jesse Helms of the Senate Foreign Relations Committee, was tied to implementing a neo-liberal economic program dictated by the International Monetary Fund. When the next president, Rene Preval (1996–2001), surprised the United States by continuing the economic policies of Aristide, refusing to privatize state utilities like the electric company and continuing subsidies to small farmers, the aid was held back.

Aristide returned to power in 2001 after easily winning the next democratic presidential election. In a phenomenon reminiscent of Chile in 1973, Australia in 1974, and Nicaragua in 1984 (see CASEs 17, 19, and 22), Aristide and Preval's Lavalas Party became increasingly popular despite the US economic warfare being visited upon their country. Aristide's return, however, coincided with the accession of George W. Bush in the

United States, and the aid screws were tightened even more after his in-auguration. They were now linked to a new set of elections in which more conservative parties might strengthen their numbers in the Haitian leg-islature. After three years of increasing economic pressure, Aristide was driven from power by US-instigated unrest. Like "Baby Doc" and General Cedras before him, Aristide was spirited out of the country—kidnapped, he claimed—on a US military transport plane on February 29, 2004.

## CASE 30. YUGOSLAVIA, 1995 AND 1999

The two US-led military interventions into the civil wars in ex-Yugosla-via—in Bosnia, 1995 and in Kosovo, 1999—will be the final case study in *American Adventurism Abroad*. As noted in the Introduction, these actions represent a return from the farther reaches of the Third World in Africa, Asia, the Middle East and Latin America to the outer periphery of the European core of global capitalism: the Balkan peninsula.

Although it often seemed halting at the time, US policy toward former Yugoslavia since the end of the Cold War can be seen in hindsight to have followed a pattern. The goal was to dismember (or to acquiesce in the dismemberment of) the former multinational communist state in a way that would be most congenial to global capitalism. In this respect it fit in with the Clinton policy of enlargement of markets and democracy, with a definite preference for markets, and where democracy took the form of a destructive variant of chauvinist self-determination.

Yugoslavia in 1990 was a country of 24 million people divided into six federal republics—Serbia, Croatia, Bosnia, Macedonia, Slovenia, and Montenegro—to account for the political aspirations of eight ethnic groups. Each of the five main ethnic groups predominated in its respective republic, with the dominant homogeneity varying between a low of 43 percent in Bosnia and a high of 95 percent in Macedonia. But there was much overlap of minorities found in other than their "natural" republic with the result of rather integrated living patterns. Finally, the largest republic, Serbia (population 11.5 million), had within it two provinces: Kosovo and Vojvodina, whose respective main ethnic groups (Albanians and Hungarians) made up about 20 percent of that republic.

The artificial "nation-state" of Yugoslavia had been created by the Great Power winners of World War I in 1919 in an effort to provide (unsuccess-fully it now turns out) a homeland for the "southern Slavic" peoples. It was held together in its first 20 years by the autocratic rule of the King of Serbia, and after World War II by the political ideology of communism enforced, until 1980, by the skillful control of its (Slovenian-Croatian) communist leader Joseph Broz Tito. But after the end of the Cold War, Yugoslavia was systematically dismembered, with its former Croatian, Bosnian, and Kosovar parts forcibly broken off in, respectively, 1992, 1995, and 1999. (Slovenia and Macedonia—two smaller (2 million each), and more ethnically homogeneous, republics—seceded more peaceably.)

US military might was crucial in the cases of Bosnia and Kosovo, and the main geostrategic beneficiaries of these secessions have been the American-dominated NATO alliance, and the European Union's economic hegemon, Germany (Zimmerman, 1999). Western capital (led by the Germany and Italy) filled the gap in restructuring ex-socialist economies and rebuilding war-torn areas in these Balkan lands. By 2000, a region previously within a Russian sphere of influence was in the Western camp, except for those minimal areas remaining in a rump-Yugoslavia composed of Serbia (9 million people), Montenegro (600,000) and Vojvodina (500,000).

In 1991–92 President George H. W. Bush followed the German lead (Joffe, 1993: 32) in recognizing the following: (1) a right-wing nationalist-secessionist regime led by former Nazi collaborators in (Catholic) Croatia (population 4.2 million, 78% Croatian); (2) a multinational, secular Bosnia (4 million people: 43% Slavic Muslim, 31% Serb, 17% Croat, 9% mixed/other); and (3) ex-communist neo-nationalists in what was left of Orthodox Christian Serbian-dominated Yugoslavia. However, the United States would not intervene to protect the government in Bosnia when it was attacked by Bosnian Serbs and Bosnian Croats receiving support from ethnic kinsmen in their respective new homelands (Croatia, Serb-controlled rump-Yugoslavia). As with Haiti (CASE 29), candidate Bill Clinton criticized incumbent president Bush during the 1992 campaign for not doing more to alleviate the situation. The Muslims of Bosnia, by the fall of 1992, were living precariously in UN-defined sanctuaries, but Bush would not condone any military use of NATO to protect them (Haas, 1997: 87).

It was not until 1994, after some 200,000 people had died in a bloody civil war that President Clinton began to act more forcefully in Bosnia (Bert, 1997: 195–202; Gow, 1997). Seizing upon a terrorist incident in which 60 Muslim civilians were killed in an outdoor market in Sarajevo in February 1994, Clinton got NATO to agree, for the first time, to use air strikes against Bosnian Serb positions. The next month, he pressured Muslims and Croats to agree to a loose "federation" between their two communities, an alliance that freed up more Muslims to fight Serbs in Bosnia.

In the summer of 1995, more massacres by Serbs of 7,000 innocent Muslims in the supposedly UN-protected cities of Srebrenica and Zepa finally provoked the United States and NATO into the decisive actions that turned the tide of the war. "Operation Deliberate Force," August 30–September 14, 1995, was 16 days of sustained bombing of Bosnian Serb positions. It was the largest military action in NATO history and, in league with Croatian ground troops moving against Serb sanctuaries in its country and in Croat areas of Bosnia, forced the Serbs to peace talks in Dayton, Ohio, later that fall (Daalder, 2000: 129–38).

The result was a peace-plus-partition plan for Bosnia that included a US military presence of some 20,000 troops as part of a NATO force policing a division between the Muslim-Croat "federation" and a reluctant Bosnian Serb "republic" (Holbrooke, 1998: 289–312). The Dayton deal saved "half-a-loaf" (i.e., the federation) in the new state of Bosnia for European and American capitalist penetration; Western influence in the remainder (the republic) would presumably come later after its protector, President Slobodan Milosevic, was ousted from power in Yugoslavia (Rieff, 1995; Rogel, 1998: 75–78).

The next stage in the evolution of Yugoslavia from multinational communism to nationality-based capitalism began four years later with the American military action in Kosovo, 1999. This operation involved a 78-day air war, which completed the job of dismembering Yugoslavia and of isolating its president. As the last ex-communist still ruling a state-run economy in Europe, Milosevic would have to go in order for Clinton's policy of enlargement of markets and democracy to succeed.

The war in Kosovo—population 2 million: 90 percent Albanian Muslim—took advantage of the tension that had been building ever since Yugoslavia removed the autonomy this province had within Serbia between 1975 and 1989. By 1999, the Kosovars were in a full campaign of civil disobedience against their Serbian rulers that included a parallel slate of government officers and their own educational system. A "Liberation Army" had even begun to make strikes against Serbian authorities in 1996. In reprisal, the Serbs killed about 2,500 Kosovars, including massacres in the town of Racak in January 1999 (Mandelbaum, 1999: 3). In this context, a NATO conference at Rambouillet, France, in March 1999 demanded that Yugoslavia make concessions for greater Kosovar control over the province. When Yugoslavia not only refused NATO's ultimatum, but also began to reinforce its own troop strength in the wayward province, more than a million refugees (half the population) fled from Kosovo into neighboring Albania and Macedonia.

The stage was set for the NATO mission. After 34,000 bombing sorties of Serbia—and 10,000 more dead Kosovars—Milosevic gave in, removed his troops, and the refugees returned home (Daalder and O'Hanlon, 2000: 173–77; LeCompte, 1999: 8). However, the province of Kosovo did not receive independence, the goal of its leaders, but only the promise of "restored autonomy within Serbia." As with the pledge to the expendable Kurds in Iraq (CASEs 16 and 27), it would be left to the indefinite future before this goal could be seriously considered.

Thus, between Bosnia, 1995 and Kosovo, 1999, NATO had replaced the UN as the United States' preferred instrument of multinational diplomacy. With the Republican takeover of Congress in 1995, President Clinton could no longer anticipate legislative approval of American action taken in concert with the United Nations. Also, after his 1996 reelection campaign, the expansion of NATO into Poland, Hungary, and the Czech Republic had become a major part of US ethnic and bureaucratic politics. With respect to ethnicity, relatives of Eastern Europeans in electorally powerful Midwestern states were energized by Clinton promises to consolidate capitalism and democracy in these former communist countries. Regarding bureaucracy, NATO in the post–Cold War era was an alliance searching for a purpose (Carpenter and Conroy, 1999). Expanding its membership into Central Europe would create new markets for American arms manufacturers, and new billets for the Pentagon.

The war in Kosovo thus satisfied both political and diplomatic objectives for the United States. Foreign policy idealists, and Eastern European-Americans—led by Czech-born Secretary of State Madeleine Albright—were particularly cheered that American power was being used for the noble Wilsonian purpose of self-determination (Fromkin, 1999: 171–74). Geostrategically, Hungary provided a convenient staging point for US/ NATO air strikes in Kosovo and welcomed American combat soldiers east of the old "Iron Curtain" for the first time. Soldiers from Poland, and even Russia (which belatedly joined in the war as a NATO "associate partner") were helpful in taking the surrender from, and policing the areas of, their Slavic Serbian kinsmen in Kosovo.

Regarding the nefarious measures that the United States has used in its past adventures, it could be argued that the bombing of Belgrade in 1999 was tantamount to an assassination attempt upon Milosevic as was the case with Qaddafi, Saddam, and Aideed (CASEs 24, 27, and 28). And, among the returning refugees protected by NATO, were members of the Kosovo Liberation Army, a group termed "terrorist" by the State Department earlier that same year. In Bosnia, a crucial ally in the expulsion of Serbs from critical areas in the west and north of that country was President Franko Tudjman and his Croatian Democratic Party of former Nazi collaborators (Doder, 1991: 5).

Overall, however, if looked at from a ten-year perspective, American foreign policy in the former Yugoslavia might be counted as successful, at least by the standard of Clinton's policy of expanding markets and democracy. The latter has certainly been consolidated in Slovenia, and even seems to have taken root in Croatia after the death of Tudjman in 1999. An uneasy peace prevails among the ethnic communities within Bosnia. And capitalism has definitely spread into all of these former communist republics of Yugoslavia. NATO forces are patrolling, and European capital is rebuilding, both Bosnia and Kosovo. In 2000, Milosevic was ousted in an election in which the promise of US "reconstruction" aid was used to affect the outcome (as in Italy, 1948 [CASE 2]). In 2001, he was given over to the Ad Hoc Tribunal at the Hague to stand trial for "war crimes," thus completing the US policy of destroying the last legacy of communism in Europe.

As in Clinton's intervention in Haiti (CASE 29), a more muddled situation was tolerated in Yugoslavia in the 1990s than in the more polarized situations presided over in the Reagan-Bush years. Although the result was increased influence for the United States and the beginnings of a market economy in the Balkans, many Americans did not see any clarity of purpose in Clinton's diplomacy. Nevertheless, the policy of "enlargement of markets and democracy," though messy in execution, proceeded inexorably. On the other hand, the price for the locals was high in terms of deaths (250,000) and the displacement of people (2.5 million, more than 10 percent of the original Yugoslav population). And "ethnic cleansing" is a phrase that has entered the political lexicon; for this Clinton and Bush bear some responsibility (Gutman, 1993: 175).

## CHAPTER 7 BIBLIOGRAPHY

### Bush/Clinton Foreign Policies

Brinkley, Douglas. 1997. "Democratic Enlargement: The Clinton Doctrine," *Foreign Policy*, No. 106 (Spring): 111–27.

Carpenter, Ted Galen. 1992. *A Search for Enemies: America's Alliances after the Cold War*. Washington, DC: Cato Institute.

Cox, Michael 1996. *US Foreign Policy after the Cold War: Superpowers without a Mission*. London: Royal Institute of International Affairs.

Duffy, Michael, and Dan Goodgame. 1992. *Marching in Place: The Status Quo Presidency of George Bush*. NY: Simon and Schuster.

Halliday, Fred. 1990. *From Kabul to Managua: Superpower Politics in the Bush-Gorbachev Era*. NY: Random House Pantheon Book.

Hyland, William G. 1999. *Clinton's World: Remaking Foreign Policy*. NY: Praeger.

Mandelbaum, Michael. 1996. "Foreign Policy as Social Work." *Foreign Affairs*, 75 (January/February): 16–32.

Mervin, David. 1998. *George Bush and the Guardianship Presidency*. NY: St. Martin's Press

Miller, Linda B. 1994. "The Clinton Years: Reinventing U.S. Foreign Policy," *International Affairs*, October: 621–34.

Rauch, Jonathan. 2000. "Father Superior: Our Greatest Modern President (Bush)," *New Republic*, May 22: 22–25.

### CASE 26. Panama, 1989

Collie, Tim. 1989. "Noriega Played All Angles in Ascent," *Tampa Tribune*, December 25.

Conniff, Michael. 1992. *Panama and the United States: The Forced Alliance*. Athens: University of Georgia Press.

Dinges, John. 1990. *Our Man in Panama*. NY: Random House.

Hogan, Michael J. 1997. "Panama and the Panama Canal," vol. 3: 355–56, in Bruce W. Jentleson and Thomas G. Paterson (eds.), *Encyclopedia of American Foreign Relations*. NY: Oxford University Press.

Independent Commission of Inquiry. 1991. *The US Invasion of Panama: The Truth behind Operation "Just Cause."* Boston: South End Press.

Kempe, Frederick. 1990. *Divorcing the Dictator: America's Bungled Affair with Noriega.* NY: G. P. Putnam's Sons.

Lapham, Lewis H. 1989. "A Political Opiate: The War on Drugs Is a Folly and a Menace," *Harper's*, December: 43–48.

McConnell, Malcolm. 1991. *Just Cause: The Real Story of America's High-Tech Invasion of Panama.* NY: St. Martin's Press.

McWilliams, Wayne C., and Harry Piotrowski. 2001. *The World Since 1945: A History of International Relations.* Boulder, CO: Lynne Rienner Publishers.

Morton, Brian. 1990. "And Just Why Did We Invade Panama?" *Dissent*, 37: 148–50.

Rockman, Bert A. 1997. "Bush, George Herbert Walker," vol. 1: 200–204, in Jentleson, *Encyclopedia* (see above, Hogan).

Sanchez Borbon, Guillermo. 1988. "Hugo Spadafora's Last Day: A Murder in Panama Undoes a Regime," *Harper's*, June: 56–62.

Scranton, Margaret E. 1991. *The Noriega Years: US-Panamanian Relations 1981–90.* Boulder, CO: Lynne Rienner Publishers.

Stiles, Kendall W. 1995. *Case Histories in International Politics.* NY: HarperCollins College Publishers.

Strong, Robert A. 1992. "Bush and the Invasion of Panama," Chapter 8: 198–225, *Decisions and Dilemmas: Case Studies in Presidential Foreign Policy Making.* Englewood Cliffs, NJ: Prentice-Hall.

"Transcript of Bush's Inaugural Address: Nation Stands Ready to Push On," *New York Times*, January 21, 1989.

Zepezauer, Mark. 1994. "Hit #39: Panama," pp. 82–83, *The CIA's Greatest Hits*, Tucson: Odonian Press.

## CASE 27. Iraq, 1991

Amin, Samir. 1994. "About the Gulf War: Reflections on the New World Order, Capitalist Utopia, Militarism and US Hegemony, and the Role of the United States," Chapter 15: 218–35, in John O'Loughlin, *Lessons from the Persian Gulf Conflict.* NY: HarperCollins.

Arnove, Anthony (ed.). 2000. *Iraq under Siege: The Deadly Impact of Sanctions and War.* Boston: South End Press.

Baker, James A., III. 1995. *The Politics of Diplomacy: Revolution, War, and Peace, 1989–1992.* NY: G. P. Putnam's Sons.

Clark, Ramsey. 1992. *The Fire This Time: US War Crimes in the Gulf.* NY: Thunder's Mouth Press.

Cordesman, Anthony. 1994. *Iran and Iraq: The Threat from the Northern Gulf.* Boulder, CO: Westview.

Draper, Theodore. 1992. "The True History of the Gulf War," *New York Review of Books*, January 30: 38–45.

Fox, Thomas C. 1991. *Iraq: Military Victory, Moral Defeat.* Kansas City, MO: Sheed and Ward.

"The Glaspie Transcript: Saddam Meets the U.S. Ambassador (July 25, 1990)," pp. 122–33 in Micah Sifry and Christopher Cerf (eds.), *The Gulf War Reader: History, Documents, Opinions.* NY: Random House Times Books, 1991.

Graubard, Stephen R. 1992. *Mr. Bush's War: Adventures in the Politics of Illusion*. NY: Hill and Wang.

Hiro, Dilip. 1991. *The Longest War: The Iran-Iraq Military Conflict*. NY: Routledge.

Human Rights Watch. 1991. *Needless Death in the Gulf War: Civilian Casualties during the Air Campaign and Violations of the Laws of War*. NY: Human Rights Watch.

Hybel, Alex Roberto. 1993. *Power over Rationality: The Bush Administration and the Gulf Crisis*. Albany: State University of New York Press.

Jentleson, Bruce W. 1994. *With Friends Like These: Reagan, Bush, and Saddam, 1982–1990*. NY: W. W. Norton.

Jones, Christopher M. 1994. "American Pre-war Technology Sales to Iraq: A Bureaucratic Politics Explanation" Chapter 19: 279–96, in Eugene R. Wittkopf (ed.), *The Domestic Sources of American Foreign Policy: Insights and Evidence*. NY: St. Martin's Press.

Pelletier, Stephen. 2001. *Iraq and the International Oil System: Why America Went to War in the Gulf*. NY: Praeger.

Salinger, Pierre, and Eric Laurent. 1991. *Secret Dossier: The Hidden Agenda behind the Gulf War*. NY: Penguin Books.

Sciolino, Elaine. 1991. *The Outlaw State: Saddam Hussein's Quest for Power and the Gulf Crisis*. NY: John Wiley and Sons.

Sklar, Holly. 1992. "Brave New World Order," Chapter 1: 3–46, in Cynthia Peters (ed.), *Collateral Damage: The New World Order at Home and Abroad*. Boston: South End Press.

Smith, Jean Edward. 1992. *George Bush's War*. NY: Henry Holt.

Sullivan, Michael J., III. 1996. *Comparing State Polities: A Framework for Analyzing 100 Governments*. Westport, CT: Greenwood Press.

## CASE 28. Somalia, 1992–94

Bowden, Mark. 1999. *Black Hawk Down: A Story of Modern War*. NY: Atlantic Monthly Press.

Brinkley, Douglas. 1997. "Democratic Enlargement" (see Bush/Clinton Foreign Policies).

Coll, Alberto R. 1997. *The Problems of Doing Good: Somalia as a Case Study in Humanitarian Intervention*. Washington, DC: Georgetown University Institute for the Study of Diplomacy, Case 518.

Cusimano, Maryann. 1995. *Operation Restore Hope: The Bush Administration's Decision to Intervene in Somalia*. Washington, DC: Georgetown University Institute for the Study of Diplomacy, Case 463.

Hirsch, John L., and Robert B. Oakley. 1995. *Somalia and Operation Restore Hope: Reflections on Peacemaking and Peacekeeping*. Washington, DC: US Institute of Peace Press.

Lake, Anthony. 1993. "From Containment to Enlargement," US Department of State *Dispatch*, September 27.

Lefebvre, Jeffrey Alan. 1991. *Arms for the Horn: US Security Policy in Ethiopia and Somalia, 1953–1991*. Pittsburgh: University of Pittsburgh Press.

Melvern, Linda. 2000. *A People Betrayed: The Role of the West in Rwanda's Genocide*. NY: Zed Books.

Menkaus, Ken. 1995. *Key Decisions in the Somalia Intervention*. Washington, DC: Georgetown University Institute for the Study of Diplomacy, Case 464.

Miller, Linda B. 1994. "The Clinton Years" (see Bush/Clinton Foreign Policies).

Power, Samantha. 2001. "Bystanders to Genocide," *Atlantic Monthly,* September: 84–110.

Prunier, Gerard. 1997. *The Rwanda Crisis: History of a Genocide.* NY: Columbia University Press.

Sloyan, Patrick J. 1994. "How the Warlord Outwitted Clinton's Spooks," *Washington Post,* April 3.

Tucker, Robert, and David Hendrickson. 1992. *The Imperial Temptation: The New World Order and America's Purpose.* NY: Council on Foreign Relations Press.

United Nations. 1996. *The United Nations and Somalia, 1992–1996.* NY: United Nations Blue Book Series, vol. 3.

Wines, Michael. 1992. "Aides Say US Role in Somalia Gives Bush a Way to Exit in Glory, *New York Times,* December 6.

## CASE 29. Haiti, 1994

Aristide, Jean-Bertrand. 2000. *Eyes of the Heart: Seeking a Path for the Poor in the Age of Globalization.* Monroe, ME: Common Courage Press.

Blum, William. 1995. "Haiti 1986–1994: Who Will Rid Me of this Man?" Chapter 55: 370–83, *Killing Hope: US Military and CIA Interventions since World War II.* Monroe, ME: Common Courage Press.

Blum, William. 2000. *Rogue State: A Guide to the World's Only Superpower.* Monroe, ME: Common Courage Press.

Farmer, Paul. 1994. *The Uses of Haiti.* Monroe, ME: Common Courage Press.

Grann, David. 2001. "Giving 'the Devil' (Emmanuel Constant) His Due," *Atlantic Monthly,* June: 55–76.

Ives, Kim. 1995. "The Unmaking of a President," Chapter 8: 65–88, in North American Congress on Latin America (NACLA) (ed.). *Haiti: Dangerous Crossroads.* Boston: South End Press.

Montague, Ludwell Lee. 1940. *Haiti and the United States, 1714–1938.* Durham, NC: Duke University Press.

Morley, Morris, and Chris McGillion. 1999. " 'Disobedient' Generals and the Politics of Redemocratization: The Clinton Administration and Haiti," pp. 113–34 in Demetrios James Caraley (ed.), *The New American Interventionism: Lessons from Successes and Failures.* NY: Columbia University Press.

Nairn, Allan. 1994. "Our Man in FRAPH: Behind Haiti's Paramilitaries," *Nation,* 29 (October 24): 13.

Nicholls, David. 1979. *From Dessalines to Duvalier: Race, Colour, and National Independence in Haiti.* Cambridge: Cambridge University Press.

Perusse, Roland I. 1995. *Haitian Democracy Restored.* Lanham, MD: University Press of America.

Schmidt, Hans. 1971. *The United States Occupation of Haiti, 1915–1934.* New Brunswick, NJ: Rutgers University Press.

Shacochis, Bob. 1998. *The Immaculate Invasion.* NY: Viking Press.

Stotzky, Irwin P. 1997. *Silencing the Guns in Haiti: The Promise of Deliberative Democracy.* IL: University of Chicago Press.

Sullivan, Michael J., III. 1996. *Comparing State Polities* (see CASE 27).

Trouillot, Michel-Rolph. 1990. *Haiti, State Against Nation: The Origins and Legacy of Duvalierism.* NY: Monthly Review Press.

Wilentz, Amy. 1989. *The Rainy Season: Haiti since Duvalier.* NY: Simon and Schuster.

## CASE 30. Yugoslavia, 1995 and 1999

Bert, Wayne. 1997. *The Reluctant Super Power: US Policy in Bosnia, 1991–95.* NY: St. Martin's Press.

Carpenter, Ted Galen, and Barbara Conroy (eds.). 1999. *NATO Enlargement: Illusion and Reality.* Washington, DC: Cato Institute.

Daalder, Ivo H. 2000. *Getting to Dayton: The Making of America's Bosnia Policy.* Washington, DC: Brookings Institution Press.

Daalder, Ivo H., and Michael E. O'Hanlon. 2000. *Winning Ugly: NATO's War to Save Kosovo.* Washington, DC: Brookings Institution Press.

Doder, Dusko. 1991. "History Repeating Itself in Rebirth of Serbian Guerrillas, Nationalism," *Baltimore Sun,* July 15.

Fromkin, David. 1999. *Kosovo Crossing: American Ideals Meet Reality on the Balkan Battlefields.* NY: Free Press.

Gow, James. 1997. *Triumph of the Lack of Will: International Diplomacy and the Yugoslav War.* NY: Columbia University Press.

Gutman, Roy. 1993. *A Witness to Genocide: The First Inside Account of the Horrors of "Ethnic Cleansing" in Bosnia.* Shaftsbury, Dorset, UK: Element Books.

Haas, Richard N. 1997. *The Reluctant Sheriff: The United States after the Cold War.* NY: Council on Foreign Relations Publications.

Holbrooke, Richard. 1998. *To End A War (Bosnia).* NY: Random House.

Joffe, Josef. 1993. "The New Europe: Yesterday's Ghosts," *Foreign Affairs,* 72(1), January–February: 29–43.

LeCompte, Eric M. 1999. "Are We Ready to Forget Another War? The Untold Story of the Destruction of Yugoslavia," *Catholic Peace Voice,* Summer: 6–8.

Mandelbaum, Michael. 1999. "A Perfect Failure: NATO's War against Yugoslavia," *Foreign Affairs,* September/October: 2–8.

Rieff, David. 1995. *Slaughterhouse: Bosnia and the Failure of the West.* NY: Touchstone.

Rogel, Carole. 1998. *The Breakup of Yugoslavia and the War in Bosnia.* Westport, CT: Greenwood Press.

Zimmerman, Warren (Ambassador). 1999. *Origins of a Catastrophe: Yugoslavia and Its Destroyers.* NY: Random House, Times Books.

# Conclusion

Since the terrorist attack upon the World Trade Center of 9-11-01, much has been written about how world politics and American foreign policy have been changed. However, from the perspective of this book, it looks a lot more like business as usual. Since 9-11-01, the United States has launched two major Third World interventions: the wars to overthrow the displeasing regimes in Afghanistan and in Iraq.

To the extent that none of the men who were on the planes that flew into the World Trade Center or the Pentagon were from either of these countries (15 were Saudi Arabian, 4 were Egyptian), it would seem that these two most recent cases of American military intervention in the periphery of the global capitalist system deserve some scrutiny.

The "war against terrorism," in whose name the massive military deployments in support of these two wars was made, has resulted in US troops being spread from Kenya and Somalia in east Africa to Uzbekistan and Tajikistan among the central Asian republics of the former Soviet Union (not to mention regional back-up presence in European-oriented Turkey and Israel to the west). It is no coincidence that this swath of territory roughly embraces the "arc of crisis" that Zbigniew Brzezinski described for President Jimmy Carter at the time of the Soviet invasion of Afghanistan. But within this realm there is little credible talk today of democracy or human rights, the justifications for American adventures in the Third World during the Cold War and the Carter years.

The US allies in the wars against Afghanistan and Iraq are some of the most dictatorial and autocratic in the world. This is especially true of

General Pervez Musharraf in Pakistan and President-for-Life Islam Karimov in Uzbekistan, frontline providers of US bases and intelligence for the war and subsequent occupation in Afghanistan. The main supporters of the war against Iraq (apart from Great Britain) are the absolute monarchies in Saudi Arabia, Kuwait, Qatar, and the other Persian Gulf sheikhdoms.

It would be too facile to say the US wars in Afghanistan and Iraq were about "oil," for more is involved than the 10 percent of world reserves in Iraq, or the pipeline across Afghanistan that would provide an exit for the natural gas of central Asia across territories other than those of Iran or Russia. What is at stake is the future development of one of the last outposts on the periphery of the capitalist world. To the extent that east Asia is now a zone of competition vis-a-vis a resurgent neo-capitalist nuclear China, and that eastern Europe is once again a focus for Russia and Germany, the "arc of crisis" represents the last fruitful area for America unlikely to be of immediate interest to any other Great Power. (Sub-Saharan Africa is at a more primitive stage of development and therefore not a factor in such calculations; but the focus of the "war on terror" on Islamic fundamentalists provides a foothold for future expansion from Africa's northern and eastern Muslim areas further into this continent at a later time.)

In this strategic pursuit, the historic imperial powers—UK, France, Germany, and Japan, along with Russia and China through the medium of the United Nations Security Council—are effectively acting as junior partners of the United States. As new global hegemon, the United States is deferred to as it makes the latest frontier stable, and sets the general parameters, for the next expansion of global capitalism.

From a longer historical perspective, it can be seen that the model is American neo-colonialism in the Western Hemisphere during the era of gunboat diplomacy around the turn of the last century (see Chapter 2). In the latest phase of its rise to global hegemony, the United States tries to stay away from genuine "nation-building" and political micromanagement in the conquered areas, contenting itself with mere "regime change." As soon as the government "harborers of terrorists," or "makers of weapons of mass destruction," or whatever the next rationale might be, are overthrown, America is content to withdraw most of its forces and to allow the newly installed local satrap to resume normal activities. The pattern of US foreign policy on the periphery prevails.

# Index

*Case discussions are in bold print.*

MICHAEL J. SULLIVAN, III, is professor of Political Science at Drexel University in Philadelphia, P.A. A graduate of the University of Virginia, he is author of *Measuring Global Values,* and *Comparing State Polities* (Greenwood). He has also published articles on arms control and nuclear nonproliferation in various scholarly journals, and is the winner of fellowships from Pew foundation, the National Endowment for the Humanities, and the North Atlantic Treaty Organization. He also holds the Lindback Award for Excellence in Teaching.